Introduction

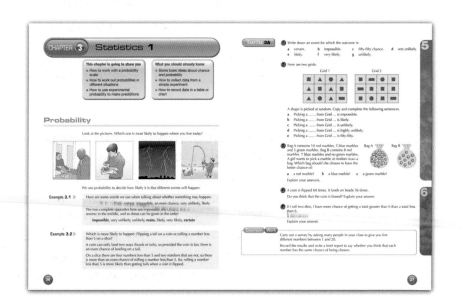

Learning objectives

See what you are going to cover and what you should already know at the start of each chapter. The purple and blue boxes set the topic in context and provide a handy checklist.

National Curriculum levels

Know what level you are working at so you can easily track your progress with the colour-coded levels at the side of the page.

Worked examples

Understand the topic before you start the exercises by reading the examples in blue boxes. These take you through how to answer a question step-by-step.

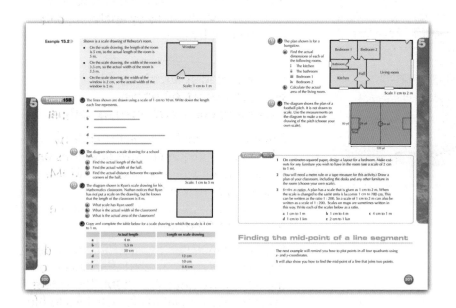

Functional Maths

Practise your Functional Maths skills to see how people use Maths in everyday life.

> **FM** Look out for the Functional Maths icon on the page.

Extension activities

Stretch your thinking and investigative skills by working through the extension activities. By tackling these you are working at a higher level.

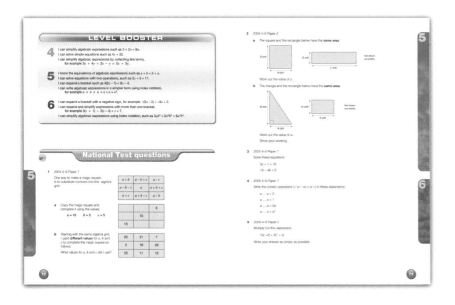

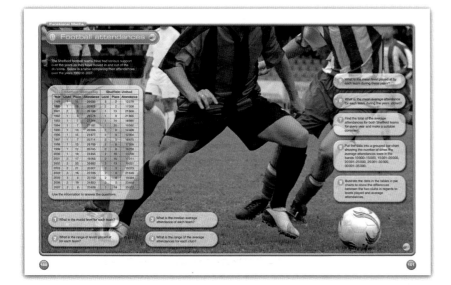

Level booster

Progress to the next level by checking the Level boosters at the end of each chapter. These clearly show you what you need to know at each level and how to improve.

National Test questions

Practise the past paper Test questions to feel confident and prepared for your KS3 National Curriculum Tests. The questions are levelled so you can check what level you are working at.

Extra interactive National Test practice

Watch and listen to the audio/visual National Test questions on the separate Interactive Book CD-ROM to help you revise as a class on a whiteboard.

 Look out for the computer mouse icon on the page and on the screen.

Functional Maths activities

Put Maths into context with these colourful pages showing real-world situations involving Maths. You are practising your Functional Maths skills by analysing data to solve problems.

Extra interactive Functional Maths questions and video clips

Extend your Functional Maths skills by taking part in the interactive questions on the separate Interactive Book CD-ROM. Your teacher can put these on the whiteboard so the class can answer the questions on the board.

See Maths in action by watching the video clips and doing the related Worksheets on the Interactive Book CD-ROM. The videos bring the Functional Maths activities to life and help you see how Maths is used in the real world.

 Look out for the computer mouse icon on the page and on the screen.

<table>
<tr><td>

This chapter is going to show you

- How to multiply and divide negative numbers
- How to find the highest common factor and the lowest common multiple of sets of numbers
- How to find the prime factors of a number
- How to generate and describe number patterns

</td><td>

What you should already know

- How to add and subtract negative integers
- How to generate terms of a simple number sequence
- Recognise the square and triangle number sequences
- How to test numbers for divisibility

</td></tr>
</table>

Multiplying and dividing negative numbers

Example 1.1 Work out the answers to: **a** $-2 \times +4$ **b** -6×-3 **c** $-15 \div -5$ **d** $+6 \times -4 \div -2$

a $2 \times 4 = 8$, and $- \times +$ is equivalent to $-$, so $-2 \times +4 = -8$

b $6 \times 3 = 18$, and $- \times -$ is equivalent to $+$, so $-6 \times -3 = +18$

c $15 \div 5 = 3$, and $- \div -$ is equivalent to $+$, so $-15 \div -5 = +3$

d $+6 \times -4 = -24$, $-24 \div -2 = +12$

Example 1.2 Find the missing number in: **a** $\boxed{} \times 3 = -6$ **b** $-12 \div \boxed{} = 3$

a The inverse problem is $\boxed{} = -6 \div +3$, so the missing number is -2.

b The inverse problem is $\boxed{} = -12 \div +3$, so the missing number is -4.

Example 1.3 Work out: **a** $-3 \times -2 + 5$ **b** $-3 \times (-2 + 5)$

a Using BODMAS do -3×-2 first, $-3 \times -2 + 5 = +6 + 5 = +11$

b This time the bracket must be done first, $-3 \times (-2 + 5) = -3 \times +3 = -9$

Exercise 1A

1. Work out the following.

   a $-7 + 8$ **b** $-2 - 7$ **c** $+6 - 2 + 3$ **d** $-6 - 1 + 7$ **e** $-3 + 4 - 9$

   f $-3 - 7$ **g** $-4 + -6$ **h** $+7 - +6$ **i** $-3 - 7 + -8$ **j** $-5 + -4 - -7$

2 In these 'walls', subtract the right-hand from the left-hand number to find the number in the brick below.

a
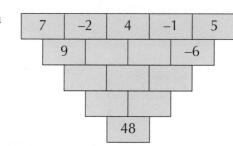

b
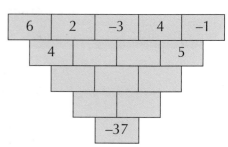

3 Copy and complete the following patterns.

a
$3 \times +3 = 9$
$2 \times +3 = 6$
$1 \times +3 = \ldots$
$0 \times +3 = \ldots$
$\ldots \times +3 = \ldots$
$\ldots \times +3 = \ldots$

b
$3 \times -2 = -6$
$2 \times -2 = -4$
$1 \times -2 = \ldots$
$0 \times -2 = \ldots$
$\ldots \times -2 = \ldots$
$\ldots \times -2 = \ldots$

c
$-2 \times +1 = -2$
$-1 \times +1 = \ldots$
$\ldots \times +1 = \ldots$
$\ldots \times +1 = \ldots$
$\ldots \times +1 = \ldots$
$\ldots \times +1 = \ldots$

4 Work out the answer to each of these.

a $+2 \times -3$ b $-3 \times +4$ c $-5 \times +2$ d -6×-3

e $-3 \times +8$ f $-4 \times +5$ g -3×-4 h -6×-1

i $+7 \times -2$ j $+2 \times +8$ k $+6 \times -10$ l $+8 \times +4$

m -15×-2 n $-6 \times -3 \times -1$ o $-2 \times +4 \times -2$

5 The answer to the question on this blackboard is −12.

Using multiplication and/or division signs write down at least five different calculations that give this answer.

6 Work out the answer to each of these.

a $+12 \div -3$ b $-24 \div +4$ c $-6 \div +2$ d $-6 \div -3$

e $-32 \div +8$ f $-40 \div +5$ g $-32 \div -4$ h $-6 \div -1$

i $+7 \div -2$ j $+12 \div +6$ k $+60 \div -10$ l $+8 \div +4$

m $-15 \div -2$ n $-6 \times -3 \div -2$ o $-2 \times +6 \div -3$

7 Copy and complete the following multiplication grids.

a

×	−2	3	−4	5
−3	6			
6				
−2				
5				

b

×	−1	−3	4	
−2		6		
		12		
	−5			
7			−42	

c

×				−8
−2		−12		
	−15		21	
4			28	
		−30		

8 Find the missing number in each calculation. (Remember that the numbers without a + or – sign in front of them are actually positive, as we do not always show every positive sign when writing a calculation.)

a $2 \times -3 = \boxed{}$ **b** $-2 \times \boxed{} = -8$ **c** $3 \times \boxed{} = -9$

d $\boxed{} \div -5 = -15$ **e** $-4 \times -6 = \boxed{}$ **f** $-3 \times \boxed{} = -24$

g $-64 \div \boxed{} = 32$ **h** $\boxed{} \times 6 = 36$ **i** $-2 \times 3 = \boxed{}$

j $\boxed{} \times -6 = -48$ **k** $-2 \times \boxed{} \times 3 = 12$ **l** $\boxed{} \div -4 = 2$

m $5 \times 4 \div \boxed{} = -10$ **n** $-5 \times \boxed{} \div -2 = -10$ **o** $\boxed{} \times -4 \div -2 = 14$

9 Work out the following.

a -2×-2 **b** -4×-4 **c** $(-3)^2$ **d** $(-6)^2$

e Explain why it is impossible to get a negative answer when you square any number.

10 Work out the following.

a $2 \times -3 + 4$ **b** $2 \times (-3 + 4)$ **c** $-2 + 3 \times -4$ **d** $(-2 + 3) \times -4$

e $-5 \times -4 + 6$ **f** $-5 \times (-4 + 6)$ **g** $-12 \div -6 + 2$ **h** $-12 \div (-6 + 2)$

11 Put brackets in each of these to make them true.

a $2 \times -5 + 4 = -2$ **b** $-2 + -6 \times 3 = -24$ **c** $9 - 5 - 2 = 6$

Extension Work

This is an algebraic magic square.

1 What is the 'Magic expression' that every row, column and diagonal adds up to?

2 Find the value in each cell when $a = 7$, $b = 9$, $c = 2$.

3 Find the value in each cell when $a = -1$, $b = -3$, $c = -5$.

$a+c$	$c-a-b$	$b+c$
$b+c-a$	c	$a+c-b$
$c-b$	$a+b+c$	$c-a$

HCF and LCM

Remember that:

HCF stands for Highest Common Factor   LCM stands for Lowest Common Multiple

Look at the diagrams. What do you think they are showing?

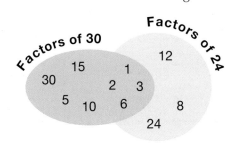

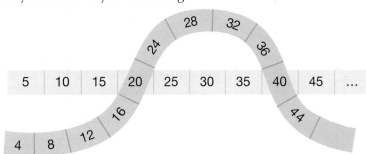

Example 1.4 ▶ Find the lowest common multiple (LCM) of the following pairs of numbers.

a 3 and 7   **b** 6 and 9

a Write out the first few multiples of each number:
3, 6, 9, 12, 15, 18, 21, 24, 27, ...
7, 14, 21, 28, 35, ...
You can see that the LCM of 3 and 7 is 21.

b Write out the multiples of each number: 6, 12, 18, 24, ...
9, 18, 27, 36,
You can see that the LCM of 6 and 9 is 18.

Example 1.5 ▶ Find the highest common factor (HCF) of the following pairs of numbers.

a 15 and 21   **b** 16 and 24

a Write out the factors of each number: 1, 3, 5, 15
1, 3, 7, 21
You can see that the HCF of 15 and 21 is 3.

b Write out the factors of each number: 1, 2, 4, 8, 16
1, 2, 3, 4, 6, 8, 12, 24
You can see that the HCF of 16 and 24 is 8.

Exercise 1B

① Write down the numbers in this list that are multiples of:

a 2   **b** 3   **c** 5   **d** 9

| 10 | 4 | 23 | 18 | 69 | 81 | 8 | 65 | 33 | 72 | 100 |

② Write down the first 10 multiples of the following numbers.

a 4   **b** 5   **c** 8   **d** 15   **e** 20

③ Write down all the factors of the following.

a 15   **b** 20   **c** 32   **d** 35   **e** 60

④ Use your answers to Question 2 to help find the LCM of the following.

a 5 and 8   **b** 4 and 20   **c** 4 and 15   **d** 8 and 15

⑤ Use your answer to Question 3 to help find the HCF of the following.

a 15 and 20   **b** 15 and 60   **c** 20 and 60   **d** 20 and 32

⑥ Find the LCM of the following.

a 5 and 9   **b** 5 and 25   **c** 3 and 8   **d** 4 and 6
e 8 and 12   **f** 12 and 15   **g** 9 and 21   **h** 7 and 11

7 Find the HCF of the following.

    a   15 and 18   **b**   12 and 32   **c**   12 and 22   **d**   8 and 12

    e   2 and 18   **f**   8 and 18   **g**   18 and 27   **h**   7 and 11

Extension Work

1 **a** Two numbers have an LCM of 24 and an HCF of 2. What are they?

     b Two numbers have an LCM of 18 and an HCF of 3. What are they?

     c Two numbers have an LCM of 60 and an HCF of 5. What are they?

2 **a** What is the HCF and the LCM of: **i** 5, 7 **ii** 3, 4 **iii** 2, 11?

     b Two numbers, x and y, have an HCF of 1. What is the LCM of x and y?

3 **a** What is the HCF and LCM of: **i** 5, 10 **ii** 3, 18 **iii** 4, 20?

     b Two numbers, x and y, (where y is bigger than x) have an HCF of x. What is the LCM of x and y?

Powers and roots

Look at these cubes. Is cube B twice as big, four times as big or eight times as big as cube A? How many times bigger is cube C than cube A?

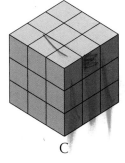

A   B   C

Example 1.6   Use a calculator to work out: **a** 4^3 **b** 5.5^2 **c** -3^4

   a $4^3 = 4 \times 4 \times 4 = 64$

   b $5.5^2 = 5.5 \times 5.5 = 30.25$ (most calculators have a button for squaring, usually marked $\boxed{x^2}$)

   c $-3^4 = -3 \times -3 \times -3 \times -3 = +9 \times +9 = 81$

Example 1.7   Use a calculator to work out: **a** $\sqrt{12.25}$ **b** $\sqrt{33\,124}$

   a Depending on your calculator, sometimes you type the square root before the number, and sometimes the number comes first. Make sure you can use your calculator. The answer is 3.5.

   b The answer is 182.

Exercise 1C

1 The diagrams at the beginning of this section show cubes made from smaller 1 cm cubes. Copy and complete this table.

Length of side	1 cm	2 cm	3 cm	4 cm	5 cm	6 cm	7 cm	8 cm	9 cm	10 cm
Area of face	1 cm²	4 cm²	9 cm²							
Volume of cube	1 cm³	8 cm³	27 cm³							

2 Use the table in Question 1 to work out the following.

a $\sqrt{4}$ b $\sqrt{64}$ c $\sqrt{81}$ d $\sqrt{100}$ e $\sqrt{25}$

f $\sqrt[3]{27}$ g $\sqrt[3]{125}$ h $\sqrt[3]{1000}$ i $\sqrt[3]{512}$ j $\sqrt[3]{729}$

3 Find two values of x that make the following equations true.

a $x^2 = 36$ b $x^2 = 121$ c $x^2 = 144$ d $x^2 = 2.25$

e $x^2 = 196$ f $x^2 = 5.76$ g $x^2 = 2.56$ h $x^2 = 3600$

4 Use a calculator to find the value of the following.

a 13^2 b 13^3 c 15^2 d 15^3 e 21^2 f 21^3

g 1.4^2 h 1.8^3 i 2.3^3 j 4.5^2 k 12^3 l 1.5^3

5 Use a calculator to find the value of the following.

a 2^4 b 3^5 c 3^4 d 2^5 e 4^4 f 5^4

g 7^4 h 8^3 i 2^7 j 2^9 k 2^{10} l 3^{10}

6 Without using a calculator write down the values of the following. (*Hint:* use the table in question 1 and some of the answers from Question 5 to help you.)

a 20^2 b 30^3 c 50^3 d 20^5 e 70^2 f 200^3

7 $10^2 = 100$, $10^3 = 1000$, copy and complete the following table.

Number	100	1000	10 000	100 000	1 000 000	10 000 000
Power of 10	10^2	10^3				

8 Work out: a 1^2 b 1^3 c 1^4 d 1^5 e 1^6

f write down the value of 1^{223}

9 Work out: a $(-1)^2$ b $(-1)^3$ c $(-1)^4$ d $(-1)^5$ e $(-1)^6$

f write down the value of: i $(-1)^{223}$ ii $(-1)^{224}$

10 You can see from the table in Question 1 that 64 is a square number (8^2) and a cube number (4^3).

a One other cube number (apart from 1) in the table is also a square number. Which is it?

b Which is the next cube number that is also a square number?

(*Hint:* Look at the pattern of cube numbers so far, e.g. 1^3, 4^3, ...)

How many squares are there on a chessboard?

The answer is not 64!

For example in this square ⊞ there are five squares:

four this size ☐ and one this size ☐

In this square ⊞ there are 14 squares:

nine this size ☐ four this size ☐ and one this size ☐

By drawing increasingly larger 'chessboards', work out how many squares there are and see if you can spot the pattern.

A computer spreadsheet is useful for this activity.

Prime factors

What are the prime factors of 120 and 210?

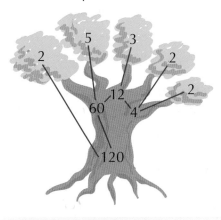
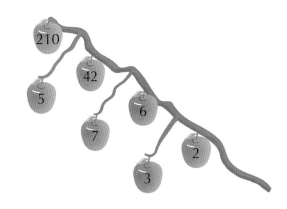

Example 1.8 ▷ Find the prime factors of 18.

Using a prime factor tree, split 18 into 3×6 and 6 into 3×2.

So, $18 = 2 \times 3 \times 3 = 2 \times 3^2$.

Note that 2×3^2 is called Index Form.

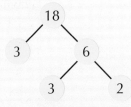

Example 1.9 ▷ Find the prime factors of 24.

Using the divide method:

```
2 | 24
2 | 12
2 |  6
3 |  3
  |  1
```

So, $24 = 2 \times 2 \times 2 \times 3 = 2^3 \times 3$.

Exercise 1D

1 These are the prime factors of some numbers. What are the numbers?

a $2 \times 2 \times 3$ b $2 \times 3 \times 3 \times 5$ c $2 \times 2 \times 3^2$ d $2 \times 3^3 \times 5$ e $2 \times 3 \times 5^2$

2 Using a prime factor tree, work out the prime factors of the following.

| a | 8 | b | 10 | c | 16 | d | 20 | e | 28 |
| f | 34 | g | 35 | h | 52 | i | 60 | j | 180 |

3 Using the division method work out the prime factors of the following.

a 42 b 75 c 140 d 250 e 480

4 Find the prime factors of all the numbers from 2 to 20.

5 a Which numbers in Question 4 only have one prime factor?

b What special name is given to these numbers?

6 The prime factors of 100 are $2 \times 2 \times 5 \times 5 = 2^2 \times 5^2$.

a Write down the prime factors of 200 in index form.

b Write down the prime factors of 50 in index form.

c Write down the prime factors of 1000 in index form.

d Write down the prime factors of one million in index form.

7 The smallest number with exactly two different prime factors is $2 \times 3 = 6$.

a What is the next smallest number with exactly two different prime factors?

b What is the smallest number with exactly three different prime factors?

8 a What are the prime factors of 32? Give your answer in index form.

b Write down the prime factors of 64 in index form.

c Write down the prime factors of 128 in index form.

d Write down the prime factors of 1024 in index form.

Extension Work

1 Using the diagrams below work out the HCF and LCM of:

a
30   72

5   2   2
          2
      3   3

30 and 72

b
50   90

5   2   3
          2
      5   3

50 and 90

c
48   84

       2   2
5   3   7
       2   2

48 and 84

2 The prime factors of 120 are $2 \times 2 \times 2 \times 3 \times 5$. The prime factors of 150 are $2 \times 3 \times 5 \times 5$.

Put these numbers into a diagram like those in Question 1.

Use the diagram to work out the HCF and LCM of 120 and 150.

3 The prime factors of 210 are $2 \times 3 \times 5 \times 7$. The prime factors of 90 are $2 \times 3 \times 3 \times 5$.

Put these numbers into a diagram like those in Question 1.

Use the diagram to work out the HCF and LCM of 210 and 90.

Sequences 1

Example 1.10

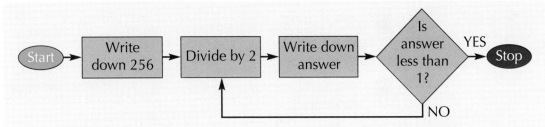

Follow the above flow diagram through and write down the numbers generated.
These are 256, 128, 64, 32, 16, 8, 4, 2, 1, 0.5

Example 1.11

For each of the following sequences:
i describe how it is being generated. **ii** find the next two terms.

a 2, 6, 10, 14, 18, 22, …

i   the sequence is going up by 4

ii next two terms are 26, 30

b 1, 3, 27, 81, 243, …

i   each term is multiplied by 3

ii next two terms are 729, 2187

Exercise 1E

1 Follow these instructions to generate sequences.

a

Start → Write down 3 → Add on 5 → Write down answer → Is answer more than 40? — YES → Stop / NO (loop back to Add on 5)

b

Start → X = 3 → Write down 1 → Add on X → Write down answer → Is answer more than 100? — YES → Stop / NO → Increase X by 2 (loop back to Add on X)

c

Start → Write down 10 → Multiply by 10 → Write down answer → Is answer more than 1 000 000? — YES → Stop / NO (loop back to Multiply by 10)

2 What is the sequence of numbers generated by the flow diagram in Question 1, part b, called?

3 Describe in words the sequence of numbers generated by the flow diagram in Question 1, part c.

4 Describe how the sequences below are generated.

    a   1, 4, 7, 10, 13, 16, …   **b**   1, 4, 16, 64, 256, 1024, …

    c   1, 4, 8, 13, 19, 26, …   **d**   1, 4, 9, 16, 25, 36, …

5 Write down four sequences beginning 1, 5, …, and explain how each of them is generated.

6 Describe how each of the following sequences is generated and write down the next two terms.

    a   40, 41, 43, 46, 50, 55, …   **b**   90, 89, 87, 84, 80, 75, …

    c   1, 3, 7, 13, 21, 31, …   **d**   2, 6, 12, 20, 30, 42, …

7 You are given a start number and a multiplier. Write down at least the first six terms of the sequences. (For example, start 2 and multiplier 3 gives 2, 6, 18, 54, 162, 486, …)

    a   start 1, multiplier 3   **b**   start 2, multiplier 2

    c   start 1, multiplier –1   **d**   start 1, multiplier 0.5

    e   start 2, multiplier 0.4   **f**   start 1, multiplier 0.3

8 The following patterns of dots generate sequences of numbers.

    i   Draw the next two patterns of dots.

    ii Write down the next four numbers in the sequence.

    a    **b** 

    c    **d** 

Extension   Work

Fibonacci numbers

You will need a calculator.

The Fibonacci sequence is: 1, 1, 2, 3, 5, 8, 13, 21, …

It is formed by adding together the previous two terms, that is 5 = 3 + 2, 8 = 5 + 3, etc.

Write down the next five terms of the sequence.

Now divide each term by the previous term, that is 1 ÷ 1 = 1, 2 ÷ 1 = 2, 3 ÷ 2 = 1.5, 5 ÷ 3 = …

You should notice something happening.

You may find a computer spreadsheet useful for this activity.

If you have access to the Internet, find out about the Italian mathematician after whom the sequence is named.

Sequences 2

Paving slabs 1 metre square are used to put borders around square ponds. Some examples are given below.

1 × 1 m² pond
8 slabs

2 × 2 m² pond
12 slabs

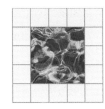

3 × 3 m² pond
16 slabs

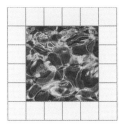

4 × 4 m² pond
20 slabs

How many slabs would fit around a 5 × 5 m² pond? What about a 100 × 100 m² pond?

Example 1.12

Generate sequences by using the rules given.

a First term 5, increase each term by a constant difference of 6.

b First term 32, multiply each term by $-\frac{1}{2}$.

c First term 3, subtract 1 then multiply by 2.

a The sequence is 5, 5 + 6 = 11, 11 + 6 = 17, …, which gives 5, 11, 17, 23, 29, 35, …

b The sequence is $32 \times -\frac{1}{2} = -16$, $-16 \times -\frac{1}{2} = 8$, etc., which gives 32, –16, 8, –4, 2, –1, $\frac{1}{2}$, $-\frac{1}{4}$, …

c The sequence is $(3 - 1) \times 2 = 4$, $(4 - 1) \times 2 = 6$, $(6 - 1) \times 2 = 10$, etc., which gives 3, 4, 6, 10, 18, 34, 66, …

We can describe sequences by giving a rule for any term. This is called the general or nth term, and is an algebraic expression.

Example 1.13

The nth term of the sequence 9, 13, 17, 21, 25, … is given by the expression $4n + 5$.

a Show this is true for the first three terms.

b Use the rule to find the 50th term of the sequence.

a Let $n = 1$, $4 \times 1 + 5 = 4 + 5 = 9$
   Let $n = 2$, $4 \times 2 + 5 = 8 + 5 = 13$
   Let $n = 3$, $4 \times 3 + 5 = 12 + 5 = 17$

b Let $n = 50$, $4 \times 50 + 5 = 200 + 5 = 205$
   So the 50th term is 205.

We can describe a sequence by finding the nth term. This is the generalisation that will allow us to find any specific term.

Example 1.14 ▶ Look at the sequence with the following patterns.

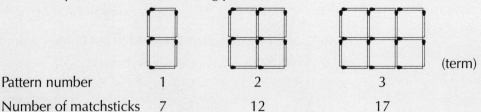

(term)

Pattern number	1	2	3
Number of matchsticks	7	12	17

a Find the generalisation (*n*th term) of the pattern.

b Find the 50th term in the sequence.

The first term is 7. For the first term $n = 1$, so $5 \times 1 + 2 = 7$, giving the *n*th term = $5n + 2$.

Example 1.15 ▶ Find the *n*th term of the sequence 3, 10, 17, 24, 31, …

The sequence goes up by 7 each time, so the *n*th term is based on $7n$.

The first term is 3, and $3 - 7 = -4$, so the *n*th term is $7n - 4$.

Exercise 1F

1 For the following arithmetic sequences, write down the first term *a*, and the constant difference *d*.

a 4, 9, 14, 19, 24, 29, …   **b** 1, 3, 5, 7, 9, 11, …
c 3, 9, 15, 21, 27, 33, …   **d** 5, 3, 1, −1, −3, −5, …

2 Given the first term *a* and the constant difference *d*, write down the first six terms of each of these sequences.

a $a = 1, d = 7$ **b** $a = 3, d = 2$ **c** $a = 5, d = 4$
d $a = 0.5, d = 1.5$ **e** $a = 4, d = -3$ **f** $a = 2, d = -0.5$

3 The following flow diagram can be used to generate sequences.

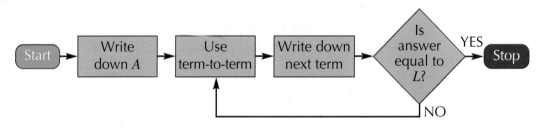

For example, if $A = 8$, the term-to-term rule is 'halve' and $L = 0.25$, the sequence is:

8, 4, 2, 1, 0.5, 0.25

Write down the sequences generated by:

	A	Term-to-term rule	L
a	1000 000	Divide by 10	1
b	1	Add 3, 5, 7, 9, 11, etc.	225
c	1	Double	1024
d	10	Subtract 5	–25
e	3	Add 2	23
f	1	Multiply by –2	1024
g	48	Halve	0.75
h	1	Double and add 1	63
i	2	Times by 3 and subtract 1	365
j	0	Add 1, 2, 3, 4, 5, 6, etc.	55

4 The nth term of sequences are given by the rules below. Use this to write down the first five terms of each sequence.

a $2n - 1$ **b** $2n + 3$ **c** $2n + 2$ **d** $2n + 1$

e What is the constant difference in each of the sequences in **a**–**d**?

5 The nth term of sequences are given by the rules below. Use this to write down the first five terms of each sequence.

a $3n + 1$ **b** $3n + 2$ **c** $3n - 2$ **d** $3n - 1$

e What is the constant difference in each of the sequences in **a**–**d**?

6 The nth term of sequences are given by the rules below. Use this to write down the first five terms of each sequence.

a $5n - 1$ **b** $5n + 2$ **c** $5n - 4$ **d** $5n + 3$

e What is the constant difference in each of the sequences in **a**–**d**?

7 Find:

i the first three terms.

ii the 100th term, of sequences whose nth term is given by:

a $n + 1$ **b** $3n - 1$ **c** $2n - 3$

d $5n - 2$ **e** $4n - 3$ **f** $9n + 1$

g $\frac{1}{2}n + 1$ **h** $6n + 1$ **i** $1\frac{1}{2}n - \frac{1}{2}$

8 For each of the patterns below:

    i find the *n*th term for the number of matchsticks.

    ii find the number of matchsticks in the 50th term of each pattern.

a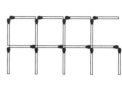

b

c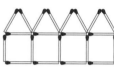

d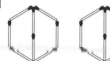

9 Find the *n*th term of each of the following sequences.

    a 4, 10, 16, 22, 28, …   **b** 9, 12, 15, 18, 21, …

    c 9, 15, 21, 27, 33, …   **d** 2, 5, 8, 11, 14, …

    e 2, 9, 16, 23, 30, …   **f** 8, 10, 12, 14, 16, …

    g 10, 14, 18, 22, 26, …   **h** 3, 11, 19, 27, 35, …

    i 9, 19, 29, 39, 49, …   **j** 4, 13, 22, 31, 40, …

10 Write down a first term *A* and a term-to-term rule that you can use in the flow diagram in Question 3 so that:

    a each term of the sequence is even.

    b each term of the sequence is odd.

    c the sequence is the five times table.

    d the sequence is the triangle numbers.

    e the numbers in the sequence all end in 1.

    f the sequence has alternating odd and even terms.

    g the sequence has alternating positive and negative terms.

Extension Work

Find:

i the first three terms.

ii the 99th term, of sequences whose *n*th term is given by:

    a $2(n + 1)^2$ **b** $(n - 1)(n + 1)$ **c** $\frac{1}{2}(n + 1)(n + 2)$

Solving problems

An Investigation

At the start of the last section you were asked to say how many slabs would be needed to go around a square pond.

1 × 1 pond
8 slabs

2 × 2 pond
12 slabs

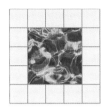

3 × 3 pond
16 slabs

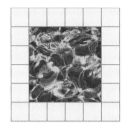

4 × 4 pond
20 slabs

To solve this problem you need to: Step 1, break the problem into simple steps;
Step 2, set up a table of results;
Step 3, predict and test a rule;
Step 4, use your rule to answer the question.

Step 1 is already done with the diagrams given.

Step 2

Pond side	Number of slabs
1	8
2	12
3	16
4	20

Step 3   Use the table to spot how the sequence is growing.
In this case, it is increasing in 4s.

So a 5 × 5 pond will need 24 slabs (see right).

We can also say that the numbers of slabs (S) is 4 times the pond side (P) plus 4, which we can write as:

$$S = 4P + 4$$

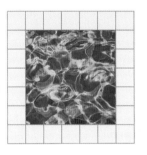

There are many other ways to write this rule, and many ways of showing that it is true.

For example: $4P + 4$ $2(P + 2) + 2P$ $4(P + 1)$

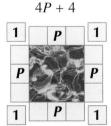

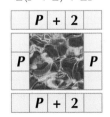

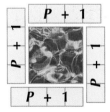

Step 4   We can now use any rule to say that for a 100 × 100 pond,
$4 \times 100 + 4 = 404$ slabs will be needed.

Exercise 1G

Do the following investigations. Make sure you follow the steps above and explain what you are doing clearly. In each investigation you are given some hints.

1 Write a rule to show how many square slabs it takes to make a border around rectangular ponds.

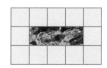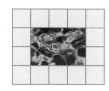

First side	Second side	Slabs
1	2	10
1	3	12
2	3	14

2 The final score in a football match was 5–4. How many different half-time scores could there have been?

For a match that ended 0–0, there is only one possible half-time result (0–0).

For a match that ended 1–2, there are six possible half-time scores (0–0, 0–1, 0–2, 1–0, 1–1, 1–2).

Take some other low-scoring matches, such as 1–1, 2–1, 2–0, etc., and work out the half-time scores for these.

Set up a table like the one in Question 1.

3 There are 13 stairs in most houses. How many different ways are there of going up the stairs in a combination of one step or two steps at a time?

Take one stair. There is only 1 way of going up it (1).

Take two stairs. There are two ways of going up (1+1, 2).

Before you think this is going to be easy, look at five stairs. There are eight ways of going up them (1+1+1+1+1, 1+1+1+2, 1+2+1+1, 1+1+2+1, 1+2+2, 2+1+2, 2+2+1, 2+1+1+1).

Work out the number of ways for three stairs and four stairs. Draw up a table and see if you can spot the rule!

LEVEL BOOSTER

4
I can write down the multiples of any whole number.
I can work out the factors of numbers under 100.

5
I can add and subtract negative numbers, for example – 7 + – 3 = –10.
I can write down and recognise the sequence of square numbers.
I know the squares of all numbers up to 15^2 and the corresponding square roots.
I can use a calculator to work out powers of numbers.
I can find any term in a sequence given the first term, say 5, and the term-to-term rule such as 'goes up by 6 each time', for example, the 20th term is 119.
I know that the square roots of positive numbers can have two values, one positive and one negative, for example $\sqrt{36}$ = +6 or –6.

6
I can multiply and divide negative numbers, for example $-5 \times +3 = -15$.
I can find the lowest common multiple (LCM) for pairs of numbers, for example, the LCM of 24 and 30 is 120.
I can find the highest common factor (HCF) for pairs of numbers, for example, the HCF of 24 and 30 is 6.
I can write a number as the product of its prime factors, for example, $24 = 2 \times 2 \times 2 \times 3 = 2^3 \times 3$.
I can find any term in a sequence given the algebraic rule for the nth term, for example, for a sequence with an nth term of $6n - 5$ has a 10th term of 55.
I can find the nth term of a sequence in the form $an + b$, for example, the nth term of 3, 7, 11, 15, 19, … is $4n - 1$.
I can investigate a mathematical problem.

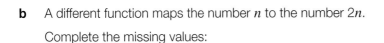

National Test questions

1 *2004 5–7 Paper 1*

a A function maps the number n to the number $n + 2$.
Complete the missing values:

n	…	$n + 2$
4	…	…
…	…	20

b A different function maps the number n to the number $2n$.
Complete the missing values:

n	…	$2n$
4	…	…
…	…	20

c Many different functions can map the number 25 to the number 5.

Copy and complete the tables by writing two different functions.

n	...	...
25	...	5

n	...	...
25	...	5

2 *2007 4–6 Paper 1*

Copy the following and write a number in each box to make the calculations correct.

$$\square + \square = -8 \qquad \square - \square = -8$$

3 *2000 Paper 1*

a Two numbers multiply together to make –15. They add together to make two.
What are the two numbers?

b Two numbers multiply together to make –15, but add together to make –2.
What are the two numbers?

c The square of 5 is 25. The square of another number is also 25.
What is that other number?

4 *2002 Paper 1*

You can often use algebra to show why a number puzzle works. Copy this puzzle and fill in the missing expressions.

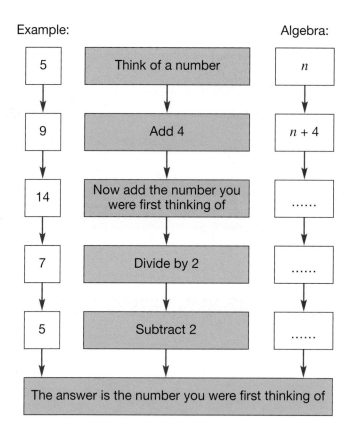

5 *2006 5–7 Paper 1*

a Put these values in order of size with the **smallest first**:

$5^2 \qquad 3^2 \qquad 3^3 \qquad 2^4$

b Look at this information:

5^5 is 3125

What is 5^7?

6 *2006 5–7 Paper 2*

Look at these pairs of number sequences.

The second sequence is formed from the first sequence by adding a number or multiplying by a number.

Work out the missing nth terms.

a 5,   9,   13,   17,   ... nth term is $4n + 1$
    6,   10,   14,   18,   ... nth term is ...

b 12,   18,   24,   30,   ... nth term is $6n + 6$
    6,   9,   12,   15,   ... nth term is ...

c 2,   7,   12,   17,   ... nth term is $5n - 3$
    4,   14,   24,   34,   ... nth term is ...

7 *2007 5–7 Paper 1*

a Copy the following and **draw lines** to match each nth term rule to its number sequence.

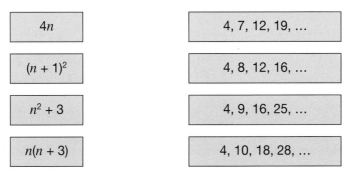

$4n$

$(n + 1)^2$

$n^2 + 3$

$n(n + 3)$

4, 7, 12, 19, ...

4, 8, 12, 16, ...

4, 9, 16, 25, ...

4, 10, 18, 28, ...

b Write the **first four** terms of the number sequence using the nth term rule below:

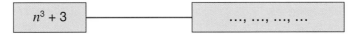

$n^3 + 3$ ..., ..., ..., ...

FM **Blackpool Tower**

Blackpool Tower is a tourist attraction in Blackpool, Lancashire, England. It opened to the public on 14 May 1894. Inspired by the Eiffel Tower in Paris, it rises to 518 ft 9 inches.

The foundation stone was laid on 29 September 1891. The total cost for the design and construction of the Tower and buildings was about £290 000. Five million bricks, 2500 tonnes of steel and 93 tonnes of cast steel were used to construct the Tower. The Tower buildings occupy a total of 6040 sq yards.

When the Tower opened, 3000 customers took the first rides to the top. Tourists paid 6 old pence for admission, a further 6 old pence for a ride in the lifts to the top, and a further 6 old pence for the circus.

Inside the Tower there is a circus, an aquarium, a ballroom, restaurants, a children's play area and amusements.

In 1998 a 'Walk of Faith' glass floor panel was opened at the top of the Tower. Made up of two sheets of laminated glass, it weighs half a tonne and is two inches thick. Visitors can stand on the glass panel and look straight down 380 ft to the promenade.

Use the information to help you answer these questions.

1 In what year did the Tower celebrate its centenary (100th birthday)?

2 How many years and months did it take to build the Tower?

3 The Tower is painted continuously. It takes seven years to paint the Tower completely. How many times has it been painted since it opened?

4 The aquarium in the Tower opened 20 years earlier than the Tower. What year did the aquarium celebrate its 100th birthday?

5 The largest tank in the aquarium holds 32 000 litres of water. There are approximately 4.5 litres to a gallon. How many gallons of water does the tank hold?

6 The water in the tropical fish tanks is kept at 75 °F. This rule is used to convert from degrees Fahrenheit to degrees Centigrade.

°F → Subtract 32 → Divide by 9 → Multiply by 5 → °C

Use this rule to convert 75°F to °C.

7 The circus in the base of the Tower first opened to the public on 14 May 1894. Admission fee was 6 old pence. Before Britain introduced decimal currency in 1971 there were 240 old pence in a pound.

   a What fraction, in its simplest form, is 6 old pence out of 240 old pence?

   b What is the equivalent value of 6 old pence in new pence?

8 Over 650 000 people visit the Tower every year. The Tower is open every day except Christmas day. Approximately how many people visit the Tower each day on average?

9
   a In January 2008, it cost €12 to visit the Eiffel Tower and £9.50 to visit Blackpool Tower. The exchange rate in January 2008 was £1 = €1.35. Which Tower was cheapest to visit and by how much (answer in pounds and pence)?

   b The Eiffel Tower is 325 m high. Blackpool Tower is 519 ft high. 1 m ≈ 3.3 ft. How many times taller is the Eiffel Tower than the Blackpool Tower?

   c The Eiffel Tower gets 6.7 million visitors a year. How many times more popular is it with tourists than the Blackpool Tower?

   d The Eiffel Tower celebrated its centenary in 1989. How many years before the Blackpool Tower did it open?

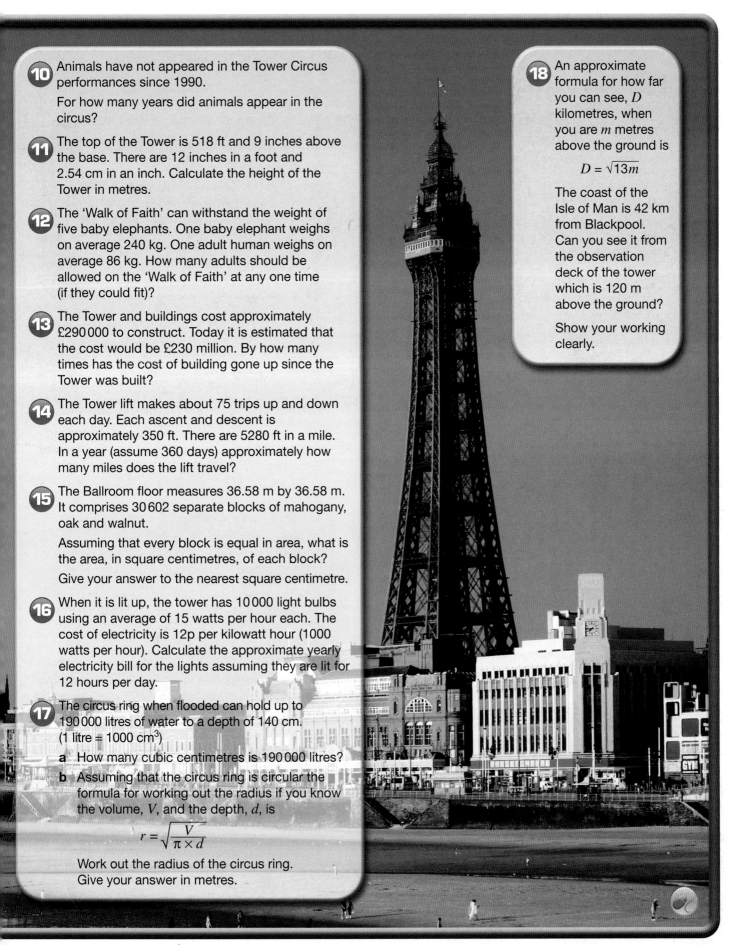

10 Animals have not appeared in the Tower Circus performances since 1990.

For how many years did animals appear in the circus?

11 The top of the Tower is 518 ft and 9 inches above the base. There are 12 inches in a foot and 2.54 cm in an inch. Calculate the height of the Tower in metres.

12 The 'Walk of Faith' can withstand the weight of five baby elephants. One baby elephant weighs on average 240 kg. One adult human weighs on average 86 kg. How many adults should be allowed on the 'Walk of Faith' at any one time (if they could fit)?

13 The Tower and buildings cost approximately £290 000 to construct. Today it is estimated that the cost would be £230 million. By how many times has the cost of building gone up since the Tower was built?

14 The Tower lift makes about 75 trips up and down each day. Each ascent and descent is approximately 350 ft. There are 5280 ft in a mile. In a year (assume 360 days) approximately how many miles does the lift travel?

15 The Ballroom floor measures 36.58 m by 36.58 m. It comprises 30 602 separate blocks of mahogany, oak and walnut.

Assuming that every block is equal in area, what is the area, in square centimetres, of each block?

Give your answer to the nearest square centimetre.

16 When it is lit up, the tower has 10 000 light bulbs using an average of 15 watts per hour each. The cost of electricity is 12p per kilowatt hour (1000 watts per hour). Calculate the approximate yearly electricity bill for the lights assuming they are lit for 12 hours per day.

17 The circus ring when flooded can hold up to 190 000 litres of water to a depth of 140 cm. (1 litre = 1000 cm³)

a How many cubic centimetres is 190 000 litres?

b Assuming that the circus ring is circular the formula for working out the radius if you know the volume, V, and the depth, d, is

$$r = \sqrt{\frac{V}{\pi \times d}}$$

Work out the radius of the circus ring. Give your answer in metres.

18 An approximate formula for how far you can see, D kilometres, when you are m metres above the ground is

$$D = \sqrt{13m}$$

The coast of the Isle of Man is 42 km from Blackpool. Can you see it from the observation deck of the tower which is 120 m above the ground?

Show your working clearly.

This chapter is going to show you	**What you should already know**
• How to identify alternate and corresponding angles • How to calculate angles in triangles and quadrilaterals • How to classify shapes using their properties • How to calculate exterior angles of polygons • How to construct angle bisectors and perpendicular lines	• How to identify parallel and perpendicular lines • How to measure angles • How to estimate acute, obtuse and reflex angles • How to measure and draw shapes accurately using a ruler and protractor

Alternate and corresponding angles

Look at the picture of the railway. Can you work out why the angle between the arms of the signals and the post are both the same?

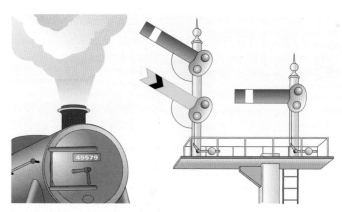

A line which intersects a set of parallel lines is called a **transversal**.

Notice in the diagram that eight distinct angles are formed by a transversal that intersects a pair of parallel lines.

The two angles marked on the diagram above are equal and are called corresponding angles.

Look for the letter F to identify **corresponding angles**.

The two angles marked on the diagram on the right are equal and are called alternate angles.

Look for the letter Z to identify **alternate angles**.

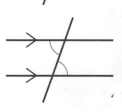

Example 2.1 ▷ Look at the diagram.

a Name pairs of angles that are alternate angles.

b Name pairs of angles that are corresponding angles.

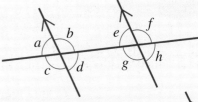

a The alternate angles are *b* and *g*, and *d* and *e*.

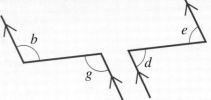

b The corresponding angles are *a* and *e*, *b* and *f*, *c* and *g*, and *d* and *h*.

   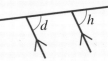

Exercise 2A

1 Copy and complete the following sentences.

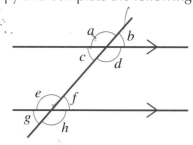 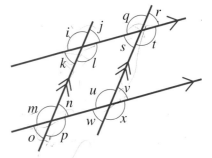

a *a* and … are corresponding angles.

b *b* and … are corresponding angles.

c *c* and … are corresponding angles.

d *d* and … are corresponding angles.

e *e* and … are alternate angles.

f *f* and … are alternate angles.

g *k* and … are corresponding angles.

h *u* and … are corresponding angles.

i *l* and … are corresponding angles.

j *r* and … are corresponding angles.

k *n* and … are alternate angles.

l *s* and … are alternate angles.

2 Work out the size of the lettered angles in these diagrams.

a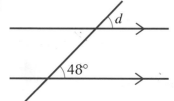

b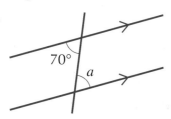

c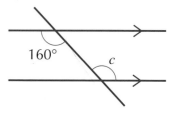

d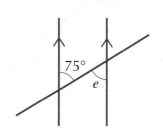

e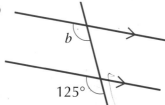

f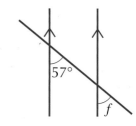

6

Work out the size of the lettered angles in these diagrams.

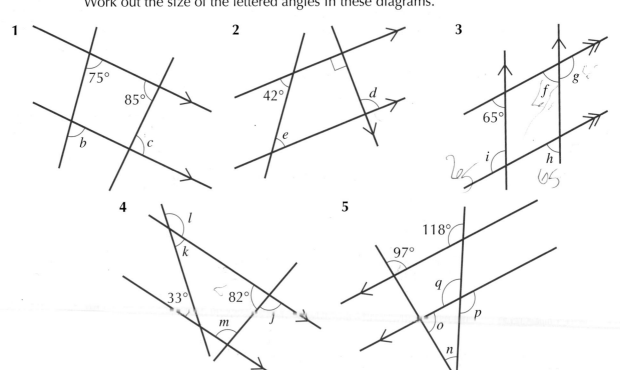

Angles in triangles and quadrilaterals

Angles in a triangle

The angles in a triangle add up to 180°.

$a + b + c = 180°$

Angles in a quadrilateral

The angles in a quadrilateral add up to 360°.

$a + b + c + d = 360°$

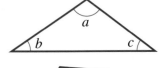

Parallel lines crop up in many different situations. Knowing their properties lets you solve all sorts of geometrical problems.

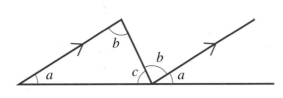

In the diagram, a is the corresponding angle and b is the alternate angle of the parallel lines. As the angles on a straight line add to 180°, $a + b + c = 180°$, and therefore the interior angles of a triangle add to 180°.

The usual name for the angle $a + b$ is an exterior angle.

Example 2.2 ▶ Work out the size of the angles marked x and y.

Angles in a triangle add up to 180°,
so x = 180 − 100 − 34
       = 46°

Angles on a straight line add up to 180°, so y = 180 − 46
                                               = 134°

Or you could say the exterior angle y = 100 + 34 (sum of the interior opposite angles)
                                      = 134°

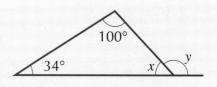

Example 2.3 ▶ Work out the size of the angles marked p and q.

Angles in a quadrilateral add up to 360°,
so p = 360 − 135 − 78 − 83
     = 64°

Angles on a straight line add up to 180°,
so q = 180 − 64
     = 116°

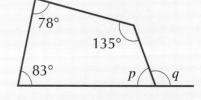

Exercise 2B

1 Calculate the size of each unknown angle.

a   b   c   d

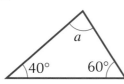 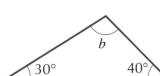

2 Calculate the size of each unknown angle.

a   b   c   d

3 Work out the size of the lettered angles in each of these diagrams.

a   b   c

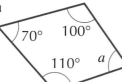 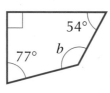 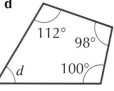

d   e   f

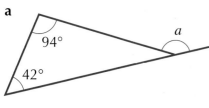 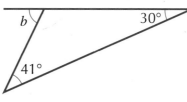 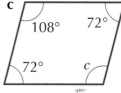

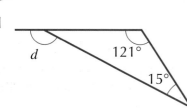 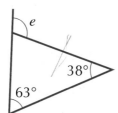 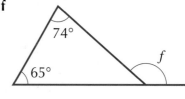

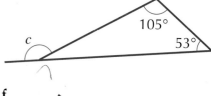

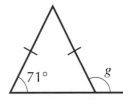

g

h

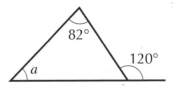

4 Work out the size of the lettered angles in each of these diagrams.

a

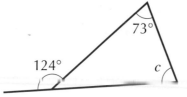

b

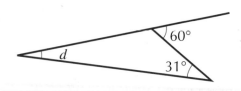

c

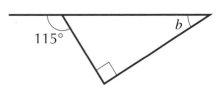

d

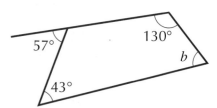

5 Work out the size of the lettered angles in each of these diagrams.

a

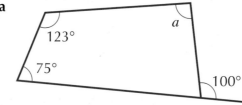

b

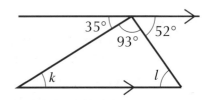

6 **a** Work out the size of angle *k*.
b Work out the size of angle *l*.
c State the value of $93 + k + l$.

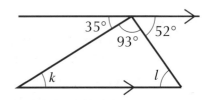

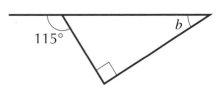

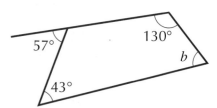

Extension **Work**

Investigate a rule for the sum of the interior angles in any polygon, for example a pentagon or a hexagon. *Hint:* Divide the polygons into triangles.

Geometric proof

The following two examples show you how to prove geometric statements. Proofs start from basic geometric facts about parallel lines and polygons which are known to be true. Algebra is used to combine the basic facts into more complex statements which must be true as well.

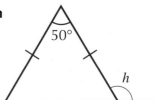

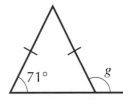

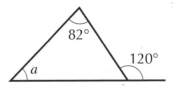

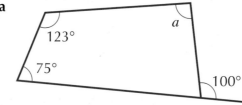

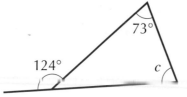

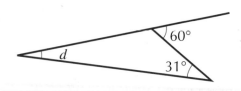

Example 2.4 ▶

The sum of the angles of a triangle is 180°.

To prove $a + b + c = 180°$:
Draw a line parallel to one side of the triangle. Let x and y be the other two angles formed on the line with a. Then $x = b$ (alternate angles), $y = c$ (alternate angles) and $a + x + y = 180°$ (angles on a line), so $a + b + c = 180°$.

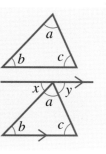

Example 2.5 ▶

The exterior angle of a triangle is equal to the sum of the two interior opposite angles.

x is an exterior angle of the triangle. To prove $a + b = x$:
Let the other interior angle of the triangle $= c$. Then $a + b + c = 180°$ (angles in a triangle) and $x + c = 180°$ (angles on a straight line), so $a + b = x$.

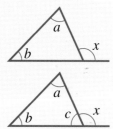

Exercise 2C

① Write a proof to show that $a + b = 90°$ in the right-angled triangle.

② Write a proof to show that the sum of the interior angles of a quadrilateral is 360°. (*Hint:* Divide the quadrilateral into two triangles.)

③ Write a proof to show that $x + y = 180°$.
(**Note:** x and y are called interior angles.)

④ Prove that the opposite angles of a parallelogram are equal. (*Hint:* Draw a diagonal on the parallelogram and use alternate angles.)

Extension Work

1 Prove that the sum of the exterior angles of a triangle is 360°.

2 Prove that the sum of the interior angles of a pentagon is 540°.

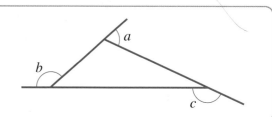

The geometric properties of quadrilaterals

Read carefully and learn all the properties of the quadrilaterals below.

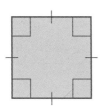

Square
- Four equal sides
- Four right angles
- Opposite sides parallel
- Diagonals bisect each other at right angles
- Four lines of symmetry
- Rotational symmetry of order four

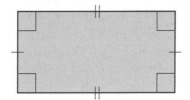

Rectangle
- Two pairs of equal sides
- Four right angles
- Opposite sides parallel
- Diagonals bisect each other
- Two lines of symmetry
- Rotational symmetry of order two

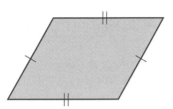

Parallelogram
- Two pairs of equal sides
- Two pairs of equal angles
- Opposite sides parallel
- Diagonals bisect each other
- No lines of symmetry
- Rotational symmetry of order two

Rhombus
- Four equal sides
- Two pairs of equal angles
- Opposite sides parallel
- Diagonals bisect each other at right angles
- Two lines of symmetry
- Rotational symmetry of order two

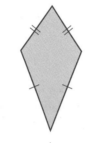

Kite
- Two pairs of adjacent sides of equal length
- One pair of equal angles
- Diagonals intersect at right angles
- One line of symmetry

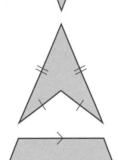

Arrowhead or Delta
- Two pairs of adjacent sides of equal length
- One pair of equal angles
- Diagonals intersect at right angles outside the shape
- One line of symmetry

Trapezium
- One pair of parallel sides
- Some trapezia have one line of symmetry

5  **Exercise 2D**

① Copy the table below and put each of these quadrilaterals in the correct column: square, rectangle, parallelogram, rhombus, kite, arrowhead and trapezium.

No lines of symmetry	One line of symmetry	Two lines of symmetry	Four lines of symmetry

2 Copy the table below and put each of these quadrilaterals in the correct column: square, rectangle, parallelogram, rhombus, kite, arrowhead and trapezium.

Rotational symmetry of order one	Rotational symmetry of order two	Rotational symmetry of order four

3 A quadrilateral has four right angles and rotational symmetry of order two. What type of quadrilateral is it?

4 A quadrilateral has rotational symmetry of order two and no lines of symmetry. What type of quadrilateral is it?

5 Rachel says:

A quadrilateral with four equal sides must be a square.

Is she right or wrong? Explain your answer.

6 Robert says:

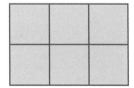

A quadrilateral with rotational symmetry of order two must be a rectangle.

Is he right or wrong? Explain your answer.

7 Sharon knows that a square is a special kind of rectangle (a rectangle with 4 equal sides). Write down the names of other quadrilaterals that could also be given to a square.

8 The three-by-two rectangle below is to be cut into squares along its grid lines:

This can be done in two different ways:

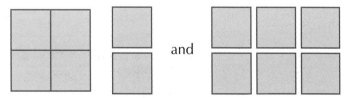

Three squares   and   Six squares

Use squared paper to show the number of ways different sizes of rectangles can be cut into squares.

1   The tree classification diagram below shows how to sort a set of triangles.

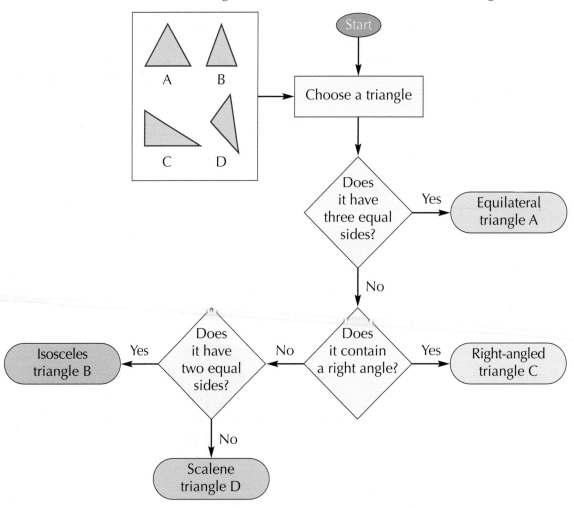

Draw a tree classification diagram to sort a given set of quadrilaterals.
Make a poster to show your diagram and display it in your classroom.

2   The instructions below are to draw the parallelogram shown.

REPEAT TWICE:

    [FORWARD 10
    TURN RIGHT 120°
    FORWARD 6
    TURN RIGHT 60°]

Write similar instructions to draw
different quadrilaterals. Choose your
own measurements for each one. If
you have access to a computer, you
may be able to draw the shapes by
using programs such as LOGO.

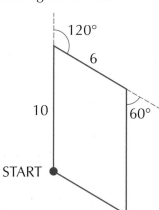

Constructions

The following examples are four important geometric constructions. Carefully work through them yourself. They are useful because they give exact measurements and are therefore used by architects and in design and technology. You will need a sharp pencil, straight edge (or ruler), compasses and a protractor. Leave all your construction lines on the diagrams.

Example 2.6 ▷ *To construct the mid-point and the perpendicular bisector of the line AB:*

- Draw a line segment AB of any length.
- Set compasses to any radius greater than half the length of AB.
- Draw two arcs, with the centre at A, one above and one below AB.
- With compasses set at the same radius, draw two arcs with the centre at B, to intersect the first two arcs at C and D.
- Join C and D to intersect AB at X. X is the mid-point of the line AB.
- The line CD is the perpendicular bisector of the line AB.

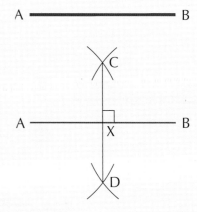

Example 2.7 ▷ *To construct the bisector of the angle ABC:*

- Draw an angle ($\angle$) ABC of any size.
- Set compasses to any radius and, with the centre at B, draw an arc to intersect BC at X and AB at Y.
- With compasses set to any radius, draw two arcs with the centres at X and Y, to intersect at Z.
- Join BZ.
- BZ is the bisector of the angle ABC.
- Then $\angle$ABZ = $\angle$CBZ.

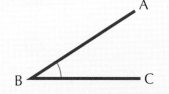

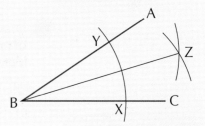

Example 2.8 ▷ *To construct the perpendicular from a point P to a line segment AB:*

- Set compasses to any suitable radius and draw arcs from P to intersect AB at X and Y.
- With compasses set at the same radius, draw arcs with the centres at X and Y to intersect at Z below AB.
- Join PZ.
- PZ is perpendicular to AB.

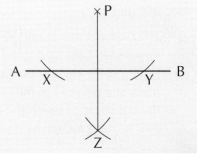

Example 2.9 ▶ *To construct the perpendicular from a point Q on a line segment XY:*

- Set compasses to a radius that is less than half the length of XY with the centre at Q. Draw two arcs on either side of Q to intersect XY at A and B. (You may have to extend the line XY slightly.)
- Set compasses to a radius that is greater than half the length of XY and, with the centres at A and B, draw arcs above and below XY to intersect at C and D.
- Join CD.
- CD is the perpendicular from the point Q.

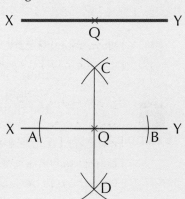

Exercise 2E

1. Draw a line AB 10 cm in length. Using compasses, construct the perpendicular bisector of the line.

2. Draw a line CD of any length. Using compasses, construct the perpendicular bisector of the line.

3. Using a protractor, draw an angle of 80°. Using compasses, construct the angle bisector of this angle. Measure the two angles formed to check that they are both 40°.

4. Using a protractor, draw an angle of 140°. Using compasses, construct the angle bisector of this angle. Measure the two angles formed to check that they are both 70°.

5. Draw a line XY that is 8 cm in length.

   a Construct the perpendicular bisector of XY.

   b By measuring the length of the perpendicular bisector, draw a rhombus with diagonals of length 8 cm and 5 cm.

6. Draw a circle of radius 6 cm and centre O. Draw a line AB of any length across the circle, as in the diagram (AB is called a chord). Construct the perpendicular from O to the line AB. Extend the perpendicular, if necessary, to make a diameter of the circle.

Extension Work

1. To construct an angle of 60°:

   Draw a line AB of any length. Set your compasses to a radius of about 4 cm. With centre at A, draw a large arc to intersect the line at X. Using the same radius and, with the centre at X, draw an arc to intersect the first arc at Y. Join A and Y: ∠YAX is 60°.

   Explain how you could use this construction to construct angles of 30° and 15°.

2. To construct the inscribed circle of a triangle:

   Draw a triangle ABC with sides of any length. Construct the angle bisectors for each of the three angles. The three angle bisectors will meet at a point O in the centre of the triangle. Using O as the centre, draw a circle to touch the three sides of the triangle.

   The circle is known as the inscribed circle of the triangle.

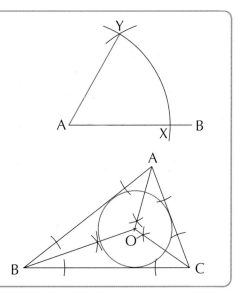

5 I know that the sum of the interior angles of a triangle is 180°.
I can identify the symmetry properties of 2-D shapes.

6 I know that the sum of the interior angles of a quadrilateral is 360°.
I know the angle properties of parallel lines.
I know how to use the properties of quadrilaterals.
I can classify the different types of quadrilaterals.
I know how to devise instructions for a computer to generate 2-D shapes.
I can construct perpendicular lines and bisect angles.

National Test questions

1 2005 3–5 Paper 1

The diagram shows triangle PQR.

Work out the sizes of angles a, b and c.

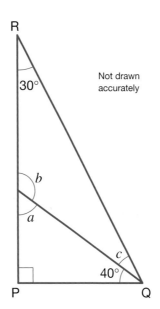

Not drawn accurately

2 *2001 Paper 1*

The diagram (not drawn accurately) shows two isosceles triangles inside a parallelogram.

a On a copy of the diagram, mark another angle that is 75°.
Label it 75°.

b Calculate the size of the angle marked k. Show your working.

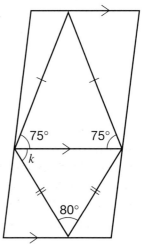

3   *2006 4–6 Paper 2*

Look at the diagram below, made from four straight lines.

The lines marked with arrows are parallel.

Work out the sizes of the angles marked with letters.

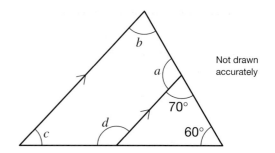

Not drawn accurately

4   *1999 Paper 1*

The shape shown has three identical white tiles and three identical grey tiles.

The sides of each tile are all the same length. Opposite sides of each tile are parallel. One of the angles is 70°.

  a Calculate the size of angle k.

  b Calculate the size of angle m.
      Show your working.

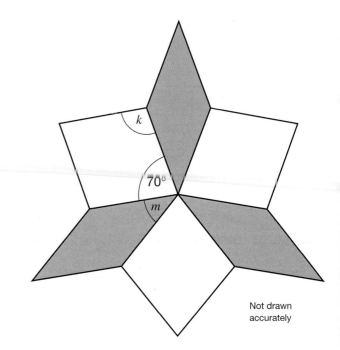

Not drawn accurately

5   *2003 4–6 Paper 1*

The drawing shows how shapes A and B fit together to make a **right-angled** triangle.

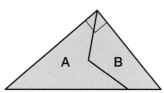

Work out the size of each of the angles in shape B.

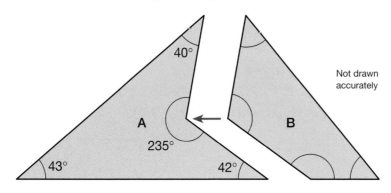

Not drawn accurately

6 *2002 Paper 2*

The diagram shows a rectangle:

Work out the size of angle a.
You must show your working.

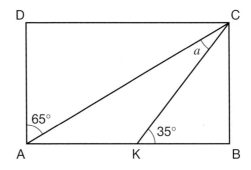

7 *2005 4–6 Paper 1*

This shape has been made from two congruent
isosceles triangles.

What is the size of angle p?

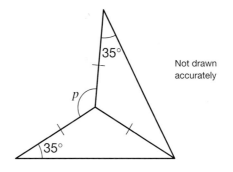

Not drawn
accurately

CHAPTER **3** Statistics **1**

This chapter is going to show you

- How to work with a probability scale
- How to work out probabilities in different situations
- How to use experimental probability to make predictions

What you should already know

- Some basic ideas about chance and probability
- How to collect data from a simple experiment
- How to record data in a table or chart

Probability

Look at the pictures. Which one is most likely to happen where you live today?

We use probability to decide how likely it is that different events will happen.

Example 3.1 ▷ Here are some words we use when talking about whether something may happen:

very likely, unlikely, certain, impossible, an even chance, very unlikely, likely

The two complete opposites here are impossible and certain, with an even chance (evens) in the middle, and so these can be given in the order:

impossible, very unlikely, unlikely, **evens**, likely, very likely, **certain**

Example 3.2 ▷ Which is more likely to happen: Flipping a tail on a coin or rolling a number less than 5 on a dice?

A coin can only land two ways (heads or tails), so provided the coin is fair, there is an even chance of landing on a tail.

On a dice there are four numbers less than 5 and two numbers that are not, so there is more than an even chance of rolling a number less than 5. So, rolling a number less than 5 is more likely than getting tails when a coin is flipped.

Exercise 3A

1. Write down an event for which the outcome is:

   a   certain.   b   impossible.   c   fifty-fifty chance.   d   very unlikely.

   e   likely.   f   very likely.   g   unlikely.

2. Here are two grids:

   Grid 1   Grid 2

   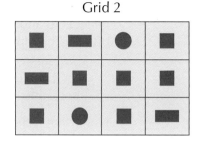

   A shape is picked at random. Copy and complete the following sentences.

   a   Picking a ...... from Grid ... is impossible.

   b   Picking a ...... from Grid ... is likely.

   c   Picking a ...... from Grid ... is unlikely.

   d   Picking a ...... from Grid ... is highly unlikely.

   e   Picking a ...... from Grid ... is fifty-fifty.

3. Bag A contains 10 red marbles, 5 blue marbles
   and 5 green marbles. Bag B contains 8 red
   marbles, 2 blue marbles and no green marbles.
   A girl wants to pick a marble at random from a
   bag. Which bag should she choose to have the
   better chance of:

   Bag A   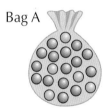   Bag B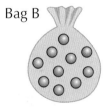

   a   a red marble?   b   a blue marble?   c   a green marble?

   Explain your answers.

4. A coin is flipped 60 times. It lands on heads 36 times.

   Do you think that the coin is biased? Explain your answer.

5. If I roll two dice, I have more chance of getting a total greater than 6 than a total less
   than 6.

   Is this correct?

   Explain your answer.

Extension   Work

Carry out a survey by asking many people in your class to give you five
different numbers between 1 and 20.

Record the results and write a brief report to say whether you think that each
number has the same chance of being chosen.

Probability scales

The probability of an event:

$$P(\text{event}) = \frac{\text{Number of outcomes in the event}}{\text{Total number of all possible outcomes}}$$

Probabilities can be written as either fractions or decimals. They always take values between 0 and 1, including 0 and 1. The probability of an event happening can be shown on the probability scale:

```
 |    |    |    |    |    |    |    |    |    |    |
 0   0.1  0.2  0.3  0.4  0.5  0.6  0.7  0.8  0.9   1
Impossible                Evens                 Certain
```

If an event is the complete opposite of another event, such as raining and not raining, then the probabilities of each event add up to 1.

Look at the probability scale and see how many pairs of decimals you can find that add up to 1.

Example 0.0 ▷

The probability that a woman washes her car on Sunday is 0.7. What is the probability that she does not wash her car?

These two events are opposites of each other, so the probabilities add up to 1. The probability that she does not wash her car is $1 - 0.7 = 0.3$.

Example 3.4 ▷

A girl plays a game of tennis. The probability that she wins is $\frac{2}{3}$. What is the probability that she loses?

Probability of not winning (losing) $= 1 - \frac{2}{3}$
$= \frac{1}{3}$

Exercise 3B

1 Here is a probability scale:

```
         A    B              C                   D
 |    |    |    |    |    |    |    |    |    |    |
 0   0.1  0.2  0.3  0.4  0.5  0.6  0.7  0.8  0.9   1
```

The probability of events A, B, C and D happening are shown on the scale. Copy the scale and mark on it the probabilities of A, B, C and D **not** happening.

2 Copy and complete the table.

Event	Probability of event occurring (p)	Probability of event not occurring ($1 - p$)
A	$\frac{1}{4}$	
B	$\frac{1}{3}$	
C	$\frac{3}{4}$	
D	$\frac{1}{10}$	
E	$\frac{2}{15}$	
F	$\frac{7}{8}$	
G	$\frac{7}{9}$	

3 A card is chosen at random from a pack of 52 playing cards. Calculate the probability that it is:

a a black card. **b** an ace. **c** not an ace. **d** a diamond.

e not a diamond. **f** not a 2. **g** not a picture. **h** not a king.

I not a red card. **j** not an even number. **k** not the ace of spades.

4 In a bus station there are 24 red buses, 6 blue buses and 10 green buses. Calculate the probability that the next bus to arrive is:

a green. **b** red. **c** red or blue. **d** yellow. **e** not green.

f not red. **g** neither red nor blue. **h** not yellow.

5 A bag contains 32 counters that are either black or white. The probability that a counter is black is $\frac{1}{4}$.

How many white counters are in the bag? Explain how you worked it out.

6 Joe has 1000 tracks on his MP3 player, which comprises the following.

    250 tracks of White rock
    200 tracks of Blues
    400 tracks of Country & western
    100 tracks of Heavy rock
     50 tracks of Quiet romantic

He sets the player to play tracks at random.
What is the probability that the next track to play is:

a White rock? **b** Blues? **c** Country & western?

d Heavy rock? **e** Quiet romantic?

Extension Work

Design a spreadsheet to convert the probabilities of events happening into the probabilities that they do not happen.

Mutually exclusive events

You have a dice and are trying to throw numbers less than 4, but you are also looking for even numbers. Which number is common to both events?

When two events **overlap** like this, we say that the events are **not mutually exclusive**. This means they can both happen at once.

Example 3.5

Here is a list of events about the old lady shown:

Event A: She chooses strawberries.
Event B: She chooses red fruit.
Event C: She chooses green apples.
Event D: She chooses red apples.
Event E: She chooses oranges.

She chooses one item only. State which of the following pairs
of events are mutually exclusive.

a A and B   **b** A and E   **c** B and C   **d** B and D

a   Strawberries are red fruit, so the events are **not mutually exclusive**.

b   Strawberries are not oranges, so the events are **mutually exclusive**.

c   Green apples are not red fruit, so the events are **mutually exclusive**.

d   Red apples are red fruit, so the events are **not mutually exclusive**.

Exercise 3C

1 A number square contains the numbers from 1 to 100.

Numbers are chosen from the number square. Here is a list of events:

Event A: A number chosen is greater than 50.

Event B: A number chosen is less than 10.

Event C: A number chosen is a square number (1, 4, 9, 16, …).

Event D: A number chosen is a multiple of 5 (5, 10, 15, 20, …).

Event E: A number chosen has at least one 6 in it.

Event F: A number chosen is a factor of 100 (1, 2, 5, 10, …).

Event G: A number chosen is a triangle number (1, 3, 6, 10, …).

1	2	3	4	5	6	7	8	9	10
11	12	13	14	15	16	17	18	19	20
21	22	23	24	25	26	27	28	29	30
31	32	33	34	35	36	37	38	39	40
41	42	43	44	45	46	47	48	49	50
51	52	53	54	55	56	57	58	59	60
61	62	63	64	65	66	67	68	69	70
71	72	73	74	75	76	77	78	79	80
82	82	83	84	85	86	87	88	89	90
91	92	93	94	95	96	97	98	99	100

State whether each of the following pairs of events are mutually exclusive or not.

a   A and B   **b**   A and C   **c**   B and C   **d**   C and D

e   B and F   **f**   C and F   **g**   C and G   **h**   D and E

i   D and G   **j**   E and F   **k**   E and G   **l**   F and G

2 A sampling bottle contains 40 different coloured beads. (A sample bottle is a plastic bottle in which only one bead can be seen at a time.)

a After 20 trials a boy has seen 12 black beads and 8 white beads. Does this mean that there are only black and white beads in the bottle? Explain your answer.

b You are told that there are 20 black beads, 15 white beads and 5 red beads in the bottle. State which of the following events are mutually exclusive.

i Seeing a black bead and seeing a white bead.

ii Seeing a black bead and seeing a bead that is not white.

iii Seeing a black bead and seeing a bead that is not black.

iv Seeing any colour and seeing a red bead.

3 British coins currently are 1p, 2p, 5p, 10p, 20p, 50p, £1 and £2 coins.

A boy has two coins in his pocket.

a List all the possible different amounts of money that he could have in his pocket.

b Is he more likely to have more than 40p than he is to have less than 40p? Explain your answer.

4 Each spinner is spun.

a Complete the table to show the different pairs of scores.

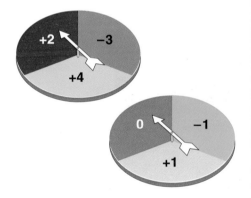

Spinner 1	Spinner 2	Total score
+2	0	2
+2	−1	1

b Gary spins both spinners. Is he:

i more likely to get a positive total than a negative total?

ii more likely to get an even total than an odd total?

Explain both your answers.

Extension Work

Imagine a horse race between two horses (called A and B). They could finish the race in two different ways, AB or BA.

Now look at a three-horse race. How many ways can they finish the race?

Extend this problem to four horses, and so on. Put your results into a table. See if you can work out a pattern to predict how many different ways a 10 horse race could finish.

When you have finished this, then you can explore what the factorial (!) button does on a calculator (this may help you to solve the horse problem).

Calculating probabilities

Look at the spinners. Which one is most likely to land on red? Remember, the answer is not how many times a colour appears, but the probability that it will appear.

$$\text{Probability of event} = \frac{\text{Number of successes}}{\text{Total number of outcomes}}$$

Sometimes you will look at more than one event happening. To do this you can use diagrams, called **sample spaces**, to help you. Look at the sample space for a coin and a dice:

	1	2	3	4	5	6
Head	H, 1	H, 2	H, 3	H, 4	H, 5	H, 6
Tail	T, 1	T, 2	T, 3	T, 4	T, 5	T, 6

You can now work out the probability of throwing both a head and a 6.

Example 3.6 ▷

An ice-cream man sells 10 different flavours of ice cream. A girl picks a tub at random (without looking). What is the probability that the girl picks her favourite flavour?

She has only one favourite, so the probability that she picks that one out of 10 flavours = $\frac{1}{10}$.

Example 3.7 ▷

The contents of Toni's shopping bags are: bag 1 – tins of spaghetti and tins of beans; bag 2 – white bread and brown bread. One item is picked from each bag. List all the combinations that could be chosen.

Beans and white bread

Spaghetti and white bread

Beans and brown bread

Spaghetti and brown bread

Exercise 3D

1. A set of cards is numbered from 1 to 50. One card is picked at random. Give the probability that it:

   a   is even.
   b   has a 7 on it.
   c   has a 3 on it.
   d   is a prime number.
   e   is a multiple of 6.
   f   is a square number.
   g   is less than 10.
   h   is a factor of 18.
   i   is a factor of 50.

2. Two pupils are chosen from a class with an equal number of boys and girls.

   a   Write down the four possible combinations that could be chosen.
   b   Jo says that the probability of choosing two boys is $\frac{1}{3}$. He is wrong. Explain why he is wrong.

3. A bag contains apples, bananas and pears. Two fruits are chosen at random. List the possible outcomes.

5

6

4 Jacket potatoes are sold either plain, with cheese or with beans. Clyde and Delroy each buy a jacket potato.

a Copy and complete the sample table:

Clyde	Delroy
plain	plain
plain	cheese

b Give the probability of:

i Clyde choosing plain.

ii Delroy choosing plain.

iii both choosing plain.

iv Clyde choosing plain and Delroy choosing beans.

v Clyde choosing beans and Delroy choosing cheese.

vi both choosing the same.

vii both not choosing plain.

viii both choosing different.

5 Two dice are rolled and the scores are added together. Copy and complete the sample space of scores.

	1	2	3	4	5	6
1	2	3				
2	3					

a What is the most likely total?

b Give the probability that the total is:

i 4   **ii** 5   **iii** 1   **iv** 12   **v** less than 7

vi less than or equal to 7   **vii** greater than or equal to 10

viii even   **ix** 6 or 8   **x** greater than 5

Extension Work

Make up your own question using two different spinners as follows. Draw the spinners and put different numbers on each section. Now make a sample space diagram and write three of your own questions followed by the answers.

Experimental probability

Will the train be late again today?

Look at the picture. How could you estimate the probability that a train will be late?

You could keep a record of the number of times that the train arrives late over a period of 10 days, and then use these results to estimate the probability that it will be late in future.

$$\text{Experimental probability} = \frac{\text{Number of events in trials}}{\text{Total number of trials carried out}}$$

Example 3.8 ▷ An electrician wants to estimate the probability that a new light bulb lasts for less than 1 month. He fits 20 new bulbs and 3 of them fail within 1 month. What is his estimate of the probability that a new light bulb fails?

3 out of 20 bulbs fail within 1 month, so his experimental probability = $\frac{3}{20}$.

Example 3.9 ▷ A dentist keeps a record of the number of fillings she gives her patients over 2 weeks. Here are her results:

Number of fillings	None	1	More than 1
Number of patients	80	54	16

Estimate the probability that a patient does not need a filling (there are 150 records altogether).

$$\text{Experimental probability} = \frac{80}{150}$$
$$= \frac{8}{15}$$

Example 3.10 ▷ A company manufactures items for computers. The number of faulty items is recorded as shown below.

Number of items produced	Number of faulty items	Experimental probability
100	8	0.08
200	20	
500	45	
1000	82	

a   Copy and complete the table.

b   Which is the best estimate of the probability of an item being faulty? Explain your answer.

a

Number of items produced	Number of faulty items	Experimental probability
100	8	0.08
200	20	0.1
500	45	0.09
1000	82	0.082

b   The last result (0.082), as the experiment is based on more results.

Exercise 3E

1 A boy decides to carry out an experiment to estimate the probability of a drawing pin landing with the pin pointing up. He drops 50 drawing pins and records the result. He then repeats the experiment several times. His results are recorded in a table as shown (on the right).

Number of drawing pins	Number pointing up
50	32
100	72
150	106
200	139
250	175

a From the results, would you say that there is a greater chance of a drawing pin landing point up or point down? Explain your answer.

b Which result is the most reliable and why?

c From these data, how could he estimate the probability of a drawing pin landing point up?

d What would his answer be?

e How could he improve the experiment?

2 A girl wishes to test whether a dice is biased. She rolls the dice 60 times. The results are shown in the table below.

Score	1	2	3	4	5	6
Frequency	6	12	10	9	15	8

a Do you think the dice is biased? Give a reason for your answer.

b How could she improve the experiment?

c From the results, estimate the probability of rolling a 1.

d From the results, estimate the probability of rolling a 1 or a 4.

3 Fay started an experiment to find the probability of spinning a coin and getting a head or a tail. Below are her results.

	Number of trials	Heads	Tails	P(H)	P(T)
First 20	20	⊮⊮ III 8	⊮⊮ ⊮⊮ II 12	$\frac{8}{20} = 0.4$	$\frac{12}{20} = 0.6$
Next 20	40	⊮⊮ ⊮⊮ I 11	⊮⊮ IIII 9	$\frac{19}{40} = 0.475$	$\frac{21}{40} = 0.525$

a Use your own coin to spin the next 20, creating the next part of Fay's tally chart.

b Complete the chart, writing down the P(H) and P(T) from all 60 trials.

c Repeat the above for the next 20 (giving a total of 80).

d What do you notice about the P(H)?

Extension Work

Decide on an experiment of your own. Write down a report of how you would carry it out and how you would record your results.

LEVEL BOOSTER

5 I can calculate probabilities using equally likely outcomes.

6 I can calculate probability from experimental data.

I know what mutually exclusive events are.

I can use the probability of an event to calculate the probability that the event does not happen.

National Test questions

1 *2005 4–6 Paper 2*

    a Aidan puts 2 white counters and 1 black counter in a bag.

       He is going to take one counter without looking.

       What is the **probability** that the counter will be **black**?

    b Aidan puts the counter back in the bag and then puts **more black** counters in the bag.

       He is going to take one counter **without** looking.

       The probability that the counter will be black is now $\frac{2}{3}$.

       How many more black counters did Aidan put in the bag?

2 *2000 Paper 2*

In each box of cereal there is a free gift of a card.

You cannot tell which card will be in a box. Each card is equally likely.

There are four different cards: A, B, C or D

    a Zoe needs card A.

       Her brother Paul needs cards C and D.

       They buy one box of cereal.

       What is the probability that the card is one that Zoe needs?

       What is the probability that the card is one that Paul needs?

    b Then their mother opens the box. She tells them the card is not card A.

       Now what is the probability the card is one that Zoe needs?

       What is the probability that the card is one that Paul needs?

3 *2007 5–7 Paper 1*

Fred had a bag of sweets.

> **Contents:**
>
> 3 yellow sweets
>
> 5 green sweets
>
> 7 red sweets
>
> 4 purple sweets
>
> 1 black sweet

He is going to take a sweet from the bag at random.

a What is the probability that Fred will get a black sweet?

b Write the missing colour from the sentence below.

The probability that Fred will get a _____ sweet is $\frac{1}{4}$.

4 *2000 Paper 1*

There are some cubes in a bag. The cubes are either red (R) or black (B). The teacher says:

> If you take a cube at random out of the bag, the probabiltiy that it will be **red** is $\frac{1}{5}$

a What is the probability that the cube will be black?

b A pupil takes one cube out of the bag. It is red.

What is the smallest number of black cubes there could be in the bag?

c Then the pupil takes another cube out of the bag. It is also red.

From this new information, what is the smallest number of black cubes there could be in the bag?

d A different bag has blue (B), green (G) and yellow (Y) cubes in it. There is at least one of each of the three colours.

The teacher says:

> If you take a cube at random out of the bag, the probabiltiy that it will be **blue** is $\frac{3}{5}$

There are 20 cubes in the bag.

What is the greatest number of yellow cubes there could be in the bag? Show your working.

Fun in the fairground

The fair has come to town.

Hoopla

You can buy 5 hoops for £1.25.

You win a prize by throwing a hoop over that prize, but it must also go over the base that the prize is standing on!

Ben spent some time watching people have a go at this stall and started to count how many goes they had and how many times someone won.

The table below shows his results.

Prize	Number of throws	Number of wins
Watch	320	1
£10 note	240	4
£1 coin	80	2

Hook a duck

This is a game where plastic ducks float around a central stall. They all have numbers stuck to their underside which cannot be seen until hooked up on a stick and presented to the stall holder.

In the game, if the number under the duck is a:

1 – you win a lollipop   2 – you win a yo-yo
5 – you win a cuddly toy

Each time a duck is hooked, it is replaced in the water.

Cindy, the stall holder, set up the stall one week with:

- 45 plastic ducks
- Only one of which had the number 5 underneath
- Nine had the number 2 underneath
- All the rest had a number 1 underneath

Cindy charged 40p for one stick, to hook up just one duck.

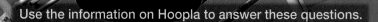
Use the information on Hoopla to answer these questions.

1 What income would these throws have made for the stall?

2 From the results shown, what is the probability of someone aiming for and winning a:
  a £1 coin?
  b £10 note?
  c watch?

3 What would you say is the chance of someone winning a prize with:
  a one hoop?
  b five hoops?

4 After watching this, Ben decided to try for a £10 note.

He bought 25 hoops and all his throws were aimed at the £10 note.
  a How much did this cost him?
  b What is his probability of winning a £10 note?

5 On a Saturday afternoon, the stall would expect about 500 people to buy a set of hoops.

Assuming that the throws would have been aimed at the various prizes in the same proportion as Ben observed:
  a how many of each prize would the stall expect to have to give away?
  b how much income would be generated from the 500 people?
  c if the watches cost £18, how much profit would the stall expect to make on a Saturday afternoon?

Use the information on Hook a duck to answer these questions.

6 What is the probability of winning:

a a cuddly toy?

b a yo-yo?

c a lollipop?

7 What is the probability of winning anything other than a lollipop?

8 Tom wanted his sister, Julie, to win a yo-yo.

a How many ducks should Julie hook to expect to have picked up at least one with a number 2 underneath?

b How much will it cost Tom to pay for the number of ducks hooked to expect Julie to win a yo-yo?

9 Before lunch on Sunday, Cindy took £100 from the stall.

a How many ducks had been hooked that morning?

b How many cuddly toys would you expect Cindy to have given away that morning?

c How many yo-yos would you expect Cindy to have given away that morning?

10 Cindy bought in the cuddly toys for £4 each and the yo-yos for 50p each. She gets the lollipops in a jar of 100 for £4.

Cindy expects to take £250 on a Friday night.

a How many ducks will she expect to be hooked that night?

b How many lollipops will she expect to give away that evening?

c How many yo-yos will she expect to give away that evening?

d How many cuddly toys will she expect to give away that evening?

e What will be the value of all the prizes she expects to give away that night?

CHAPTER 4 Number 2

<table>
<tr><td>

This chapter is going to show you

- More about working with fractions, decimals and percentages
- How to calculate percentage increase and decrease
- How to compare proportions using fractions and decimals

</td><td>

What you should already know

- The equivalences of common fractions, decimals and percentages
- How to add and subtract simple fractions with a common denominator
- How to calculate fractions and percentages of quantities

</td></tr>
</table>

Fractions and decimals

These diagrams show shapes with various fractions of them shaded. Can you write them as a decimal, fraction and percentage?

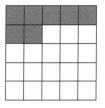 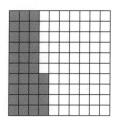 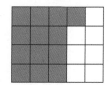

Example 4.1

Work out the following decimals as fractions.

  a   0.65   **b**   0.475

  a $0.65 = \frac{65}{100} = \frac{13}{20}$ (cancel by 5)   **b** $0.475 = \frac{475}{1000} = \frac{19}{40}$

Example 4.2

Work out the following fractions as decimals.

  a $\frac{2}{5}$ **b** $\frac{13}{16}$ **c** $\frac{4}{7}$

  a $\frac{2}{5} = 0.4$ (you should know this)

  b $\frac{13}{16} = 13 \div 16 = 0.8125$ (this is a terminating decimal because it ends without repeating itself)

  c $\frac{4}{7} = 4 \div 7 = 0.571428571 \ldots = 0.\dot{5}7142\dot{8}$ (this is a recurring decimal because the six digits 5, 7, 1, 4, 2, 8 repeat infinitely; a recurring decimal is shown by the dots over the first and last recurring digits)

1. Write the following decimals as fractions with a denominator of 10, 100 or 1000 and then cancel to their simplest form if possible.

   a 0.24   b 0.45   c 0.125   d 0.348

   e 0.8   f 0.555   g 0.55   h 0.875

2. Without using a calculator, work out the value of these fractions as decimals.

   a $\frac{3}{5}$ b $\frac{3}{8}$ c $\frac{13}{20}$ d $\frac{18}{25}$

3. Use a calculator to work out, and then write down, the following terminating decimals.

   a $\frac{1}{2}$ b $\frac{1}{4}$ c $\frac{1}{5}$ d $\frac{1}{8}$

   e $\frac{1}{10}$ f $\frac{1}{16}$ g $\frac{1}{20}$ h $\frac{1}{25}$

   i $\frac{1}{40}$ j $\frac{1}{50}$

4. Use a calculator to work out, and then write down, the following recurring decimals.

   a $\frac{1}{3}$ b $\frac{1}{6}$ c $\frac{1}{7}$ d $\frac{1}{9}$

   e $\frac{1}{11}$ f $\frac{1}{12}$ g $\frac{1}{13}$ h $\frac{1}{14}$

   i $\frac{1}{15}$ j $\frac{1}{18}$

5. By looking at the denominators of the fractions in Questions 3 and 4, predict if the following fractions will be terminating or recurring decimals (and then work them out to see if you were correct).

   a $\frac{2}{3}$ b $\frac{4}{5}$ c $\frac{3}{7}$ d $\frac{2}{9}$

   e $\frac{3}{16}$ f $\frac{5}{8}$ g $\frac{7}{12}$ h $\frac{11}{14}$

   i $\frac{4}{15}$ j $\frac{39}{50}$

6. Give the larger of these pairs of fractions.

   a $\frac{7}{20}$ and $\frac{1}{3}$ b $\frac{5}{9}$ and $\frac{11}{20}$ c $\frac{7}{8}$ and $\frac{4}{5}$ d $\frac{2}{3}$ and $\frac{16}{25}$

7. Write the following lists of fractions in increasing order of size.

   a $\frac{2}{9}, \frac{13}{50}, \frac{6}{25}$ and $\frac{1}{4}$ b $\frac{5}{8}, \frac{3}{5}, \frac{17}{25}$ and $\frac{2}{3}$

8. a Use a calculator to work out $\frac{1}{9}, \frac{2}{9}, \frac{3}{9}$ and $\frac{4}{9}$ as recurring decimals.

   b Write down $\frac{5}{9}, \frac{6}{9}, \frac{7}{9}$ and $\frac{8}{9}$ as recurring decimals.

9. Work out the 'sevenths' (that is, $\frac{1}{7}, \frac{2}{7}, \frac{3}{7}, \frac{4}{7}, \frac{5}{7}, \frac{6}{7}$) as recurring decimals. Describe any patterns that you can see in the digits.

10. Work out the 'elevenths' (that is, $\frac{1}{11}, \frac{2}{11}, \frac{3}{11}, \frac{4}{11}, \frac{5}{11}, \frac{6}{11}, \frac{7}{11}, \frac{8}{11}, \frac{9}{11}, \frac{10}{11}$) as recurring decimals. Describe any patterns that you can see in the digits.

Extension **Work**

1. Describe, in words, a rule for the denominator of a terminating decimal.

2. Describe, in words, a rule for the denominator of a recurring decimal.

Adding and subtracting fractions

All of the grids below contain 100 squares. Some of the squares have been shaded in. The fraction shaded is shown below the square in its lowest terms. Use the diagrams to work out $1 - (\frac{1}{5} + \frac{7}{20} + \frac{22}{50} + \frac{1}{25})$.

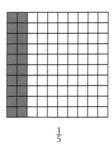
$\frac{1}{5}$

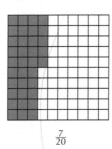
$\frac{7}{20}$

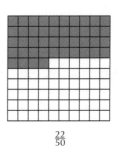
$\frac{22}{50}$

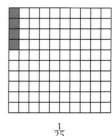
$\frac{1}{25}$

Example 4.3 ▷

Add the following.

   a $\frac{2}{5} + \frac{1}{4}$ **b** $\frac{2}{3} + \frac{2}{7}$ **c** $\frac{1}{3} + \frac{5}{6} + \frac{3}{4}$

   a The common denominator is 20, as this is the lowest common multiple of 4 and 5, hence $\frac{2}{5} + \frac{1}{4} = \frac{8}{20} + \frac{5}{20} = \frac{13}{20}$

   b The common denominator is 21, hence $\frac{2}{3} + \frac{2}{7} = \frac{14}{21} + \frac{6}{21} = \frac{20}{21}$

   c The common denominator is 12, hence $\frac{1}{3} + \frac{5}{6} + \frac{3}{4} = \frac{4}{12} + \frac{10}{12} + \frac{9}{12} = \frac{23}{12} = 1\frac{11}{12}$

       Note that the last answer is a top-heavy fraction so should be written as a mixed number.

Example 4.4 ▷

Subtract the following.

   a $\frac{2}{3} - \frac{1}{4}$ **b** $\frac{5}{6} - \frac{4}{9}$

   a Common denominator is 12, so $\frac{2}{3} - \frac{1}{4} = \frac{8}{12} - \frac{3}{12} = \frac{5}{12}$

   b Common denominator is 18, so $\frac{5}{6} - \frac{4}{9} = \frac{15}{18} - \frac{8}{18} = \frac{7}{18}$

Exercise 4B

① Find the lowest common multiple of the following pairs of numbers.

   a (3, 4)   **b** (5, 6)   **c** (3, 5)   **d** (2, 3)

   e (4, 5)   **f** (2, 4)   **g** (6, 9)   **h** (4, 6)

② Add the following fractions.

   a $\frac{2}{3} + \frac{1}{4}$ **b** $\frac{2}{5} + \frac{1}{6}$ **c** $\frac{1}{3} + \frac{2}{5}$ **d** $\frac{1}{3} + \frac{1}{2}$

   e $\frac{1}{5} + \frac{1}{4}$ **f** $\frac{1}{2} + \frac{1}{4}$ **g** $\frac{5}{6} + \frac{1}{9}$ **h** $\frac{1}{6} + \frac{1}{4}$

③ Subtract the following fractions.

   a $\frac{1}{3} - \frac{1}{4}$ **b** $\frac{2}{5} - \frac{1}{6}$ **c** $\frac{2}{5} - \frac{1}{3}$ **d** $\frac{1}{2} - \frac{1}{3}$

   e $\frac{2}{5} - \frac{1}{4}$ **f** $\frac{1}{2} - \frac{1}{4}$ **g** $\frac{5}{6} - \frac{1}{9}$ **h** $\frac{5}{6} - \frac{3}{4}$

4 Convert the following fractions to equivalent fractions with a common denominator, and then work out the answer, cancelling down or writing as a mixed number if appropriate.

a $\frac{1}{3} + \frac{1}{4}$ b $\frac{1}{6} + \frac{1}{3}$ c $\frac{3}{10} + \frac{1}{4}$ d $\frac{1}{8} + \frac{5}{6}$

e $\frac{4}{15} + \frac{3}{10}$ f $\frac{7}{8} + \frac{5}{6}$ g $\frac{7}{12} + \frac{1}{4}$ h $\frac{3}{4} + \frac{1}{3} + \frac{1}{2}$

i $\frac{2}{3} - \frac{1}{8}$ j $\frac{5}{6} - \frac{1}{3}$ k $\frac{3}{10} - \frac{1}{4}$ l $\frac{8}{9} - \frac{1}{6}$

m $\frac{4}{15} - \frac{1}{10}$ n $\frac{7}{8} - \frac{5}{6}$ o $\frac{7}{12} - \frac{1}{4}$ p $\frac{3}{4} + \frac{1}{3} - \frac{1}{2}$

5 Convert the following fractions to equivalent fractions with a common denominator, and then work out the answer, cancelling down or writing as a mixed number if appropriate.

a $1\frac{1}{3} - \frac{7}{8}$ b $2\frac{2}{3} + \frac{4}{7}$ c $1\frac{2}{3} + 2\frac{1}{4}$ d $3\frac{2}{3} - 1\frac{1}{5}$

6 Copy the diagram shown and shade in (using separate parts of the diagram): $\frac{1}{12}$, $\frac{5}{24}$, $\frac{1}{8}$, $\frac{1}{4}$ and $\frac{1}{6}$ Write down the answer, in its simplest form, to $1 - (\frac{1}{12} + \frac{5}{24} + \frac{1}{8} + \frac{1}{4} + \frac{1}{6})$.

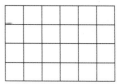

Extension Work

The ancient Egyptians only used unit fractions, that is fractions with a numerator of 1. So they would write $\frac{5}{8}$ as $\frac{1}{2} + \frac{1}{8}$.

1 Write the following as the sum of two unit fractions.

a $\frac{3}{8}$ b $\frac{3}{4}$

c $\frac{7}{12}$ d $\frac{2}{3}$

2 Write the following as the sum of three unit fractions.

a $\frac{7}{8}$ b $\frac{5}{6}$

c $\frac{5}{8}$ d $\frac{23}{24}$

Multiplying and dividing fractions

You can use grids to work out fractions of quantities.

This grid shows that $\frac{1}{4}$ of 24 is equal to 6:

This grid shows that $\frac{2}{3}$ of 24 is equal to 16:

Example 4.5 ▶ Use this grid to work out the following.

a $\frac{1}{3}$ of 30 **b** $\frac{3}{10}$ of 30

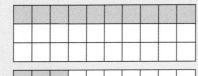

a

$\frac{1}{3}$ of 30 = 10

b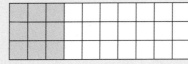

$\frac{3}{10}$ of 30 = 9

Example 4.6 ▶ Work out the following.

a $\frac{3}{4}$ of £28 **b** $5 \times \frac{2}{3}$ **c** $\frac{2}{3} \div 6$

a $\frac{1}{4}$ of £28 = £7. So $\frac{3}{4}$ of £28 = 3 × £7 = £21

b $5 \times \frac{2}{3} = \frac{10}{3} = 3\frac{1}{3}$

c $\frac{2}{3} \div 6 = \frac{2}{18}$

Exercise 4C

1 Use grids to work out the following.

a $\frac{1}{8}$ of 32 **b** $\frac{3}{8}$ of 32 **c** $\frac{1}{4}$ of 32 **d** $\frac{2}{4}$ of 32

e $\frac{1}{5}$ of 25 **f** $\frac{3}{5}$ of 25 **g** $\frac{2}{3}$ of 45 **h** $\frac{5}{6}$ of 120

2 Work out the following.

a $\frac{5}{8}$ of £32 **b** $\frac{3}{16}$ of 64 kg **c** $\frac{2}{3}$ of £45 **d** $\frac{5}{6}$ of 240 cm

e $\frac{6}{7}$ of £28 **f** $\frac{9}{10}$ of 40 grams **g** $\frac{3}{8}$ of £72 **h** $\frac{3}{4}$ of 48 km

3 Work out (cancelling down or writing as a mixed number as appropriate) the following.

a $5 \times \frac{3}{4}$ **b** $7 \times \frac{4}{5}$ **c** $9 \times \frac{2}{3}$ **d** $4 \times \frac{7}{8}$

e $8 \times \frac{9}{10}$ **f** $6 \times \frac{3}{7}$ **g** $9 \times \frac{5}{6}$ **h** $10 \times \frac{3}{4}$

4 Work out the following.

a $\frac{3}{4} \div 5$ **b** $\frac{4}{5} \div 8$ **c** $\frac{2}{3} \div 6$ **d** $\frac{5}{9} \div 7$

e $\frac{2}{7} \div 5$ **f** $\frac{8}{9} \div 2$ **g** $\frac{3}{5} \div 7$ **h** $\frac{7}{8} \div 6$

5 Copy and complete the following sentence.

Multiplying by a fraction between 0 and 1 makes the answer ......

6 Copy and complete the following sentence.

Dividing a fraction between 0 and 1 by a whole number makes the answer ......

Extension Work

1 Put these in order of size, smallest to biggest.

$24 \times \frac{5}{8}$ $36 \times \frac{1}{4}$ $35 \times \frac{2}{7}$

2 Put these in order of size, smallest to biggest.

$\frac{3}{8} \div 4$ $\frac{1}{4} \div 3$ $\frac{2}{7} \div 5$

Percentages

Example 4.7 ▷ Without using a calculator find:

    a   the percentage of 25 that 18 is.   **b**   the percentage of 300 that 39 is.

    a   Write as a fraction $\frac{18}{25}$. Multiply the top and bottom by 4, which gives $\frac{72}{100}$. So 18 is 72% of 25.

    b   Write as a fraction $\frac{39}{300}$. Cancel the top and bottom by 3, which gives $\frac{13}{100}$. So 39 is 13% of 300.

Example 4.8 ▷ Find:

    a   what percentage of 80 is 38.   **b**   what percentage of 64 is 14.

    a   Write as a fraction $\frac{38}{80}$. Convert to a percentage by dividing through and multiplying by 100, which gives $47\frac{1}{2}\%$.

    b   Write as a fraction $\frac{14}{64}$. Convert to a percentage by dividing through and multiplying by 100, which gives 22% (rounded off from 21.875).

Example 4.9 ▷ Ashram scored 39 out of 50 in a Physics test, 56 out of 70 in a Chemistry test and 69 out of 90 in a Biology test. In which science did he do best?

Convert each mark to a percentage:

    Physics   = 78%

    Chemistry = 80%

    Biology   = 77% (rounded off)

So Chemistry was the best mark.

Exercise 4D

1 Without using a calculator, work out what percentage the first quantity is of the second for the following.

    a   32 out of 50   **b**   17 out of 20   **c**   24 out of 40   **d**   16 out of 25

    e   122 out of 200   **f**   93 out of 300   **g**   640 out of 1000   **h**   18 out of 25

2 Use a calculator to work out what percentage the first quantity is of the second (round off to the nearest percent if necessary).

    a   33 out of 60   **b**   18 out of 80   **c**   25 out of 75   **d**   26 out of 65

    e   56 out of 120   **f**   84 out of 150   **g**   62 out of 350   **h**   48 out of 129

3 In the SATs test, Trevor scored 39 out of 60 in Maths, 42 out of 70 in English and 54 out of 80 in Science. Convert all these scores to a percentage. In which test did Trevor do best?

4 In a Maths exam worth 80 marks, 11 marks are allocated to Number, 34 marks are allocated to Algebra, 23 marks are allocated to Geometry and 12 marks are allocated to Statistics. Work out the percentage allocated to each topic (round the answers off to the nearest percent) and add these up. Why is the total more than 100%?

5 A table costs a carpenter £120 to make. He sells it for £192.
  a How much profit did he make?
  b What percentage was the profit of the cost price?

 6 A dealer buys a painting for £5500. He sells it at a loss for £5000.
  a How much did he lose?
  b What percentage of the original price was the loss?

 7 Mr Wilson pays £60 a month to cover his electricity, gas and oil bills. Electricity costs £24, gas costs £21 and the rest is for oil. What percentage of the total does each fuel cost?

 8 My phone bill last month was £45. Of this, £13 went on Internet calls, £24 went on long-distance calls and the rest went on local calls. What percentage of the bill was for each of these types of call?

 9 Last week the Smith family had a bill of £110.57 at the supermarket. £65.68 was spent on food, £35.88 on drinks and £9.01 on cleaning products. Work out what percentage of the total bill was for food, drinks and cleaning products (round off the answers to the nearest percent). Add the three percentages up. Why do they not total 100%?

 10 Fred drove from Barnsley to Portsmouth. The total distance was 245 miles. 32 miles of this was on B roads, 145 miles on A roads and 68 miles on motorways. What percentage of the journey was on each type of road?

Extension Work

1 Write down 20% of 100.

2 Write down 20% of 120.

3 If £100 is increased by 20%, how much do you have?

4 If £120 is decreased by 20%, how much do you have?

5 Draw a poster to explain why a 20% increase followed by a 20% decrease does not return you to the value you started with.

Percentage increase and decrease

SPORTY SHOES
$\frac{1}{3}$ off all trainers

SHOES-FOR-YOU
30% off all trainers

Which shop gives the better value?

Example 4.10

a A clothes shop has a sale and reduces its prices by 20%. How much is the sale price of:

   i a jacket originally costing £45?   **ii** a dress originally costing £125?

   i 20% of 45 is 2 × 10% of 45 = 2 × 4.5 = 9. So the jacket costs
£45 – £9 = £36.

   ii 20% of 125 is 2 × 10% of 125 = 2 × 12.50 = 25. So the dress costs
£125 – £25 = £100.

b A company gives all its workers a 5% pay rise. How much is the new wage of:

   i Joan, who originally earned £240 per week?

   ii Jack, who originally earned £6.60 per hour?

   i 5% of 240 is $\frac{1}{2}$ × 10% of 240 = $\frac{1}{2}$ × 24 = 12. So Joan now earns
£240 + £12 = £252 per week.

   ii 5% of 6.60 is $\frac{1}{2}$ × 10% of 6.60 = $\frac{1}{2}$ × 66p = 33p. So Jack gets
£6.60 + 33p = £6.99 per hour.

Exercise 4E

Do not use a calculator for the first four questions.

1 A bat colony has 40 bats. Over the breeding season the population increases by 30%.

   a How many new bats were born?

   b How many bats are there in the colony after the breeding season?

2 In a wood there are 20 000 midges. During the evening bats eat 45% of the midges.

   a How many midges were eaten by the bats?

   b How many midges were left after the bats had eaten?

   c What percentage of midges remain?

3 Work out the final amount when:

   a £45 is increased by 10%   **b** £48 is decreased by 10%

   c £120 is increased by 20%   **d** £90 is decreased by 20%

   e £65 is increased by 15%   **f** £110 is decreased by 15%

   g £250 is increased by 25%   **h** £300 is decreased by 25%

   i £6.80 is increased by 235%   **j** £5.40 is decreased by 15%

4 a In a sale all prices are reduced by 15%. Give the new price of items that previously cost:

   i £17.40   **ii** £26   **iii** £52.80   **iv** £74

   b An electrical company increases its prices by 5%. Give the new price of items that previously cost:

   i £230   **ii** £130   **iii** £385   **iv** £99

You may use a calculator for the rest of this exercise.

5 A petri dish contains 2400 bacteria. These increase overnight by 23%.

   a How many extra bacteria are there?

   b How many bacteria are there the next morning?

6 A rabbit colony has 230 rabbits. As a result of disease, 47% die.

    a How many rabbits die from disease?

    b How many rabbits are left after the disease?

    c What percentage of the rabbits remain?

 7 Work out the final price in euros when:

    a €65 is increased by 12%   **b** €65 is decreased by 14%

    c €126 is increased by 22%   **d** €530 is decreased by 28%

    e €95 is increased by 132%   **f** €32 is decreased by 31%

    g €207 is increased by 155%   **h** €421 is decreased by 18%

    i €6.82 is increased by 236%   **j** €5.40 is decreased by 28%

FM **8 a** In a sale all prices are reduced by $12\frac{1}{2}$%. Give the new price of items that previously cost:

      i £23.50   **ii** £66   **iii** £56.80   **iv** £124

   b An electrical company increases its prices by $17\frac{1}{2}$% so that they include value-added tax (VAT). Give the price with VAT of items that previously cost:

      i £250   **ii** £180   **iii** £284   **iv** £199

Extension **Work**

FM The government charges you VAT at $17\frac{1}{2}$% on most things you buy. Although this seems like an awkward percentage to work out, there is an easy way to do it without a calculator! We already know that it is easy to find 10%, which can be used to find 5% (divide the 10% value by 2), which can in turn be used to find $2\frac{1}{2}$% (divide the 5% value by 2), and 10% + 5% + $2\frac{1}{2}$% = $17\frac{1}{2}$%.

Find the VAT on an item that costs £24 before VAT is added.

10% of £24 = £2.40, 5% of £24 is £1.20, and $2\frac{1}{2}$% of £24 is £0.60.

So $17\frac{1}{2}$% of £24 = £2.40 + £1.20 + £0.60 = £4.20.

Work out the VAT on items that cost:

a £34   **b** £44   **c** £56   **d** £75   **e** £120   **f** £190

Real-life problems

Percentages occur in everyday life in many situations. You have already met percentage increase and decrease. Percentages are also used when buying goods on credit, working out profit and/or loss and paying tax.

Example 4.11 ▷ A car that costs £5995 can be bought on credit by paying a 25% deposit and then 24 monthly payments of £199.

    a How much will the car cost on credit?

    b What is the extra cost as a percentage of the usual price?

    a The deposit is 25% of £5995 = £1498.75. The payments are 24 × £199 = £4776. Therefore, the total paid = £1498.75 + £4776 = £6274.75.

    b The extra cost = £6274.75 − £5995 = £279.75. This as a percentage of £5995 is (279.75 ÷ 5995) × 100 = 4.7%.

Example 4.12 ▷ A jeweller makes a brooch for £250 and sells it for £450. What is the percentage profit?

The profit is £450 − £250 = £200, which as a percentage of £250 is
200 ÷ 250 × 100 = 80%.

Example 4.13 ▷ Jeremy earns £18 000. His tax allowance is £3800. He pays tax on the rest at 22%. How much tax does he pay?

Taxable income = £18 000 − £3800 = £14 200. The tax paid is 22% of £14 200, that is (£14 200 × 22) ÷ 100 = £3124.

Exercise 4F

FM **1** A mountain bike that normally costs £479.99 can be bought using three different plans.

Plan	Deposit	Number of payments	Each payment
A	20%	24	£22
B	50%	12	£20
C	10%	36	£18

a Work out how much the bike costs using each plan.
b Work out the percentage of the original price that each plan costs.

2 A shop buys a radio for £55 and sells it for £66. Work out the percentage profit made by the shop.

3 A CD costs £10.99. The shop paid £8.50 for it. What is the percentage profit?

FM **4** A car that costs £6995 can be bought by paying a 15% deposit, followed by 23 monthly payments of £189 and a final payment of £1900.
a How much will the car cost using the credit scheme?
b What percentage of the original cost is the extra cost on the credit scheme?

FM **5** Work out the tax paid by the following people.

Person	Income	Tax allowance	Tax rate
Ada	£25 000	£4700	22%
Bert	£32 000	£5300	25%
Carmine	£10 000	£3850	15%
Derek	£12 000	£4000	22%
Ethel	£45 000	£7000	40%

6 A shop sells a toaster for £19.99 in a sale. It cost the shop £25. What is the percentage loss?

FM **7** **a** What is £10 decreased by 10%?
b Decrease your answer to **a** by 10%.

c What is £10 decreased by 20%?

d A shirt in a clothes shop is reduced from its original price by 20% because it has a button missing. The shop is offering a further 15% off all marked prices in a sale. John the shop assistant says:

> I don't need to work out the two reductions one after the other, I can just take 35% off the original price.

Is John correct? Explain your answer.

(FM) **8** An insurance policy for a motorbike is £335. It can be paid for by a 25% deposit and then five payments of £55.25.

    a How much does the policy cost using the scheme?

    b What percentage is the extra cost of the original cost of the policy?

(FM) **9** Mrs Smith has an annual income of £28 000. Her tax allowance is £4500. She pays tax at 22%.

    a How much tax does she pay?

    b It is discovered that her tax allowance should have been £6000. How much tax does she get back?

(FM) **10** A TV costs £450. The shop has an offer '40% deposit and then 12 equal payments, one each month, for a year'.

    a How much is the deposit?   **b** How much is each payment?

(FM) **11** Which of these schemes to buy a three-piece suite worth £999 is cheapest?

    Scheme A: No deposit followed by 24 payments of £56.

    Scheme B: 25% deposit followed by 24 payments of £32.

Give a reason why someone might prefer scheme A.

LEVEL BOOSTER

5
I can work out lowest common multiples.
I can calculate a fraction of a quantity.
I can calculate percentages of a quantity.
I can multiply a fraction by a whole number (integer).

6
I can change fractions to decimals.
I can add and subtract fractions with different denominators.
I can calculate one quantity as a percentage of another.
I can use percentages to solve real-life problems.

1 *2007 5–7 Paper 1*

a Write down the missing numbers from the following:

50% of 80 = ...

5% of 80 = ...

1% of 80 = ...

b Work out 56% of 80.

You can use part **a** to help you.

FM **2** *2006 5–7 Paper 1*

a Work out the missing values:

10% of 84 = ...

5% of 84 = ...

$2\frac{1}{2}$% of 84 = ...

b The cost of a CD player is £84 **plus** $17\frac{1}{2}$% tax.

What is the **total** cost of the CD player?

You can use part **a** to help you.

3 *2004 6–8 Paper 2*

In 2001 the average yearly wage was **£21 842**.
On average, people spent **£1644** on their family holiday.

What percentage of the average yearly wage is that?

Show your working.

4 *2006 6–8 Paper 2*

Kate asked people if they read a daily newspaper.
Then she wrote this table to show her results.

The values in the table **cannot** all be correct.

No	80 people = 40%
Yes	126 people = 60%

a The error could be in the number of people.

Copy and complete each table to show what the correct numbers could be.

No	80 people = 40%
Yes	... people = 60%

No	... people = 40%
Yes	126 people = 60%

b The error could be in the percentages.

Copy and complete the table with the correct percentages.

No	80 people = ... %
Yes	126 people = ... %

Going on holiday

1 This table shows the outgoing flights from Leeds to Tenerife.

Flight	Mon	Tue	Wed	Thu	Fri	Sat	Sun	Departs	Arrives
LS223		✈			✈	✈		13:55	18:30
LS225					✈			07:45	12:30

This table shows the return flights from Tenerife to Leeds.

Flight	Mon	Tue	Wed	Thu	Fri	Sat	Sun	Departs	Arrives
LS224		✈			✈	✈		19:15	23:50
LS226					✈			13:30	18:05

Mr and Mrs Brown and their two children are planning a week's holiday to Tenerife.

Mr Brown goes on the Internet to find the times of the planes from Leeds to Tenerife.

a On which days can they fly out to Tenerife?

b The family decides to fly out on Friday morning and return on the latest flight on the following Friday. What are the flight numbers for the two flights?

c How long are these two flights?

d When Mr Brown books the flights, he is informed that he needs to check in at Leeds airport at least $2\frac{1}{2}$ hours before the departure time of the flight. What is the latest time the family can arrive at the airport?

e The return cost for an adult is £289 and for a child is £210. What is the total cost of the tickets for the family?

f Each member of the family also has to pay a fuel supplement tax at £6.08, a baggage allowance at £5.99 and £3 to book a seat. Find the total cost for the family.

2 Mr Brown decides to take some euros (€) for the holiday. The exchange rate at the bank is £1 = €1.25.

a Mr Brown changes £450 at the bank. How many euros will he receive? Give your answer to the nearest five euros.

b Mr Brown also has 120 dollars ($) from a previous holiday to change into euros at the bank. The exchange rate at the bank is $1 = £0.50. How many euros will he receive?

c Mr Brown returns from the holiday with €50. How much is this in pounds?

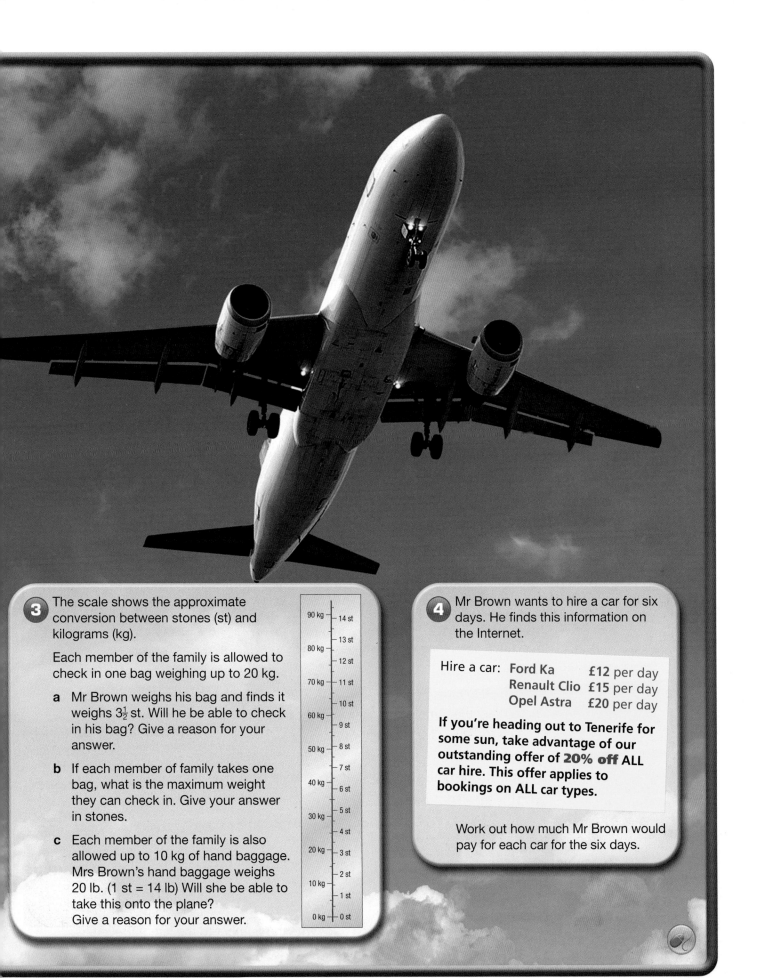

3 The scale shows the approximate conversion between stones (st) and kilograms (kg).

Each member of the family is allowed to check in one bag weighing up to 20 kg.

a Mr Brown weighs his bag and finds it weighs $3\frac{1}{2}$ st. Will he be able to check in his bag? Give a reason for your answer.

b If each member of family takes one bag, what is the maximum weight they can check in. Give your answer in stones.

c Each member of the family is also allowed up to 10 kg of hand baggage. Mrs Brown's hand baggage weighs 20 lb. (1 st = 14 lb) Will she be able to take this onto the plane?
Give a reason for your answer.

Scale (from bottom to top):
0 kg — 0 st
10 kg — 1 st
— 2 st
20 kg — 3 st
— 4 st
30 kg — 5 st
40 kg — 6 st
— 7 st
50 kg — 8 st
60 kg — 9 st
— 10 st
70 kg — 11 st
80 kg — 12 st
— 13 st
90 kg — 14 st

4 Mr Brown wants to hire a car for six days. He finds this information on the Internet.

Hire a car: Ford Ka   **£12** per day
Renault Clio **£15** per day
Opel Astra   **£20** per day

If you're heading out to Tenerife for some sun, take advantage of our outstanding offer of 20% off ALL car hire. This offer applies to bookings on ALL car types.

Work out how much Mr Brown would pay for each car for the six days.

This chapter is going to show you	What you should already know
• How to simplify expressions in algebra • How to expand brackets • How to use index notation with algebra	• How to substitute into algebraic expressions • How to add, subtract and multiply with negative numbers

Algebraic shorthand

In algebra we try not to use the $\times$ sign as it is easily confused with the variable x, so we use shorthand, for example:

$3 \times m = 3m$; $a \times b = ab$; $w \times 7 = 7w$; $d \times 4c = 4cd$, $n \times (d + t) = n(d + t)$

The use of the equals sign

When we use the = sign, each side of the sign must have the same value. The two sides may look different, but will still be equal.

Example 5.1 ▷

Which of the following expressions are equal to each other? Write correct mathematical statements for those that equal each other.

$a + b$		$b - a$		ab		$\dfrac{b}{a}$
	ba		$\dfrac{a}{b}$		$b + a$		$a - b$

We can pick out $a + b$ as being equal to $b + a$ ($a + b = b + a$) and ab as being equal to ba ($ab = ba$). None of the others are the same.

Example 5.2 ▷

Solve the equation $3x + 2 = 23$.

We subtract the same value, 2, from both sides to keep the sides equal:

$\quad 3x + 2 - 2 = 23 - 2$

So: $3x = 21$

We now divide both sides by 3, again to keep both sides equal:

$\quad \dfrac{3x}{3} = \dfrac{21}{3}$

So: $x = 7$

Example 5.3 ▷

Simplify the following expressions.

a $4a \times b$ **b** $9p \times 2$ **c** $3h \times 4i$

Leave out the multiplication sign and write the number to the left of the letters.

a $4a \times b = 4ab$ **b** $9p \times 2 = 18p$ **c** $3h \times 4i = 12hi$

1 Write each of these expressions in as simple a way as possible.

a $3 \times n$	**b** $5 \times n$	**c** $7 \times m$	**d** $8 \times t$
e $a \times b$	**f** $m \times n$	**g** $p \times 5$	**h** $m \times 6$
i $a \times (b + c)$	**j** $m \times (p + q)$	**k** $(a + b) \times c$	**l** $a \times b \times c$
m $m \div 3$	**n** $5 \div n$	**o** $(a + b) \div c$	**p** $7 \div (m + n)$
q $2f \times g$	**r** $5e \times j$	**s** $b \times (a + 3)$	**t** $(5 + g) \div 3$

2 Simplify the following expressions.

a $h \times 4p$	**b** $4s \times t$	**c** $2m \times 4n$	**d** $5w \times 5x$
e $b \times 9c$	**f** $3b \times 4c \times 2d$	**g** $4g \times f \times 3a$	

3 Find the pairs of expressions in each box that are equal to each other and write them down; the first one is done for you.

$$\boxed{\begin{array}{l} a + b \\ b + a \\ ab \end{array}} \quad a + b = b + a$$

a
$$\boxed{\begin{array}{l} m \times n \\ m + n \\ mn \end{array}}$$

b
$$\boxed{\begin{array}{l} p - q \\ q - p \\ -p + q \end{array}}$$

c
$$\boxed{\begin{array}{l} a \div b \\ b \div a \\ \frac{a}{b} \end{array}}$$

d
$$\boxed{\begin{array}{l} 6 + x \\ 6x \\ x + 6 \end{array}}$$

e
$$\boxed{\begin{array}{l} 3y \\ 3 + y \\ 3 \times y \end{array}}$$

4 Solve the following equations, making correct use of the equals sign.

a $2x + 1 = 11$	**b** $4x - 3 = 5$	**c** $5x + 4 = 19$
d $2x - 1 = 13$	**e** $4x + 3 = 9$	**f** $6x - 3 = 12$
g $10x + 7 = 12$	**h** $2x - 5 = 10$	**i** $3x - 12 = 33$
j $7x + 3 = 80$	**k** $5x + 8 = 73$	**l** $9x - 7 = 65$

5 Only some of the statements below are true. Write a list of those that are.

a $b + c = d + e$ is the same as $d + e = b + c$

b $a - b = 6$ is the same as $6 = a - b$

c $5x = x + 3$ is the same as $x = 5x + 3$

d $5 - 2x = 8$ is the same as $8 = 2x - 5$

e $ab - bc = T$ is the same as $T = ab - bc$

Extension Work

Show by the use of substitution which of the following are either not true or may be true.

1 $m(b + c) = mb + mc$

2 $(m + n) \times (p + q) = mp + nq$

3 $(m + n) \times (m - n) = (m \times m) - (n \times n)$

4 $a(b + c) + d(b + c) = (a + d) \times (b + c)$

Like terms

5 apples + 3 apples can be simplified to 8 apples. Similarly, we can simplify $5a + 3a$ to $8a$. $5a$ and $3a$ are called **like terms**, which can be combined because they contain exactly the same letters.

5 apples + 3 bananas cannot be simplified. Similarly, $5a + 3b$ cannot be simplified, because $5a$ and $3b$ are **unlike** terms so they canot be combined. Work through Example 5.4.

Example 5.4 ▷

a $5p - 2p = 3p$ **b** $5ab + 3ab = 8ab$
c $3x^2 + 6x^2 = 9x^2$ **d** $7y - 9y = -2y$ (because $7 - 9 = -2$)
e $-3u - 6u = -9u$ (because $-3 - 6 = -9$) **f** $5a + 2a + 3b = 7a + 3b$
g $5p - 2p + 7y - 9y = 3p - 2y$ **h** $8t + 3i - 6t - i = 8t - 6t + 3i - i$
$\qquad\qquad\qquad\qquad\qquad\qquad\qquad\qquad\qquad\qquad = 2t + 2i$
$\qquad\qquad\qquad\qquad\qquad\qquad\qquad\qquad$ (put the like terms together
$\qquad\qquad\qquad\qquad\qquad\qquad\qquad\qquad$ before combining)

Exercise 5B

1 Make a list of the terms in each of the following.

a $4a + 2d - 6c$ **b** $5x - 3 = 7$ **c** $3x^2 + 4x + 5$ **d** $9 - 2u - 7$

2 Simplify the following expressions.

a $5h + 6h$ **b** $4p + p$ **c** $9u - 3u$
d $3b - 8b$ **e** $-2j + 7j$ **f** $-6r - 6r$
g $2k + k + 3k$ **h** $9y - y$ **i** $7d - 2d + 5d$
j $10i + 3i - 6i$ **k** $2b - 5b + 6b$ **l** $-2b + 5b - 7b$
m $3xy + 6xy$ **n** $4p^2 + 7p^2$ **o** $5ab - 10ab$
p $5a^2 + 2a^2 - 3a^2$ **q** $4fg - 6fg - 8fg$

3 Simplify the following expressions.

a $6h + 2h + 5g$ **b** $4g - 2g + 8m$ **c** $8f + 7d + 3d$
d $4x + 5y + 7x$ **e** $6q + 3r - r$ **f** $4 + 5s - 3s$
g $c + 2c + 3$ **h** $12b + 7 + 2b$ **i** $7w - 7 + 7w$
j $2bf + 4bf + 5g$ **k** $7d + 5d^2 - 2d^2$ **l** $6st - 2st + 5t$
m $4s - 7s + 2t$ **n** $-5h + 2i + 3h$ **o** $4y - 2w - 7w$

4 Simplify the following expressions.

a $9e + 4e + 7f + 2f$ **b** $10u - 4u + 9t - 2t$ **c** $b + 3b + 5d - 2d$
d $4a + 5c + 3a + 2c$ **e** $f + 2g + 3g + 5f$ **f** $9h + 4i - 7h + 2i$
g $7p + 8q - 6p - 3q$ **h** $14j - 5k + 5j + 9k$ **i** $4u - 5t - 6u + 7t$
j $2s + 5t - 9t + 3s$ **k** $5p - 2q - 7p + 3q$ **l** $-2d + 5e - 4d - 9e$

Extension **Work**

1 Show that two consecutive integers multiplied together always give an even number. (*Hint:* Start with the first number as n.)

2 Show that any three consecutive integers always multiply together to give a multiple of 6.

Expanding brackets

When a number multiplies a bracket, it multiplies every term inside the bracket. This is called **multiplying out** or **expanding** the bracket.

Example 5.5

   a $3(a + b) = 3a + 3b$

   b $4(2s - 3) = 8s - 12$

   c $m(2n + 4) = 2mn + 4m$

When a negative number multiplies a bracket, it changes all the signs in the bracket.

Example 5.6

   a $-2(x + y) = -2x - 2y$

   b $-5(2d - 4e) = -10d + 20e$

   c $-(2a + 4b) = -2a - 4b$

   d $-(3x - 2) = -3x + 2$

After expanding brackets, it is often possible to simplify the answer.

Example 5.7

   a $4m + 2(m - 3n) = 4m + 2m - 6n = 6m - 6n$

   b $3(2w + 3v) + 2(4w - v) = 6w + 9v + 8w - 2v = 14w + 7v$

   c $4(u - 3t) - 2(4u - t) = 4u - 12t - 8u + 2t = -4u - 10t$

Exercise 5C

1 Expand the following brackets.

   a $5(p + q)$ **b** $9(m - n)$ **c** $s(t + u)$

   d $4(3d + 2)$ **e** $a(2b + c)$ **f** $3(5j - 2k)$

   g $e(5 + 2f)$ **h** $10(13 - 5n)$ **i** $6(4g + 3h)$

   j $8(a + b + c)$

2 Expand the following brackets.

   a $-(a + b)$ **b** $-(q - p)$ **c** $-(3p + 4)$

   d $-(7 - 2x)$ **e** $-3(g + 2)$ **f** $-2(d - f)$

   g $-5(2h + 3i)$ **h** $-4(6d - 3f)$ **i** $-3(-2j + k)$

3 Expand and simplify the following expressions.

   a $3w + 2(w + x)$ **b** $7(d + f) - 2d$ **c** $4h + 5(2h + 3s)$

   d $12x + 4(3y + 2x)$ **e** $2(2m - 3n) - 8n$ **f** $16p + 3(3q - 4p)$

4 Expand and simplify the following expressions.

   a $4(a + b) + 2(a + b)$ **b** $3(2i + j) + 5(3i + 4j)$

   c $6(5p + 2q) + 3(3p + q)$ **d** $5(d + f) + 3(d - f)$

   e $7(2e + t) + 2(e - 3t)$ **f** $2(3x - 2y) + 6(2x + y)$

   g $5(m - x) + 3(2m + x)$ **h** $7(4u - 3k) + 5(2u - k)$

5 Expand and simplify the following expressions.

a $8h - (3h + 2k)$ **b** $6v - (t + 2v)$ **c** $9 - (a + 2)$

d $7p - (3p - 5q)$ **e** $12 - (3e - 4)$ **f** $4a - (5b - 6a)$

6 Expand and simplify the following expressions.

a $5(m + n) - (3m + 2n)$ **b** $8(g + 3h) - 2(2g + h)$

c $7(d + 2e) - 3(2d - 3e)$ **d** $6(2 - 3x) - 3(2 - 5x)$

Extension **Work**

1 Show that $a(b + c) + b(a + c) + c(a + b)$ always equals the same as $2(ab + bc + ac)$.

2 Show that an even number multiplied with another even number always makes an even number.

Using algebra with shapes

Example 5.8   State:

a the perimeter and

b the area of the rectangle.

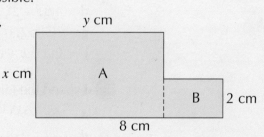

a The perimeter $= 2(k + p) = 2k + 2p$

b The area $= k \times p = kp$

Example 5.9   State the area of the shape as simply as possible:

First, split the shape into two parts A and B, as shown.

Shape A has the area xy cm^2.

Shape B has the area $2(8 - y)$ cm^2 $= (16 - 2y)$ cm^2.

The total area is $(xy + 16 - 2y)$ cm^2.

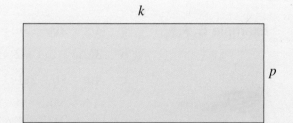

Exercise 5D   **1** Write down as simply as possible the length of the perimeter of each of these shapes.

a   **b**   **c**

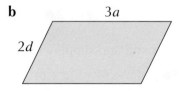 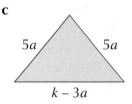

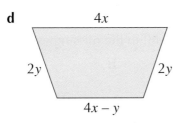

d

4x

2y 2y

4x − y

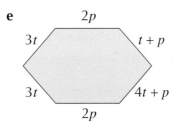

e

2p

3t t + p

3t 4t + p

2p

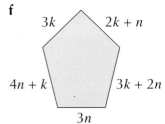

f

3k 2k + n

4n + k 3k + 2n

3n

2 What is the total area of each of the following shapes?

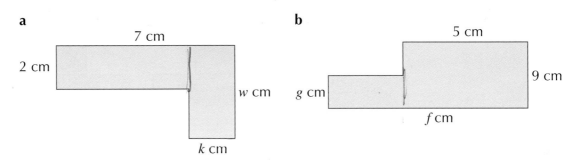

a

7 cm

2 cm

w cm

k cm

b

5 cm

9 cm

g cm

f cm

3 **a** What is the area of this rectangle?

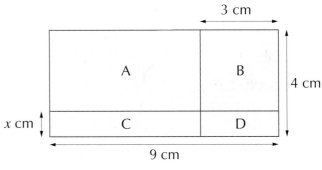

9 cm

4 cm

The rectangle has been divided into four separate rectangles below:

b Show that the area of A is $(24 − 6x)$ cm².

c Find the areas of:
  i rectangle B.
  ii rectangle C.
  iii rectangle D.

x cm

3 cm

A B

4 cm

C D

9 cm

d Show that when you add up the areas of the four rectangles A, B, C and D, it comes to the same answer that you had in **a**.

4 Write down the area of each smaller rectangle in the larger rectangle.

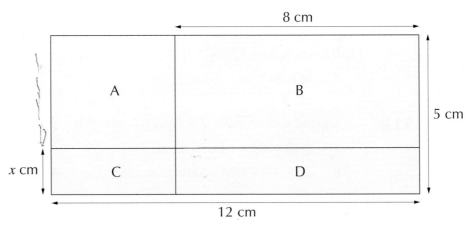

8 cm

A B

5 cm

x cm C D

12 cm

5 The expression in each box is made by adding the expressions in the two boxes it stands on. Copy the diagrams and fill in the missing expressions.

a

?

| $3x + 4y$ | $5x + 3y$ |

| ? | $x + 2y$ | ? |

b

?

| $2p + 6t$ | $3p - 2t$ |

| $p + 4t$ | ? | ? |

c

$3n + 5c$

| $2n - c$ | ? |

| $n + c$ | ? | ? |

d

$6a + 4b$

| ? | $4a + b$ |

| ? | $2a - b$ | ? |

Extension Work

1 Use a spreadsheet to verify that $3a + 3b$ is always the same as $3(a + b)$.

A	B	C	D
put any number in A	put any number in B	put in the formula 3*A1 + 3*B1	put in the formula 3*(A1 + B1)

Copy the formula from C1 and D1 down to about C20 and D20. Put a variety of numbers in each row of columns A and B. Check that for any type of number, negative and decimal, the value in cell C = cell D for each row.

2 Use a spreadsheet to verify that $(a + b) \times (a - b)$ is always the same as $a^2 - b^2$.

Use of index notation with algebra

You can save time by writing $5 \times 5 \times 5$ as 5^3 using index notation.

In the same way, $m \times m \times m$ or mmm can be written briefly as m^3.

Example 5.10

a $x \times x = x^2$

b $4m \times 3m = 12mm = 12m^2$

c $2a \times 3a \times 5a = 30aaa = 30a^3$

Example 5.11

Expand and simplify: **a** $3m(2m - 4n)$ **b** $a(a + 4b) - b(2a - 5b)$

a $3m(2m - 4n) = 6m^2 - 12mn$

b $a(a + 4b) - b(2a - 5b) = a^2 + 4ab - 2ba + 5b^2$

$$= a^2 + 2ab + 5b^2$$

1 Write the following expressions using index form.

a $a \times a \times a \times a \times a$

b $r \times r \times r \times r \times r \times r \times r$

c $b \times b \times b \times b \times b \times b \times b \times b \times b$

d $m \times m \times m \times m \times m \times m \times m \times m \times m \times m \times m \times m \times m$

e $4a \times 3a$

f $p \times 2p$

g $2g \times 3g \times 2g$

h $9k \times 4 \times 2k \times k \times 3k$

2 Write the following expressions as briefly as possible.

a $f + f + f + f + f$

b $w \times w \times w \times w$

c $c + c + c + c + c + c + c$

d $k \times k \times k \times k \times k \times k \times k \times k \times k \times k$

e $D + D + D + D + D + D$

3 Explain the difference between $5j$ and j^5.

4 Expand the following brackets.

a $d(d + 1)$

b $a(4a - 3)$

c $p(4 + p)$

d $w(6 - 3w)$

e $f(3f + g)$

f $u(2u - 3s)$

g $q(h + 4q)$

h $A(9C - 5A)$

5 Expand and simplify the following expressions.

a $4mn + m(2n + 3)$

b $i(3i + 7r) - 3ir$

c $3vt + v(5v - 7t)$

d $6jk - j(3k + j)$

e $3st - s(2t - 5s)$

f $4cq - q(3q + 7c)$

6 Expand and simplify the following expressions.

a $d(d + h) + h(2h + d)$

b $m(3m + 7n) + n(2m - 4n)$

c $e(5e + 4f) - f(2e + 3f)$

d $y(4x - 2y) + x(7y + 5x)$

e $k(4k - 2t) - t(3k + 7t)$

f $j(j + 7r) - r(2r - 9j)$

7 Expand and simplify the following expressions.

a $4d^2 + d(2d - 5)$

b $a(a + 1) + a(2a + 3)$

c $t(3t + 5) + t(2t - 3)$

d $w(5w + 4) - w(2w + 3)$

e $u(5u - 3) - u(3u - 1)$

f $d(2d - 5) - d(7 - 3d)$

Extension Work

1 Simplify the following expressions.

a $d^3 \times d^2$ **b** $d^5 \times d$ **c** $d^6 \times d^3$ **d** $d \times d^8$

2 a Write down a rule for multiplying two powers of the same quantity, as you were doing in Question 1.

b Copy and complete the following: $d^m \times d^n = d$

3 Use your rule to simplify the following expressions.

a $d^3 \times d^3$ **b** $a^{10} \times a^6$ **c** $e^{20} \times e^{25}$ **d** $99 \times w$ **e** $r^4 \times r^7 \times r^5$

4 Simplify the following expressions.

a $5a^7 \times 3a^5$ **b** $j^7 \times j^7 \times k^6 \times k^4$

c $8m^6n^3 \times 3m^9n^8$ **d** $s^3 \times t^4 \times t^7 \times s^8 \times t^3$

4
I can simplify algebraic expressions such as $3 \times 2n = 6n$.

I can solve simple equations such as $4x = 32$.

I can simplify algebraic expressions by collecting like terms,
   for example $3x + 4y + 2x - y = 5x + 3y$.

5
I know the equivalence of algebraic expressions such as $a + b = b + a$.

I can solve equations with two operations, such as $2x + 5 = 11$.

I can expand a bracket such as $4(2x - 1) = 8x - 4$.

I can write algebraic expressions in a simpler form using index notation,
   for example $n \times n \times n \times n \times n = n^5$.

6
I can expand a bracket with a negative sign, for example $-(3x - 2) = -3x + 2$.

I can expand and simplify expressions with more than one bracket,
   for example $3(x + 1) - 2(x - 4) = x + 7$.

I can simplify algebraic expressions using index notation, such as $3ab^2 \times 2a^3b^2 = 6a^4b^4$.

National Test questions

1 *2004 4–6 Paper 1*

One way to make a magic square is to substitute numbers into this algebra grid.

$a + b$	$a - b + c$	$a - c$
$a - b - c$	a	$a + b + c$
$a + c$	$a + b - c$	$a - b$

a Copy the magic square and complete it using the values:

$a = 10$ $b = 3$ $c = 5$

		5
	10	
15		

b Starting with the same algebra grid, I used **different values** for a, b and c to complete the magic square as follows:

What values for a, b and c did I use?

20	21	7
3	16	29
25	11	12

2 *2004 4–6 Paper 2*

a The square and the rectangle below have the **same area**.

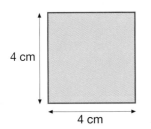
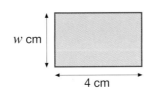

Not drawn accurately

Work out the value of y.

b The triangle and the rectangle below have the **same area**.

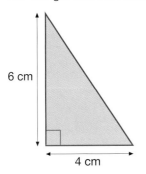

w cm

4 cm

Not drawn accurately

Work out the value of w.

Show your working.

3 *2005 4–6 Paper 1*

Solve these equations:

$3y + 1 = 16$

$18 = 4k + 6$

4 *2006 4–6 Paper 1*

Write the correct operations (+ or – or × or ÷) in these statements:

$a \ldots a = 0$

$a \ldots a = 1$

$a \ldots a = 2a$

$a \ldots a = a^2$

5 *2006 4–6 Paper 2*

Multiply out this expression.

$5(x + 2) + 3(7 + x)$

Write your answer as simply as possible.

6 *2005 4–6 Paper 2*

Look at this equation:

$$14y - 51 = 187 + 4y$$

Is **y = 17** the solution to the equation?

Show how you know.

7 *2005 4–6 Paper 2*

Write these expressions as simply as possible.

$$9 - 3k + 5k = \ldots\ldots$$
$$k^2 + 2k + 4k = \ldots\ldots$$

8 *2006 4–6 Paper 1*

Solve this equation:

$$3y + 14 = 5y + 1$$

9 *2007 4–6 Paper 1*

Solve this equation:

$$2(2n + 5) = 12$$

10 *2007 4–6 Paper 2*

Jenny wants to multiply out the brackets in the expression $3(2a + 1)$.

She writes: **3(2a + 1) = 6a + 1**

Show why Jenny is **wrong**.

CHAPTER 6

Geometry and Measures **2**

This chapter is going to show you	What you should already know
● How to calculate the area of triangles, parallelograms and trapezia ● How to calculate the area of compound shapes ● How to calculate the surface area and volume of a cuboid ● How to convert imperial units to metric units	● How to find the perimeter and area of a rectangle ● How to calculate the surface area of a cuboid ● How to convert one metric unit to another

Area of a triangle

To find the area of a triangle, we need to know the length of its base and its height. The height of the triangle is sometimes known as its **perpendicular height**. The diagram shows that the area of the triangle is half of the area of a rectangle.

Area 1 = Area 2

and

Area 3 = Area 4

So the area of a triangle is $\frac{1}{2} \times$ base $\times$ height. The formula for the area of a triangle is given by:

$$A = \tfrac{1}{2} \times b \times h = \tfrac{1}{2}bh = \frac{b \times h}{2}$$

Example 6.1 ▸ Calculate the area of this triangle.

$$A = \frac{8 \times 3}{2} = \frac{24}{2} = 12 \text{ cm}^2$$

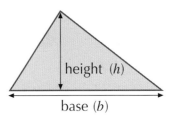

Sometimes the perpendicular height may be shown outside the triangle, as in the example below.

Example 6.2 ▸ Calculate the area of this triangle.

$$A = \frac{6 \times 5}{2} = \frac{30}{2} = 15 \text{ cm}^2$$

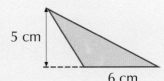

To find the area of a compound shape, made from rectangles and triangles, find the area of each one separately and then add together all the areas to obtain the total area of the shape.

Example 6.3 ▶ Calculate the area of this shape.

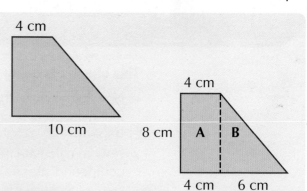

Divide the shape into a rectangle A and a triangle B:

Area of A = 8 × 4 = 32 cm²

Area of B = $\frac{6 \times 8}{2}$ = $\frac{48}{2}$ = 24 cm²

Area of shape = 32 + 24 = 56 cm²

Exercise 6A

① Calculate the area of each of the following triangles.

a
6 cm
8 cm

b
10 cm
14 cm

c
5 cm
5 cm

d
5 m
3 m
4 m

e
9 m
7 m
8 m

② Calculate the area of each of the following triangles.

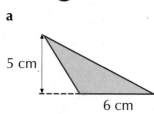
a
5 cm
6 cm

b
12 cm
10 cm

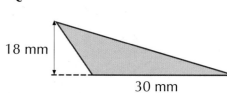
c
18 mm
30 mm

③ Calculate the area of each of the following triangles.

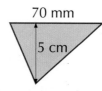
a
70 mm
5 cm

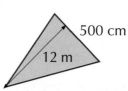
b
500 cm
12 m

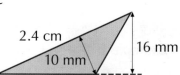
c
2.4 cm
10 mm
16 mm

④ Copy and complete the table for triangles **a** to **e**.

Triangle	Base	Height	Area
a	5 cm	4 cm	
b	7 cm	2 cm	
c	9 m	5 m	
d	12 mm		60 mm²
e		8 m	28 m²

5 On centimetre-squared paper, draw axes for x and y from 0 to 6 for each of the following questions, and then plot the coordinates and find the area of each triangle below.

    a $\triangle$ABC with A(2, 0), B(5, 0) and C(4, 4)

    b $\triangle$DEF with D(1, 1), E(6, 1) and F(3, 5)

    c $\triangle$PQR with P(2, 1), Q(2, 5) and R(5, 3)

    d $\triangle$XYZ with X(0, 5), Y(6, 5) and Z(4, 1)

6 Calculate the area of each compound shape below.

    a 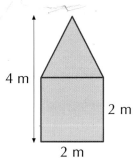   **b** 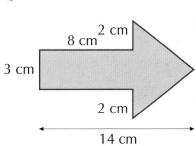   **c**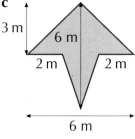

7 Find the area of this computer worktop.

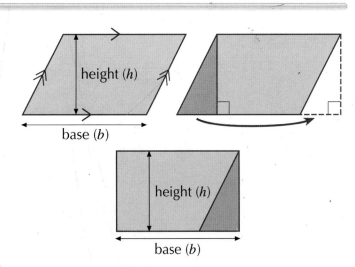

Extension **Work**

The right-angled triangle shown has an area of 36 cm². Find other right-angled triangles, with different measurements, that also have an area of 36 cm².

8 cm
9 cm

Area of a parallelogram

To find the area of a parallelogram, we need to know the length of its base and its height. The height of the parallelogram is sometimes known as its **perpendicular height**. The diagrams show that the parallelogram has the same area as that of a rectangle with the same base and height. So the area of a parallelogram is base × height.

The formula for the area of a parallelogram is given by:

$A = b \times h = bh$

Example 6.4 ▶ Calculate the area of this parallelogram.

$A = 6 \times 10 = 60 \text{ cm}^2$

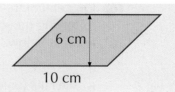

6 cm

10 cm

Exercise 6B

1 Calculate the area of each of the following parallelograms.

a
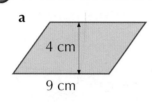
4 cm

9 cm

b
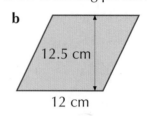
12.5 cm

12 cm

c
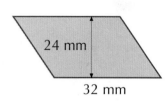
24 mm

32 mm

2 Calculate the area of each of the following parallelograms.

a
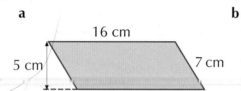
16 cm

5 cm

7 cm

b
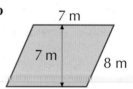
7 m

7 m

8 m

c
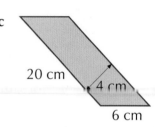
20 cm

4 cm

6 cm

3 Calculate the area of each of the following parallelograms.

a
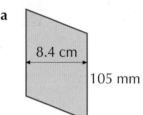
8.4 cm

105 mm

b
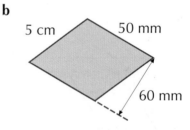
5 cm

50 mm

60 mm

4 Copy and complete the table below for parallelograms **a** to **e**.

Parallelogram	Base	Height	Area
a	8 cm	4 cm	
b	17 cm	12 cm	
c	8 m	5 m	
d	15 mm		60 mm²
e		8 m	28 m²

5 On centimetre-squared paper, draw axes for x and y from 0 to 8 for each of the following questions, and then plot the coordinates and find the area of each parallelogram below.

a Parallelogram ABCD: A(2, 0), B(6, 0), C(8, 5) and D(4, 5)

b Parallelogram EFGH: E(1, 2), F(4, 2), G(7, 7) and H(4, 7)

c Parallelogram PQRS: P(1, 8), Q(7, 5), R(7, 1) and S(1, 4)

6 The area of the parallelogram is 27 cm². Calculate the perpendicular height of the parallelogram.

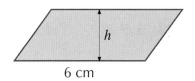

6 cm

Extension Work

1 Calculate the value of h in the given diagram.

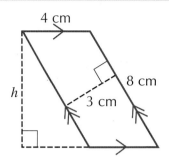

4 cm

8 cm

h

3 cm

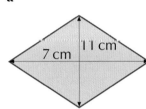

2 A formula to find the area of a rhombus is given here. The lengths of the two diagonals of the rhombus are AC = a and BD = b. The formula for the area of the rhombus is:

$$A = \frac{ab}{2}$$

Use the formula to calculate the area of each of the following rhombuses.

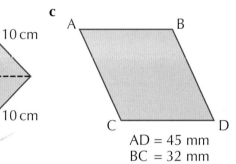

a

7 cm 11 cm

b

10 cm 10 cm

8 cm

12 cm

10 cm 10 cm

c

A B

C D

AD = 45 mm
BC = 32 mm

Area of a trapezium

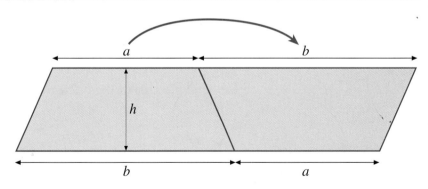

a

h

b

a b

h

b a

To find the area of a trapezium, we need to know the length of its two parallel sides, a and b, and the perpendicular height, h, between the parallel sides. The diagram shows how two equivalent trapezia fit together to form a parallelogram. So the area of a trapezium is $\frac{1}{2} \times$ the sum of the lengths of the parallel sides $\times$ the height. The formula for the area of a trapezium is therefore given by:

$$A = \tfrac{1}{2} \times (a + b) \times h = \tfrac{1}{2}(a + b)h = \frac{(a + b)h}{2}$$

Example 6.5 ▸ Calculate the area of this trapezium.

$A = \frac{1}{2} \times (9 + 5) \times 4$

$= \frac{14 \times 4}{2}$

$= 28 \text{ cm}^2$

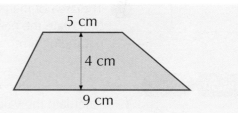

5 cm
4 cm
9 cm

Exercise 6C

1 Calculate the area of each of the following trapezia.

a
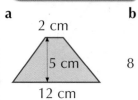
2 cm
5 cm
12 cm

b
4 cm
8 cm
10 cm

c
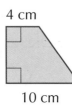 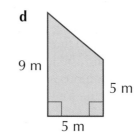
5 m
2 m
3 m

d
9 m
5 m
5 m

e
7 mm
16 mm
13 mm

2 Copy and complete the table below for trapezia **a** to **f**.

Trapezium	Length a	Length b	Height h	Area A
a	4 cm	6 cm	3 cm	
b	10 cm	12 cm	6 cm	
c	9 m	3 m	5 m	
d	5 cm	5 cm		20 cm^2
e	8 cm	12 cm		100 cm^2
f	6 m		4 m	32 m^2

3 The diagram shows the end wall of a garden shed. The shaded area is the door.

a Find the area of the door.

b Find the area of the brick wall.

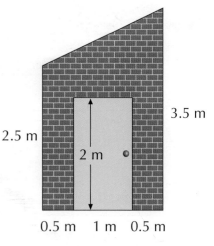

3.5 m
2.5 m
2 m
0.5 m   1 m   0.5 m

4 The side of a swimming pool is a trapezium, as shown in the diagram below. Calculate its area.

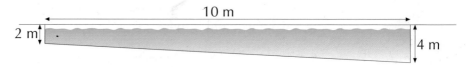

10 m
2 m
4 m

5 The diagram shows the measurements of a sauce bottle label. Calculate its area.

25 mm

52 mm

20 mm

30 mm

6 Find the solid area of this mathematical stencil, which has the shapes cut out.

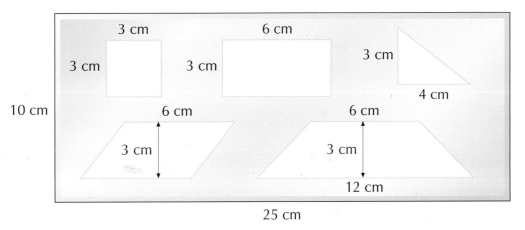

3 cm

6 cm

3 cm

3 cm

3 cm

3 cm

4 cm

10 cm

6 cm

6 cm

3 cm

3 cm

12 cm

25 cm

7 The area of this trapezium is 8 cm². Find different values of *a*, *b* and *h*, with *b* > *a*.

a

h

b

Extension Work

1 A formula to find the area of a kite is given here. The lengths of the two diagonals of the kite are AC = *a* and BD = *b*. The formula for the area of the kite is:

$$A = \frac{ab}{2}$$

Use the formula to calculate the area of each of the following kites.

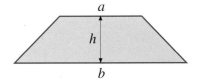

A

a

B

b

D

C

a

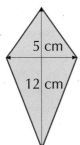

5 cm

12 cm

b

15 cm

18 cm

c

P

Q

S

R

PR = 5.2 m

QS = 2.4 m

2 The shapes below are drawn on a 1 cm grid of dots.

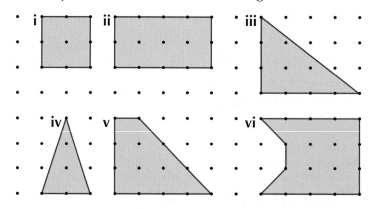

Shape	Number of dots on perimeter of shape	Number of dots inside shape	Area of shape (cm²)
i			
ii			
iii			
iv			
v			
vi			

a Copy and complete the table for each shape.

b Find a formula that connects the number of dots on the perimeter P, the number of dots inside I and the area A of each shape.

c Check your formula by drawing different shapes on a 1 cm grid of dots.

Volume of a cuboid

Volume is the amount of space inside a three-dimensional (3-D) shape.

The diagram shows a cuboid that measures 4 cm by 3 cm by 2 cm. The cuboid is made up of cubes of edge length 1 cm. The top layer consists of 12 cubes and, since there are two layers, altogether the cuboid has 24 cubes. The volume of the cuboid is therefore found by calculating $4 \times 3 \times 2 = 24$ cubes.

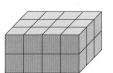

The volume of a cuboid is found by multiplying its length by its width by its height:

Volume of a cuboid = length × width × height

$$V = l \times w \times h = lwh$$

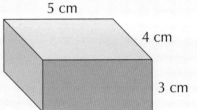

The metric units of volume in common use are the:

- cubic millimetre (mm³)
- cubic centimetre (cm³)
- cubic metre (m³)

The **capacity** of a 3-D shape is the volume of liquid or gas it can hold. The metric unit of capacity is the litre (l) with:

- 100 centilitres (cl) = 1 litre
- 1000 millilitres (ml) = 1 litre

The following metric conversions between capacity and volume should be learnt:

- 1 l = 1000 cm³
- 1 ml = 1 cm³
- 1000 l = 1 m³

Example 6.6 ▷ Calculate the total surface area and volume of the following cuboid.

The formula for the total surface area S of a cuboid is:

$$S = 2lw + 2lh + 2wh$$
$$= (2 \times 5 \times 4) + (2 \times 5 \times 3) + (2 \times 4 \times 3)$$
$$= 40 + 30 + 24$$
$$= 94 \text{ cm}^2$$

The formula for the volume of a cuboid is:

$$V = lwh$$
$$= 5 \times 4 \times 3$$
$$= 60 \text{ cm}^3$$

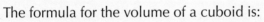

Example 6.7 ▷ Calculate the volume of the tank shown and then work out the capacity of the tank in litres.

$$V = 50 \times 30 \times 10 = 15\,000 \text{ cm}^3$$

Since 1000 cm³ = 1 l, the capacity of the tank = 15 000 ÷ 1000 = 15 l.

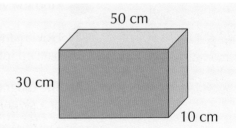

Example 6.8 ▷ Calculate the volume of the shape shown.

The shape is made up of two cuboids with measurements 7 m by 3 m by 2 m and 2 m by 3 m by 6 m. So the volume of the shape is given by:

$$V = (7 \times 3 \times 2) + (2 \times 3 \times 6)$$
$$= 42 + 36$$
$$= 78 \text{ m}^3$$

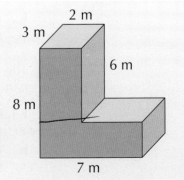

1 For each of the following cuboids, find: **i** the surface area.   **ii** the volume.

a

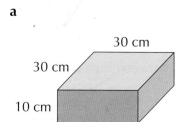

10 cm
4 cm
8 cm

b

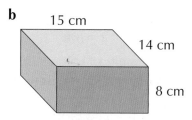

15 cm
14 cm
8 cm

c

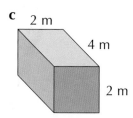

2 m
4 m
2 m

2 Find the capacity, in litres, of each of the following cuboid containers.

a

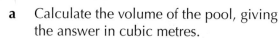

30 cm
30 cm
10 cm

b

12 cm
6 cm
25 cm

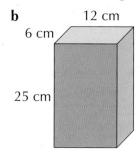

c

7 cm
16 cm
5 cm

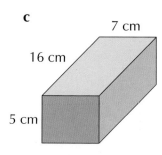

3 Copy and complete the table of cuboids **a** to **e**.

	Length	Width	Height	Volume
a	6 cm	4 cm	1 cm	
b	3.2 m	2.4 m	0.5 m	
c	8 cm	5 cm		120 cm³
d	20 mm	16 mm		960 mm³
e	40 m	5 m		400 m³

4 Calculate the volume for each of the cubes with the following edge lengths.

   a   2 cm   **b**   5 cm   **c**   12 cm

5 Find the volume of a hall that is 30 m long, 20 m wide and 10 m high.

6 How many packets of sweets that each measure 8 cm by 5 cm by 2 cm can be packed into a cardboard box that measures 32 cm by 20 cm by 12 cm?

7 The diagram shows the dimensions of a swimming pool.

   a   Calculate the volume of the pool, giving the answer in cubic metres.

   b   How many litres of water does the pool hold when it is full?

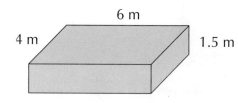

6 m
4 m
1.5 m

8 The diagram shows the dimensions of a rectangular carton of orange juice.

   a   Calculate the volume of the carton, giving your answer in cubic centimetres.

   b   How many glasses can be filled with orange juice from four full cartons, if each glass holds 240 ml?

10 cm
6 cm
18 cm
Orange Juice

9 Find the volume of this block of wood, giving your answer in cubic centimetres.

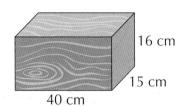

16 cm

15 cm

40 cm

10 Calculate the volume of each of the following 3-D shapes.

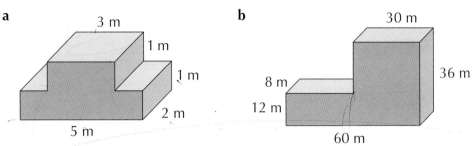

a

3 m

1 m

1 m

2 m

5 m

b

30 m

36 m

8 m

12 m

60 m

1 Estimate the volume for various cuboid objects in your classroom. Then copy and complete the table below (some examples have already been filled in).

Object	Estimate for volume	Actual volume
Book		
Storage box		
Cupboard		

2 The diagram shows the areas of the faces of a cuboid. Use this information to calculate the volume of the cuboid.

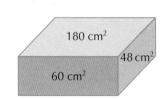

180 cm²

48 cm²

60 cm²

Imperial units

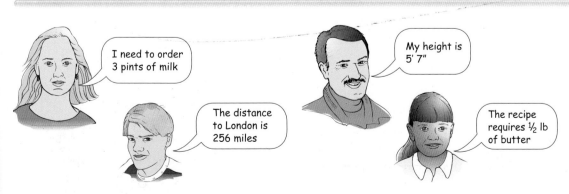

I need to order 3 pints of milk

The distance to London is 256 miles

My height is 5' 7"

The recipe requires ½ lb of butter

In Britain we are gradually changing to the metric system of units, but people still often prefer to use the Imperial system of units in certain cases, as the examples show.

The following Imperial units are still commonly used and it is a good idea to be familiar with them.

Imperial units of length	Imperial units of mass	Imperial units of capacity
12 inches (in) = 1 foot (ft) 3 feet = 1 yard (yd) 1760 yards = 1 mile	16 ounces (oz) = 1 pound (lb) 14 pounds = 1 stone (st) 2240 pounds = 1 ton	8 pints (pt) = 1 gallon (gall)

Example 6.9

Express 5 ft 6 in in inches.

5 ft = 5 × 12 = 60 in

So, 5 ft 6in = 60 + 6 = 66 in

Example 6.10

Express 100 lb in stones and pounds.

100 lb ÷ 14 = 7 stone with 2 pounds left over

So, 100 lb = 7 st 2 lb

Note: If a calculator is used, the answer will be a decimal.

Rough metric equivalents of Imperial units

As we are changing to the metric system, you need to be able to convert from Imperial units to metric units by using suitable approximations. It is useful to know the following rough metric equivalents of Imperial units, although if better accuracy is required the exact conversion factor should be used. The symbol ≈ means 'is approximately equal to'.

Units of length	Units of mass	Units of capacity
1 in ≈ 2.5 cm 1 yard ≈ 1 metre 5 miles ≈ 8 km	1 oz ≈ 30 g 1 lb ≈ 500 g	$1\frac{3}{4}$ pints ≈ 1 l 1 gallon ≈ 4.5 l

Example 6.11

Approximately how many kilometres are there in 20 miles?

5 miles ≈ 8 km

So, 20 miles ≈ 4 × 8 ≈ 32 km

Example 6.12

Approximately how many gallons are there in 18 litres?

1 gallon ≈ 4.5 l

So, 18 l ≈ 18 ÷ 4.5 ≈ 4 gallons

Exercise 6E

1 Express each of the following in the units given in brackets.

    a 6 ft 2 in (in)   **b** 22 yd (ft)   **c** 2 lb 10 oz (oz)

    d 6 st 5 lb (lb)   **e** $3\frac{1}{2}$ gallons (pints)

5

2 Express each of the following in the units given in brackets.

    a   30 in (ft and in)   **b**   20 ft (yd and ft)   **c**   72 oz (lb and oz)

    d   35 lb (st and lb)   **e**   35 pints (gallons and pints)

3 How many inches are there in:

    a   a yard?   **b**   a mile?

4 How many ounces are there in:

    a   a stone?   **b**   a ton?

5 Convert each of the following Imperial quantities into the metric quantity given in brackets.

    a   6 in (cm)   **b**   10 yd (m)   **c**   25 miles (km)

    d   8 oz (g)   **e** $1\frac{1}{2}$ lb (g)   **f**   7 pints (l)

    g   8 gallons (l)

6 Convert each of the following metric quantities into the Imperial quantity given in brackets.

    a   30 cm (in)   **b**   200 m (ft)   **c**   80 km (miles)

    d   150 g (oz)   **e**   3 kg (lb)   **f**   6 l (pints)

    g   54 l (gallons)

FM **7** Pièrre is on holiday in England and he sees this sign near to his hotel. Approximately how many metres is it from his hotel to the beach?

FM **8** Mike is travelling on a German autobahn and he sees this road sign. He knows that it means that the speed limit is 120 kilometres per hour. What is the approximate speed limit in miles per hour?

FM **9** Steve needs 6 gallons of petrol to fill the tank of his car. The pump only dispenses petrol in litres. Approximately how many litres of petrol does he need?

10 A metric tonne is 1000 kg. Approximately how many pounds is this?

FM **11** Anne's height is 5 ft 6 in. She is filling in an application form for a passport and needs to know her height in metres. What height should she enter on the form?

1   Working in pairs or groups, draw a table to show each person's height and weight in Imperial and in metric units.

2   Other Imperial units are less common, but are still used in Britain. For example:
   - furlongs to measure distance in horse racing
   - fathoms to measure the depth of sea water
   - nautical miles to measure distance at sea.

   Use reference material or the Internet to find metric approximations for these units. Can you find other Imperial units for measuring length, mass and capacity that are still in use?

3   How long is 1 million seconds? Give your answer in days, hours, minutes and seconds.

LEVEL BOOSTER

5   I know how to convert one metric unit into another.
   I know how to convert Imperial units into metric units using rough equivalents.

6   I can use the approximate formulae to find the area of triangles, parallelograms and trapezia.
   I can find the volume of a cuboid.

National Test questions

FM 1   *2000 Paper 2*

How many kilometres are there in 5 miles?

Copy and complete the missing part of the sign.

Footpath to Hightown
5 miles or ..... kilometres

2   *2002 Paper 1*

A scale measures in grams and in ounces.

Use the scale to answer these questions:

a   About how many ounces is 400 grams?

b   About how many grams is 8 ounces?

c   About how many ounces is 1 kilogram? Explain your answer.

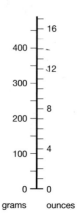

3 *2006 3–5 Paper 2*

Find the missing numbers from the statements below:

120 mm is the same as …… cm.

120 mm is the same as …… m.

120 mm is the same as …… km.

4 *2001 4–6 Paper 2*

a On a copy of the cm² grid below, draw a **right-angled triangle** with an area of **12 cm²**.

Use line AB as one side of the triangle.

b Now draw an **isosceles triangle** with an area of **12 cm²**.

Use line AB as one side of the triangle.

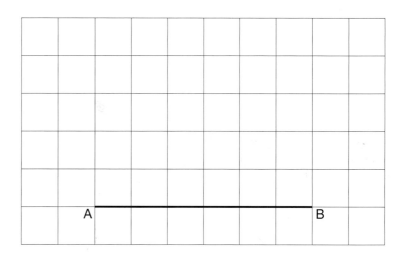

5 *2002 Paper 2*

The drawing shows two cuboids that have the same volume:

a What is the volume of cuboid A?

Remember to state your units.

b Work out the value of the length marked x in Cuboid B.

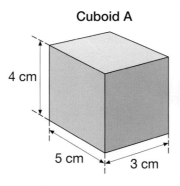

Cuboid A

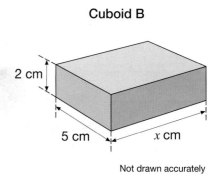

Cuboid B

4 cm

5 cm   3 cm

2 cm

5 cm x cm

Not drawn accurately

6 *2007 4–6 Paper 2*

The diagram shows a shaded parallelogram drawn inside
a rectangle.

What is the area of the shaded parallelogram?

You must give the correct unit with your answer.

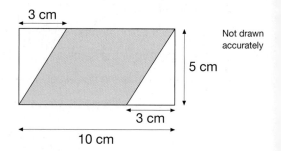

CHAPTER 7 Algebra 3

This chapter is going to show you

- How to draw mapping diagrams from functions
- How to identify a function from inputs and outputs
- Special features of a linear graph

What you should already know

- How to use a function
- How to plot coordinates
- How to calculate with negative numbers

Linear functions

A linear function is a simple rule that involves any of the following:

addition	subtraction	multiplication	division

Mapping diagrams can illustrate these functions as shown in Example 7.1.

Example 7.1 ▷ Draw a mapping diagram to illustrate:

$$x \rightarrow 2x + 3$$

We draw two number lines; usually the top one is for the starting points and the bottom one shows where the numbers map to with the function. The starting number line is often from −2 to 5. We can see that if:

$$x \rightarrow 2x + 3$$

then:
$$-2 \rightarrow -1$$
$$-1 \rightarrow 1$$
$$0 \rightarrow 3$$
$$1 \rightarrow 5$$

We illustrate the function by drawing arrows between the two number lines to show where each number maps to:

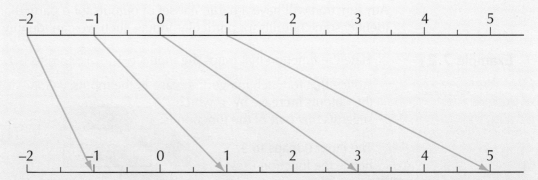

The illustration shows, of course, only part of a very long pair of number lines that contain hundreds of numbers. We only draw this part to illustrate what the pattern looks like.

Exercise 7A

1 a Copy the mapping diagram for the function $x \rightarrow x + 3$.
b Complete the mapping diagram for all the integer values from −2 to 2.
c Complete the mapping diagram for the following values.
i 1.5 **ii** 0.5 **iii** −0.5 **iv** −1.5

2 a Using two number lines from −5 to 10, draw mapping diagrams to illustrate the following functions.
i $x \rightarrow x + 2$ **ii** $x \rightarrow 2x + 1$ **iii** $x \rightarrow x - 2$ **iv** $x \rightarrow 2x - 1$
b In each of your mapping diagrams from **2a**, draw the lines from −1.5, 0.5 and 1.5.

3 a Using number lines from −5 to 15, draw mapping diagrams to illustrate the following functions.
i $x \rightarrow 3x + 1$ **ii** $x \rightarrow 4x - 1$ **iii** $x \rightarrow 2x + 5$ **iv** $x \rightarrow 3x - 5$
b In each of your mapping diagrams from **3a**, draw the lines from −0.5, 1.5 and 2.5.

4 Write down the similarity between all the mapping diagrams of functions such as the following.
a $x \rightarrow x + 2$ **b** $x \rightarrow x + 1$ **c** $x \rightarrow x + 5$ **d** $x \rightarrow x + 7$

Extension Work

1 Using number lines from 0 to 10, draw a mapping diagram of the function $x \rightarrow 2x$.

2 For each of the arrows drawn on your mapping diagram, extend the line backwards towards the line that joins both zeros. They should all meet at the same place on this line.

3 Repeat the above for the mapping $x \rightarrow 3x$. Does this also join together at a point on the line joining the zeros?

4 Can you explain why this works for all similar functions?

Finding a function from its inputs and outputs

Any function will have a particular set of outputs for a particular set of inputs. If we can identify some outputs for particular inputs, then we can identify the function.

Example 7.2

State the function that maps the inputs {−1, 0, 1, 2, 3} to { 1, 3, 7, 11, 15}.

Notice that for each integer increase in the inputs, the outputs **increase by 4**, which suggests that part of the function is: 　　× 4

The input **0 maps to 3**, hence the function uses: 　　+ 3

This leads to the function: 　　$x \rightarrow 4x + 3$

A quick check that this does map 1 to 7 and 2 to 11 confirms the function is correct.

1 State the function that maps the following inputs to their respective outputs.

a $\{-1, 0, 1, 2, 3\}$ ⟶ $\{4, 5, 6, 7, 8\}$
b $\{-1, 0, 1, 2, 3\}$ ⟶ $\{-2, -1, 0, 1, 2\}$
c $\{-1, 0, 1, 2, 3\}$ ⟶ $\{-1, 1, 3, 5, 7\}$
d $\{-1, 0, 1, 2, 3\}$ ⟶ $\{3, 5, 7, 9, 11\}$
e $\{-1, 0, 1, 2, 3\}$ ⟶ $\{2, 5, 8, 11, 14\}$

2 What are the functions that generate the following mixed outputs from the given mixed inputs? (*Hint:* Put the numbers in sequence first.)

a $\{2, 5, 3, 0, 6, 4\}$ ⟶ $\{6, 8, 9, 3, 7, 5\}$
b $\{5, 9, 6, 4, 10, 8\}$ ⟶ $\{15, 17, 12, 16, 11, 13\}$
c $\{5, 1, 8, 4, 0, 6\}$ ⟶ $\{5, 13, 15, 3, 19, 11\}$
d $\{3, 1, 7, 5, 8, 2\}$ ⟶ $\{9, 1, 13, 5, 15, 3\}$
e $\{9, 5, 10, 6, 3, 7\}$ ⟶ $\{16, 10, 28, 19, 31, 22\}$

3 This question looks at using the simple functions:

By using any two, you can create six different combined functions, such as:

$\{2, 3, 4, 5\}$ ⟶ $\boxed{+ 2}$ ⟶ $\boxed{- 3}$ ⟶ $\{1, 2, 3, 4\}$

Draw a diagram like the one above for the other five possible combined functions.

Graphs from functions

There are different ways to write functions down. For example, the function:

$x \rightarrow 4x + 3$

can also be written as:

$y = 4x + 3$

with the inputs as x and the outputs as y.

This latter way of writing functions is simpler when it comes to drawing graphs.

Every function has a graph associated with it, which we find by finding ordered pairs, or coordinates, from the function and plotting them. Every graph of a linear function is a straight line.

Example 7.3

Draw a graph of the function:

$$y = 3x + 1$$

First, we draw up a table of simple values for x:

x	−2	−1	0	1	2	3
$y = 3x + 1$	−5	−2	1	4	7	10

Then we plot each point on a grid, and join up all the points.

Notice that the line we have drawn is actually hundreds of other coordinates too – *all* of these obey the same rule of the function, that is $y = 3x + 1$. Choose any points on the line that have not been plotted and show that this is true.

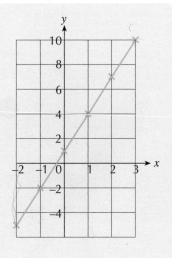

Exercise 7C

1 a Complete the table below for the function $y = x + 3$.

x	−2	−1	0	1	2	3
$y = x + 3$			3			

b Draw a grid with its x-axis from −2 to 3 and y-axis from −1 to 7.
c Use the table to help draw, on the grid, the graph of the function $y = x + 3$.

2 a Complete the table below for the function $y = x − 2$.

x	−2	−1	0	1	2	3
$y = x − 2$			−2			

b Draw a grid with its x-axis from −2 to 3 and y-axis from −4 to 2.
c Use the table to help draw, on the grid, the graph of the function $y = x − 2$.

3 a Complete the table below for the function $y = 4x + 1$.

x	−2	−1	0	1	2	3
$y = 4x + 1$			1			

b Draw a grid with its x-axis from −2 to 3 and y-axis from −7 to 13.
c Use the table to help draw, on the grid, the graph of the function $y = 4x + 1$.

4 a Complete the table below for the function $y = 4x − 1$.

x	−2	−1	0	1	2	3
$y = 4x − 1$			−1			

b Draw a grid with its x-axis from −2 to 3 and y-axis from −9 to 11.
c Use the table to help draw, on the grid, the graph of the function $y = 4x − 1$.

5 **a** Complete the table below for the functions shown.

x	-2	-1	0	1	2	3
$y = 2x + 5$	1					11
$y = 2x + 3$		1			7	
$y = 2x + 1$			1	3		
$y = 2x - 1$			-1	1		
$y = 2x - 3$		-5			1	

b Draw a grid with its x-axis from -2 to 3 and y-axis from -7 to 11.

c Draw the graph for each function in the table above.

d What two properties do you notice about each line?

e Use the properties you have noticed to draw the graphs of the following functions.

  i $y = 2x + 2.5$ **ii** $y = 2x - 1.5$

6 **a** Complete the table below for the functions shown.

x	-2	-1	0	1	2	3
$y = 3x + 4$	-2					13
$y = 3x + 2$		-1			8	
$y = 3x$			0	3		
$y = 3x - 2$			-2	1		
$y = 3x - 4$		-7			2	

b Draw a grid with its x-axis from -2 to 3 and y-axis from -10 to 13.

c Draw the graph for each function in the table above.

d What two properties do you notice about each line?

e Use the properties you have noticed to draw the graphs of the following two functions.

  i $y = 3x + 2.5$ **ii** $y = 3x - 2.5$

Extension Work

1 Draw the graphs of:

  $y = 0.5x - 2$ and $y = 0.5x + 2$

2 Now draw, without any further calculations, the graphs of:

  $y = 0.5x - 1$ and $y = 0.5x + 3$

Gradient of a straight line (steepness)

The gradient of a straight line is:

The increase in the y ordinate for an increase of 1 in the x ordinate.

Examples of gradients:

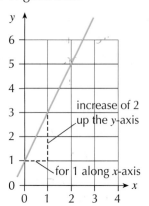
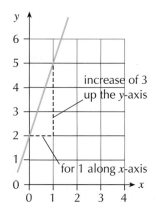

For any linear equation of the form $y = mx + c$, you might have found out the following from the previous exercise:

$y = mx + c$

The m is the same as the gradient of the line (steepness).

The c is the number on the y-axis where the line cuts through.

Example 7.4

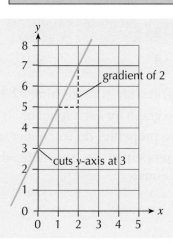

Graph of $y = 2x + 3$

gradient of 2

cuts y-axis at 3

Exercise 7D

(1) State the gradient of each of the following lines.

a
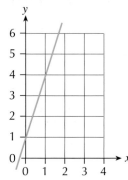

b
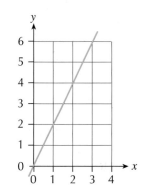

c
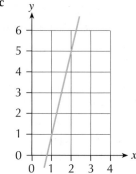

d
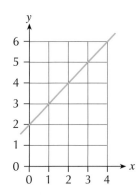

2 State the equation of the straight line with:

    a   a gradient of 3 passing through the *y*-axis at (0, 5).

    b   a gradient of 2 passing through the *y*-axis at (0, 7).

    c   a gradient of 1 passing through the *y*-axis at (0, 4).

    d   a gradient of 7 passing through the *y*-axis at (0, 15).

3 For each of the following graphs:

    i   find the gradient of the coloured line.

    ii   write down the coordinates of where the line crosses the *y*-axis.

    iii   write down the equation of the line.

a 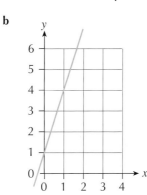   **b** 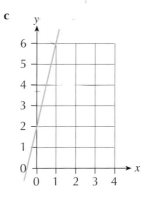   **c** 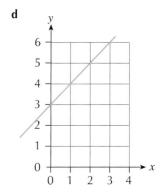   **d**

Extension Work

Find the equations of the graphs that pass through the following points.

Hint: Plot each pair of points on a coordinate grid. Work out the gradient and extend the line to cross the *y*-axis if necessary.

  1 (0, 3) and (1, 4)   **2** (0, 2) and (1, 5)   **3** (1, 2) and (2, 3)

  4 (1, 3) and (2, 7)   **5** (2, 3) and (4, 7)   **6** (3, 5) and (5, 11)

Real-life graphs

Graphs are all around us. They are found in newspapers, adverts, on TV, and so on.

Most of these graphs show a relationship between what is given on one axis and what is given on the other.

A distance–time graph (as shown on the right) can be used to describe a journey.

When you draw graphs from data such as time and distance, you need to find key coordinates to plot to identify the line or lines that make up the graph. The axes need to be labelled, and need to be accurate.

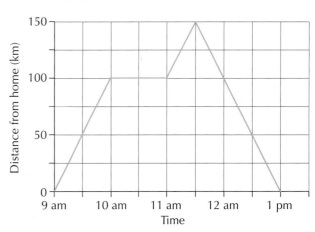

Example 7.5 ▶ I set off from home to pick up a dog from the vet. I travelled $1\frac{1}{2}$ hours at an average speed of 60 km/hour. It took me 30 minutes to get the dog settled into my car. I then travelled back home at an average speed of 40 km/hour as I didn't want to jolt the dog. Draw a distance–time graph of the journey.

The key coordinates (time, distance from home) are:

- the start from home at (0, 0)
- arrive at the vets at $(1\frac{1}{2}, 90)$
- set off from the vet at (2, 90)
- arrive back home at $(4\frac{1}{4}, 0)$

Note: $90 \div 40 = 2\frac{1}{4}$ hours for the return journey.

Now plot the points and draw the graph:

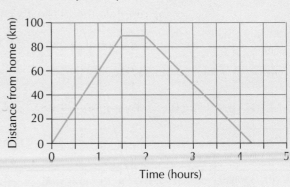

Exercise 7E

1 a Draw a grid with the following scale:
horizontal, time, showing 0 to 5 hours, with 1 cm to 30 minutes;
vertical, distance from home, showing 0 to 100 km, 1 cm to 20 km.

b Draw on the grid the travel graph that shows the following:
I travelled from home to Manchester Airport, at an average speed of 50 km/hour. It took me 2 hours. I stopped there for 30 minutes, and picked up Auntie Freda. I brought her straight back home, driving this time at an average of 40 km/hour.

c I set off to the airport at 9 am. Use the graph to determine what time I arrived back home.

2 a Draw a grid with the following scale:
horizontal, time showing 0 to 2 hours, 1 cm to 20 minutes;
vertical, distance from home, showing 0 to 60 km, 1 cm to 10 km.

b Draw on the grid the travel graph showing the following:
Elise travelled to meet Ken who was 60 km away. She left home at 11 am and travelled the first 40 km in 1 hour. She stopped for 30 minutes to buy a present, and then completed her journey in 20 minutes.

c What was Elise's average speed over the last 20 minutes?

3 a Draw a grid with the following scale:
horizontal, time showing 0 to 60 minutes, 1 cm to 5 minutes;
vertical, depth showing 0 to 200 cm, 2 cm to 50 cm.

b A swimming pool, 2 m deep, was filled with water from a hose. The pool was empty at the start and the depth of water in the pool increased at the rate of 4 cm/minute. Complete the following table (on next page), showing the depth of water after various times.

Time (minutes)	0	10	25	40	50
Depth (cm)					

   c   Draw a graph to show the increase in depth of water against time.

4 Draw a graph for the depth of water in the same swimming pool if the water was poured in with a different hose that filled the pool quicker, at the rate of 5 cm/minute.

5 A different swimming pool that contained water was emptied by a pump at the rate of 30 gallons/minute. It took 3 hours for the pool to be emptied.

   a   Complete the following table that shows how much water is in the pool.

Time (minutes)	0	30	60	90	120	150	180
Water left (gallons)	5400						

   b   Draw a graph to show the amount of water left in the pool against time.

Extension Work

At 11 am, Billy and Leon set off towards each other from different places 32 km apart. Billy cycled at 20 km/hour and Leon walked at 5 km/hour.

Draw distance–time graphs of their journeys on the same grid to find out:

a the time at which they meet.

a when they are 12 km apart.

LEVEL BOOSTER

5 I can complete a mapping diagram to represent a linear function, for example $x \rightarrow 2x + 1$.

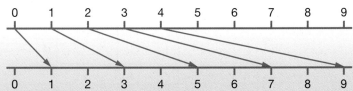

6 I can find the linear function that connect two sets of data,
for example $x = \{1, 2, 3, 4, 5\} \rightarrow y = \{2, 5, 8, 11, 14\}$ is $y = 3x - 1$.

I can complete a table of values for a linear relationship and use this to draw a graph of the relationship.

I can calculate the gradient of a straight line drawn on a coordinate grid and can distinguish between a positive and a negative gradient.

I can draw and interpret graphs that describe real-life situations.

1 *2000 Paper 2*

The graph shows my journey in a lift.
I got in the lift at floor number 10.

a The lift stopped at two different floors before I got to floor number 22. What floors did the lift stop at?

b For how long was I in the lift while it was moving?

c After I got out of the lift at floor number 22, the lift went directly to the ground floor.

It took 45 seconds.

On a copy of the graph, show the journey of the lift from floor 22 to the ground floor.

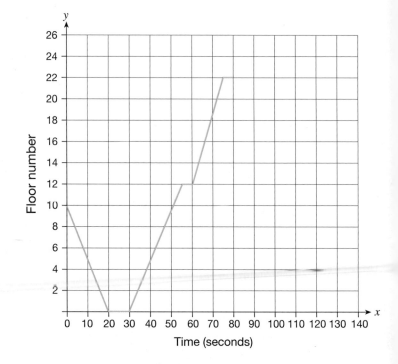

2 *2007 5–7 Paper 1*

Look at this equation: $y = 2x + 10$

a When $x = 4$, what is the value of y?

b When $x = -4$, what is the value of y?

c Which of the equations below gives the **same** value of y for both **$x = 4$** and **$x = -4$**?

$$y = 2x \qquad y = 2 + x \qquad y = x^2 \qquad y =$$

3 *2002 Paper 1* The graph shows a straight line. The equation of the line is $y = 3x$.

Does the point (25, 75) lie on the straight line $y = 3x$?

Explain how you know.

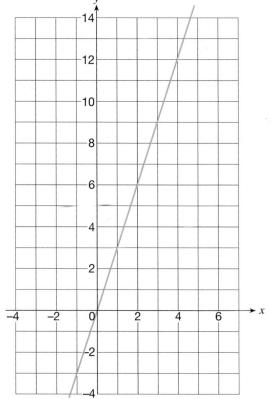

4 *2003 5–7 Paper 1*

The diagram below shows a square drawn on a square grid.

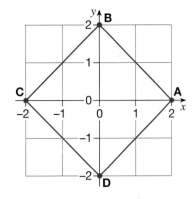

a The points A, B, C and D are at the vertices of the square.

Match the correct line to each equation. One is done for you.

$y = 0$

$x = 0$

$x + y = 2$

$x + y = -2$

| Line through C and D |

| Line through A and C |

| Line through A and D |

| Line through B and D |

| Line through B and C |

| Line through A and B |

The mid-points of each side, E, F, G and H, join to make a different square:

b Write the equation of the straight line through **E** and **H**.

c Is $y = -x$ the equation of the straight line through **E** and **G**?

Explain how you know.

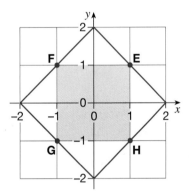

FM The M25

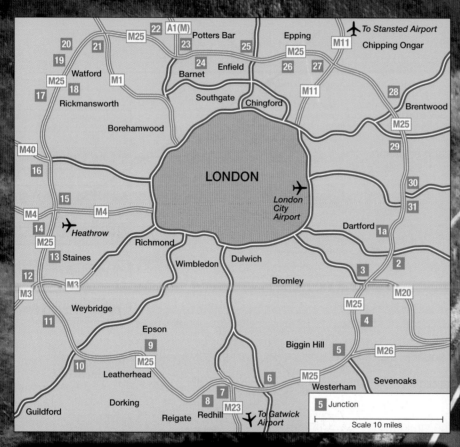

The M25 motorway is an orbital motorway, 117 miles long, that encircles London.

Construction of the first section began in 1973. Construction of the M25 continued in stages until its completion in 1986.

For most of its length, the motorway has six lanes (three in each direction), although there are a few short stretches which are four-lane and perhaps one-sixth is eight-lane, around the south-western corner. The motorway was widened to 10 lanes between junctions 12 and 14, and 12 lanes between junctions 14 and 15, in November 2005. The Highways Agency has plans to widen almost all of the remaining stretches of the M25 to eight lanes.

It is one of Europe's busiest motorways, with 205 000 vehicles a day recorded in 2006 between junctions 13 and 14 near London Heathrow Airport. This is, however, significantly fewer than the 257 000 vehicles a day recorded in 2002 on the A4 motorway at Saint-Maurice, in the suburbs of Paris, or the 216 000 vehicles a day recorded in 1998 on the A 100 motorway near the Funkturm in Berlin.

The road passes through several counties. Junctions 1–5 are in Kent, 6–14 in Surrey, 15–16 in Buckinghamshire, 17–24 in Hertfordshire, 25 in Greater London, 26–28 in Essex, 29 in Greater London and 30–31 in Essex.

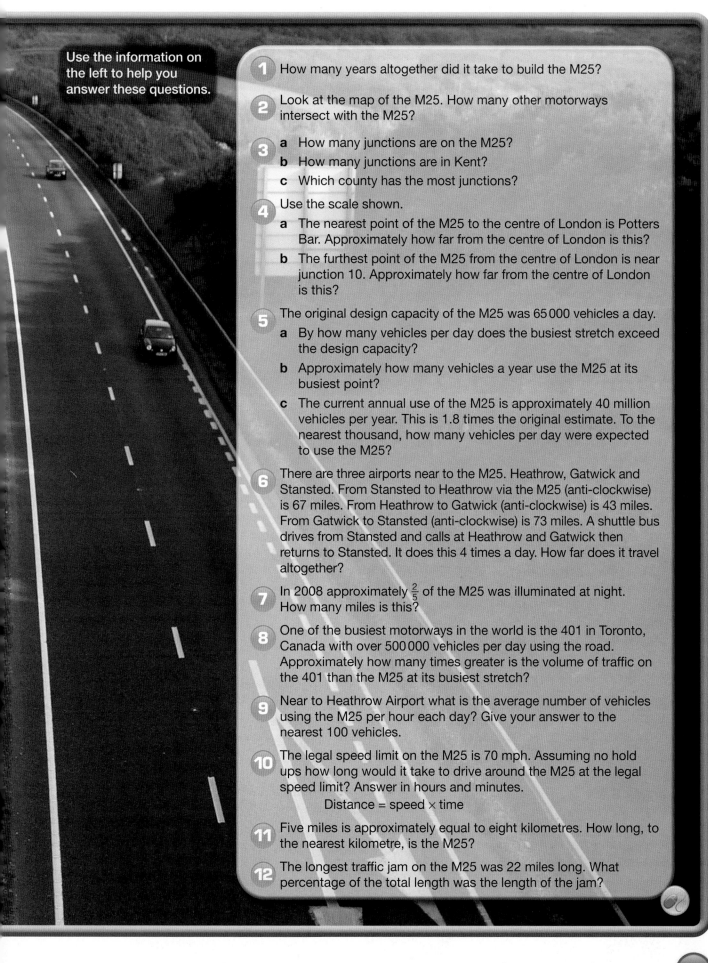

Use the information on the left to help you answer these questions.

1 How many years altogether did it take to build the M25?

2 Look at the map of the M25. How many other motorways intersect with the M25?

3
a How many junctions are on the M25?
b How many junctions are in Kent?
c Which county has the most junctions?

4 Use the scale shown.
a The nearest point of the M25 to the centre of London is Potters Bar. Approximately how far from the centre of London is this?
b The furthest point of the M25 from the centre of London is near junction 10. Approximately how far from the centre of London is this?

5 The original design capacity of the M25 was 65 000 vehicles a day.
a By how many vehicles per day does the busiest stretch exceed the design capacity?
b Approximately how many vehicles a year use the M25 at its busiest point?
c The current annual use of the M25 is approximately 40 million vehicles per year. This is 1.8 times the original estimate. To the nearest thousand, how many vehicles per day were expected to use the M25?

6 There are three airports near to the M25. Heathrow, Gatwick and Stansted. From Stansted to Heathrow via the M25 (anti-clockwise) is 67 miles. From Heathrow to Gatwick (anti-clockwise) is 43 miles. From Gatwick to Stansted (anti-clockwise) is 73 miles. A shuttle bus drives from Stansted and calls at Heathrow and Gatwick then returns to Stansted. It does this 4 times a day. How far does it travel altogether?

7 In 2008 approximately $\frac{2}{5}$ of the M25 was illuminated at night. How many miles is this?

8 One of the busiest motorways in the world is the 401 in Toronto, Canada with over 500 000 vehicles per day using the road. Approximately how many times greater is the volume of traffic on the 401 than the M25 at its busiest stretch?

9 Near to Heathrow Airport what is the average number of vehicles using the M25 per hour each day? Give your answer to the nearest 100 vehicles.

10 The legal speed limit on the M25 is 70 mph. Assuming no hold ups how long would it take to drive around the M25 at the legal speed limit? Answer in hours and minutes.
Distance = speed × time

11 Five miles is approximately equal to eight kilometres. How long, to the nearest kilometre, is the M25?

12 The longest traffic jam on the M25 was 22 miles long. What percentage of the total length was the length of the jam?

This chapter is going to show you	What you should already know
● How to multiply and divide by powers of 10 ● How to round numbers to one or two decimal places ● How to check calculations by approximations ● How to use a calculator efficiently	● How to multiply and divide by 10, 100 and 1000 ● How to round to the nearest 10, 100 and 1000 ● How to use brackets and memory keys on a calculator ● How to use standard column methods for the four operations

Powers of 10

The nearest star, Proxima Centauri, is 40 653 234 200 000 kilometres from Earth. An atom is 0.000 000 0001 metres wide. When dealing with very large and very small numbers it is easier to round them and work with powers of 10. You will meet this concept later when you do work on Standard Form. In this section you will multiply and divide by powers of 10 and round numbers to one or two decimal places.

Example 8.1

Multiply the following.

   a   0.937   **b**   2.363   **c**   0.002 81

   by **i** 10   **ii** 10^2 **iii** 10^4

   a **i** $0.937 \times 10 = 9.37$ **ii** $0.937 \times 10^2 = 93.7$ **iii** $0.937 \times 10^4 = 9370$

   b **i** $2.363 \times 10 = 23.63$ **ii** $2.363 \times 10^2 = 236.3$ **iii** $2.363 \times 10^4 = 23630$

   c **i** $0.00281 \times 10 = 0.0281$ **ii** $0.00281 \times 10^2 = 0.281$ **iii** $0.00281 \times 10^4 = 28.1$

Example 8.2

Multiply and divide the following.

   a   6   **b**   50   **c**   7.8

     by **i** 0.1   **ii** 0.01

   a **i** $6 \times 0.1 = 0.6, 6 \div 0.1 = 60$ **ii** $6 \times 0.01 = 0.06, 6 \div 0.01 = 600$

   b **i** $50 \times 0.1 = 5, 50 \div 0.1 = 500$ **ii** $50 \times 0.01 = 0.5, 50 \div 0.01 = 5000$

   c **i** $7.8 \times 0.1 = 0.78, 7.8 \div 0.1 = 78$ **ii** $7.8 \times 0.01 = 0.078, 7.8 \div 0.01 = 780$

Example 8.3 ▷ Round each of these numbers to:

    i   one decimal place (1 dp).   **ii**   two decimal places (2 dp).

    a   7.215

    b   0.384

    a   **i**   7.215 is 7.2 to 1 dp   **ii**   7.215 is 7.22 to 2 dp

    b   **i**   0.384 is 0.4 to 1 dp   **ii**   0.384 is 0.38 to 2 dp

Example 8.4 ▷ Work out:

    a 0.00737×10^2

    b $54.1 \div 10^3$

Round the answers to two decimal places (2 dp).

    a $0.00737 \times 10^2 = 0.737$

        0.737 is 0.74 to two decimal places

    b $54.1 \div 10^3 = 0.0541$

        0.0541 is 0.05 to two decimal places

Exercise 8A

1   Multiply the numbers given below by: **i**   10 and   **ii** 10^2

    a   5.3   **b**   0.79   **c**   24   **d**   5.063   **e**   0.003

2   Divide the numbers below by: **i**   10 and   **ii** 10^3

    a   83   **b**   4.1   **c**   457   **d**   6.04   **e**   34 781

3   Write down the answers to the following.

    a 3.1×10 **b** 6.78×10^2 **c** 0.56×10^3 **d** $34 \div 10^3$

    e $823 \div 10^2$ **f** $9.06 \div 10^3$ **g** 57.89×10^2 **h** $57.89 \div 10^2$

    i 0.038×10^3 **j** $0.038 \div 10$ **k** 0.05×10^5 **l** $543 \div 10^5$

4   Multiply the numbers below by: **i**   0.1 and   **ii**   0.01

    a   4.5   **b**   56.2   **c**   0.04   **d**   400   **e**   0.7

5   Divide the numbers below by: **i**   0.1 and   **ii**   0.01

    a   6.3   **b**   300   **c**   7   **d**   81.3   **e**   29

6   This grid represents a 1 cm × 1 cm square that has been split into 100 equal smaller squares. Give all your answers to the questions below in centimetres.

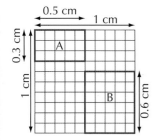

    a   What is the area of each small square?

    b   How many small squares are there inside rectangle A, and what is its area?

    c   Use your answer to **b** to write down the answer to 0.3 × 0.5.

    d   Rectangle B has an area of 0.3 cm². Use this fact and the diagram to write down the answer to 0.3 ÷ 0.6.

6

7 Round the numbers given below to: **i** one decimal place **ii** two decimal places

a	4.722	**b**	3.097	**c**	2.634	**d**	1.932	**e**	0.784
f	0.992	**g**	3.999	**h**	2.604	**i**	3.185	**j**	3.475

8 Multiply the numbers given below by: **i** 10 **ii** 10^2

a 0.4717   **b** 2.6345   **c** 0.0482

Round each answer to one decimal place.

9 Divide the numbers given below by: **i** 10 **ii** 10^2

a 12.34   **b** 136.71   **c** 10.05

Round each answer to one decimal place.

Extension Work

1 Write down the answers to the following.
   a 5×10 **b** 70×10 **c** 0.8×10 **d** 6.3×10

2 Write down the answers to the following.
   a $5 \div 10$ **b** $70 \div 10$ **c** $0.8 \div 10$ **d** $6.3 \div 10$

3 Write down the answers to the following.
   a $5 \div 0.1$ **b** $70 \div 0.1$ **c** $0.8 \div 0.1$ **d** $6.3 \div 0.1$

4 Write down the answers to the following.
   a 5×0.1 **b** 70×0.1 **c** 0.8×0.1 **d** 6.3×0.1

5 Explain the connection between the answers to the above problems, particularly the connection between multiplying by 10 and dividing by 0.1.

6 What is a quick way to calculate $73 \div 0.01$?

Large numbers

Example 8.5

Write down the two numbers shown in the table in words. Consider the numbers in blocks of three digits, that is:

6 058 702
1 700 056

	10^6	10^5	10^4	10^3	10^2	10	1
a	6	0	5	8	7	0	2
b	1	7	0	0	0	5	6

a   6 058 702 = Six million, fifty-eight thousand, seven hundred and two
b   1 700 056 = One million, seven-hundred thousand, and fifty-six.

Example 8.6

The United Kingdom is said to have a population of 61 million. What is the largest and smallest population this could mean?

As the population is given to the nearest million, the actual population could be as much as half a million either way, so the population is between $60\frac{1}{2}$ million and $61\frac{1}{2}$ million or 60 500 000 and 61 500 000.

Example 8.7

a The bar chart shows the annual profits for a large company over the previous five years. Estimate the income each year.

b The company chairman says, 'Income in 2002 was nearly 50 million pounds.' Is the chairman correct?

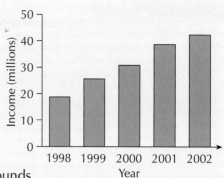

a In 1998 the profits were about 19 million pounds.
In 1999 they were about 25 million pounds.
In 2000 they were about 31 million pounds.
In 2001 they were about 39 million pounds.
In 2002 they were about 43 million pounds.

b The chairman is wrong, as in 2002 the income is nearer 40 million pounds.

Exercise 8B

1 Write the following numbers in words.

   a 3 452 763   **b** 2 047 809   **c** 12 008 907   **d** 3 006 098

2 Write the following numbers using figures.

   a Four million, forty-three thousand, two hundred and seven
   b Nineteen million, five hundred and two thousand and thirty-seven
   c One million, three hundred and two thousand and seven

3 The bar chart shows the population of some countries in the European Community. Estimate the population of each country.

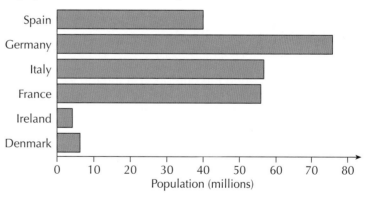

4 Round off the following numbers to: **i** the nearest ten thousand. **ii** the nearest hundred thousand. **iii** the nearest million.

   a 3 547 812   **b** 9 722 106   **c** 3 042 309   **d** 15 698 999

(FM) 5 There are 2 452 800 people out of work. The government says, 'Unemployment is just over two million'. The opposition says, 'Unemployment is still nearly three million'. Who is correct and why?

6 There are 8 million people living in London. What are the highest and lowest figures that the population of London could be?

Standard Form is a way of writing large numbers in a more manageable form.
For example, 3.1×10^6 means $3.1 \times 1\,000\,000 = 3\,100\,000$, and
$4.54 \times 10^9 = 4\,540\,000\,000$.

Write these Standard Form numbers out in full.

a 2.9×10^7 **b** 3.56×10^5 **c** 1.17×10^8 **d** 2.2×10^6

e 9.5×10^8 **f** 8.3×10^6 **g** 2.31×10^{10} **h** 5.04×10^5

Estimations

You should have an idea if the answer to a calculation is about the right size or not. Here are some ways of checking answers.

- First, when it is a multiplication, you can check that the final digit is correct.
- Second, you can round off numbers and do a mental calculation to see if an answer is about right.
- Third, you can check by doing the inverse operation.

Example 8.8

Explain why these calculations must be wrong.

a $23 \times 45 = 1053$ **b** $19 \times 59 = 121$

a The last digit should be 5, because the product of the last digits is 15.
That is, $23 \times 45 = \ldots 5$

b The answer is roughly $20 \times 60 = 1200$.

Example 8.9

Estimate the answers to each of these calculations.

a $\dfrac{21.3 + 48.7}{6.4}$ **b** 31.2×48.5 **c** $359 \div 42$

a Round the numbers on the top to $20 + 50 = 70$. Round off 6.4 to 7.
Then $70 \div 7 = 10$.

b Round to 30×50, which is $3 \times 5 \times 100 = 1500$.

c Round to $360 \div 40$, which is $36 \div 4 = 9$.

Example 8.10

By using the inverse operation, check if each calculation is correct.

a $450 \div 6 = 75$ **b** $310 - 59 = 249$

a By the inverse operation, $450 = 6 \times 75$. This is true and can be checked mentally: $6 \times 70 = 420$, $6 \times 5 = 30$, $420 + 30 = 450$.

b By the inverse operation, $310 = 249 + 59$.
This addition must end in 8 as $9 + 9 = 18$, so the calculation cannot be correct.

Example 8.11 ▷ Estimate the answers to the following.

    a 12% of 923   **b** $\dfrac{11.2 + 53.6}{18.7 - 9.6}$ **c** 324 ÷ 59

    a Round to 10% of 900 = 90

    b Round to $\dfrac{10 + 50}{20 - 10} = \dfrac{60}{10} = 6$

    c Round to 300 ÷ 60 = 5

Exercise 8C

1 Explain why these calculations must be wrong.

    a 24 × 42 = 1080   **b** 51 × 73 = 723   **c** $\dfrac{34.5 + 63.2}{9.7} = 20.07$

    d 360 ÷ 8 = 35   **e** 354 − 37 = 323

2 Estimate the answer to each of these problems.

    a 2768 − 392   **b** 231 × 18   **c** 792 ÷ 38   **d** $\dfrac{36.7 + 23.2}{14.1}$

    e 423 × 423   **f** 157.2 ÷ 38.2   **g** $\dfrac{135.7 - 68.2}{15.8 - 8.9}$ **h** $\dfrac{38.9 \times 61.2}{39.6 - 18.4}$

FM 3 Delroy had £10. In his shopping basket he had a magazine costing £2.65, some batteries costing £1.92, and a tape costing £4.99. Without adding up the numbers, how could Delroy be sure he had enough to buy the goods in the basket? Explain a quick way for Delroy to find out if he could afford a 45p bar of chocolate as well.

FM 4 Amy bought 6 bottles of pop at 46p per bottle. The shopkeeper asked her for £3.16. Without working out the correct answer, explain why this is wrong.

FM 5 A first class stamp is 27p. I need eight. Will £2 be enough to pay for them? Explain your answer clearly.

FM 6 In a shop I bought a 53p comic and a £1.47 model car. The till said £54.47. Why?

7 Estimate the value the arrow is pointing at in each of these.

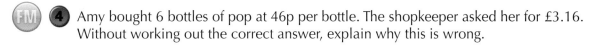
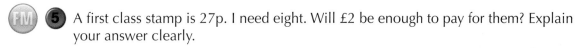

a   0.7   3.7   **b**   0   6.3   **c**   −20   10

8 Estimate the answers to the following.

    a 23% of 498   **b** 6.72^2 **c** 523 × 69   **d** $\frac{1}{3}$ of 320

    e 1.75 × 16   **f** 287 × 102   **g** $\dfrac{18.3 - 5.2}{10.7 + 8.6}$ **h** $\dfrac{178 \times 18}{21}$

Extension Work

1 Without working out areas or counting squares, explain why the area of the square shown must be between 36 and 64 grid squares.

2 Now calculate the area of the square.

3 Using an 8 × 8 grid, draw a square with an area of exactly 50 grid squares.

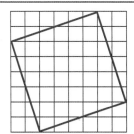

Adding and subtracting decimals

Example 8.12

Work out the following.

a　$64.062 + 178.9 + 98.27$　　　**b**　$20 - 8.72 - 6.5$

The numbers need to be lined up in columns with the decimal point in line. Blank places can be filled with zeros if needed. Part **b** needs to be done in two stages.

a
```
   64.062
  178.900
+  98.270
  341.232
    2 1  1
```

b
```
   ¹²⁰.⁹⁰⁰       ⁰¹
   2̸0̸.0̸0       1̸1̸.28
 -  8.72      -  6.50
   11.28         4.78
```

Example 8.13

In a Science lesson a student adds 0.45 kg of water and 0.72 kg of salt to a beaker that weighs 0.092 kg. He then pours out 0.6 kg of the mixture. What is the total mass of the beaker and mixture remaining?

This has to be set up as an addition and subtraction problem, that is:
$0.092 + 0.45 + 0.72 - 0.6$

The problem has to be done in two stages:

```
   0.092        ⁰¹
   0.450       1̸.262
+  0.720     - 0.600
   1.262       0.662
    1 1
```

0·72 kg

−0·6 kg

0·45 kg　+

0·092 kg

? kg

So the final mass is 0.662 kg or 662 grams.

Exercise 8D

1 Work out the following.

a　$4.32 + 65.098 + 172.3$　　　　**b**　$8.7 + 9 + 14.02 + 1.035$

c　$11.423 + 15.72 - 12.98$　　　　**d**　$42.7 + 67.3 - 35.27$

e　$19.87 + 2.8 - 13.46 - 12.873 + 8.9$　**f**　$12 - 5.096 + 3.21$

g　$23.907 + 8 - 9.25$　　　　　　**h**　$7.05 + 2.9 + 7 + 0.64$

i　$7.25 + 19.3 - 12.06 - 0.008$

j　$21.35 + 6.72 - 12.36 - 9.476 + 16.406 - 7.64$

2 There are 1000 metres in a kilometre. Work out the following (work in kilometres).

a　7.45 km + 843 m + 68 m　　　　**b**　3.896 km + 723 m + 92 m

c　8.76 km + 463 m − 892 m　　　　**d**　16 km − 435 m − 689 m

e　7.8 km + 5.043 km − 989 m

3 There are 1000 grams in a kilogram. Calculate the mass of the following shopping baskets (work in kilograms).

a　3.2 kg of apples, 454 g of jam, 750 g of lentils, 1.2 kg of flour

b　1.3 kg of sugar, 320 g of strawberries, 0.65 kg of rice

4 In an experiment a beaker of water has a mass of 1.104 kg. The beaker alone weighs 0.125 kg. What is the mass of water in the beaker?

5 A rectangle is 2.35 m by 43 cm. What is its perimeter (in metres)?

6 A piece of string is 5 m long. Pieces of length 84 cm, 1.23 m and 49 cm are cut from it. How much string is left (in metres)?

7 A large container of oil contains 20 litres. Over five days the following amounts are poured from the container:

2.34 l, 1.07 l, 0.94 l, 3.47 l, 1.2 l

How much oil is left in the container?

Extension Work

Much as fractions and decimals show the same thing, centimetres and millimetres both show lengths. The first length shown on the rule below, AB, can be given as 1.6 cm, 16 mm or $1\frac{3}{5}$ cm.

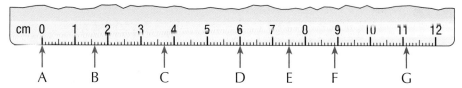

Write the distances shown:
i in centimetres as a decimal **ii** in millimetres **iii** in centimetres as a fraction
a AC **b** BD **c** CE **d** DE **e** EF **f** EG

Efficient calculations

It is important that you know how to use your calculator. You should be able to use the basic functions (×, ÷, +, −) and the square, square root and brackets keys. You have also met the memory and sign-change keys. This exercise introduces the fraction and power keys.

Example 8.14 ▷ Use a calculator to work out:

a $(1\frac{3}{10} - \frac{4}{5}) \times \frac{3}{4}$ **b** $\dfrac{1\frac{2}{5} + 1\frac{1}{4}}{2\frac{1}{2} - 1\frac{7}{8}}$

a Using the fraction button ▤ and the arrows ◀ ▲ ▶ ▼, type in the calculation as:

(SHIFT ▤ 1 ▶ 3 ▼ 1 0 ▶ − ▤ 4 ▼ 5) × ▤ 3 ▼ 4 =

The display should show $\frac{3}{8}$.

b Using brackets and the fraction buttons gives an answer of $4\frac{6}{25}$ (may also display as $\frac{106}{25}$).

To convert from improper ($\frac{106}{25}$) to a mixed number ($4\frac{6}{25}$), press SHIFT S↔D .

Example 8.15

Use a calculator to work out the following.

a 5^6 b $\sqrt[3]{729}$ c $\sqrt{19.5^2 - 7.5^2}$

a   Using the power button, $\boxed{x^\blacksquare}$, the answer should be 15 625.

b   This can be keyed in as:

   $\boxed{\text{SHIFT}}$ $\boxed{x^\blacksquare}$ $\boxed{3}$ $\boxed{\blacktriangleright}$ $\boxed{7}$ $\boxed{2}$ $\boxed{9}$ $\boxed{=}$

   The answer is 9. Make sure you can use your calculator to find this answer.

c   Using the square root, bracket and square keys the answer should be 18. For example, the following are two ways to key the problem in to the calculator:

   or $\boxed{\sqrt{}}$ $\boxed{(}$ $\boxed{1}$ $\boxed{9}$ $\boxed{.}$ $\boxed{5}$ $\boxed{x^2}$ $\boxed{-}$ $\boxed{7}$ $\boxed{.}$ $\boxed{5}$ $\boxed{x^2}$ $\boxed{)}$ $\boxed{=}$

   $\boxed{(}$ $\boxed{1}$ $\boxed{9}$ $\boxed{.}$ $\boxed{5}$ $\boxed{x^2}$ $\boxed{-}$ $\boxed{7}$ $\boxed{.}$ $\boxed{5}$ $\boxed{x^2}$ $\boxed{)}$ $\boxed{\sqrt{}}$ $\boxed{=}$

Exercise 8E

1 Use the bracket and/or memory keys on your calculator to work out each of these.

a $\dfrac{38.7 - 23.1}{3.82 + 1.38}$ b $\sqrt{4.1^2 - 0.9^2}$ c $9.75 \div (3.2 - 1.7)$

2 Use the fraction key on your calculator to work out each of these (give your answer as a mixed number or a fraction in its simplest form).

a $\frac{1}{8} + \frac{3}{5} + \frac{3}{16}$ b $1\frac{2}{3} + 2\frac{2}{9} - \frac{5}{6}$ c $\frac{3}{8} \times \frac{4}{15} \div \frac{4}{5}$

d $(2\frac{1}{5} + 3\frac{3}{4}) \times 2\frac{1}{7}$ e $\dfrac{2\frac{1}{4} - 1\frac{2}{7}}{1\frac{1}{2} + 1\frac{1}{14}}$ f $\dfrac{4\frac{3}{5} - 3\frac{2}{3}}{3\frac{3}{8} - 1\frac{4}{5}}$

g $(1\frac{3}{4})^2$ h $\sqrt{3\frac{11}{16} - 1\frac{7}{16}}$ i $(2\frac{2}{3} + 1\frac{1}{8}) \div \frac{7}{8}$

3 Use the power, cube and cube root keys on your calculator to work out each of these (round your answers to one decimal place if necessary).

a 4^6 b 2.3^3 c $\sqrt[3]{1331}$

d $\sqrt{3^4 + 4^3}$ e 2^{10} f $4 \times (5.78)^3$

g 3×7.2^2 h $(3 \times 7.2)^2$ i $\sqrt{8.9^2 - 3.1^2}$

4 A time given in hours and minutes can be put into a calculator as a fraction. For example, 3 hours and 25 minutes is $3\frac{25}{60}$, which is entered as

   $\boxed{\text{SHIFT}}$ $\boxed{\frac{\blacksquare}{\square}}$ $\boxed{3}$ $\boxed{\blacktriangleright}$ $\boxed{2}$ $\boxed{5}$ $\boxed{\blacktriangledown}$ $\boxed{6}$ $\boxed{0}$

Using the fraction button on your calculator and remembering that $\frac{1}{3}$ hour = 20 minutes, $\frac{1}{5}$ hour = 12 minutes, and so on, do the following time problems (give your answers in hours and minutes).

a   Add 2 hours and 25 minutes to 3 hours and 55 minutes.

b   Subtract 1 hour 48 minutes from 3 hours 24 minutes.

c   Multiply 1 hour 32 minutes by 5.

5 Most square and cube roots cannot be given as an exact value, so we have to approximate them. The following are a selection of square and cube roots of whole numbers. Unfortunately, you do not know if the number is a square root or a cube root. Use your calculator to find out if it is a square root or a cube root and the number for which it is either of these (**a** and **b** are done for you).

a 1.41421	**b** 2.15443	**c** 3.41995	**d** 2.23607
e 4.47214	**f** 1.44225	**g** 2.28943	**h** 5.47723

a $1.41421^2 = 1.999396$, so $\sqrt{2} \approx 1.41421$

b $2.15443^3 = 9.9995$, so $\sqrt[3]{10} \approx 2.15443$

Extension Work

On your calculator you may have a key or a function above a key marked x^{-1}.

Find out what this key does. For example, on some calculators you can key:

3 **SHIFT** x^{-1}

3 and the display shows 6,

and you can key:

7 **SHIFT** x^{-1}

7 and the display shows 5040.

Similarly, investigate what the key marked x^{-1} does.

Multiplying and dividing decimals

Example 8.16

Work out the following.

a 8.6×6.5 **b** 1.43×3.4

a Firstly, estimate the answer, that is $9 \times 6 = 54$. This problem is done using a box method, breaking the two numbers into their whole number and fractions. Each are multiplied together and the totals added:

×	8	0.6
6	48	3.6
0.5	4	0.3

Sum of multiplications

```
  48
   4
 3.6
 0.3
─────
55.9
```

The answer is 55.9.

b Firstly, estimate the answer, that is $1.5 \times 3 = 4.5$, to show where the decimal point will be. This problem is then done using standard column methods without decimal points:

```
   143
 ×  34
 ─────
   572
  4290
 ─────
  4862
```

The position of the decimal point is shown by the estimate, and so the answer is 4.862

Note that the number of decimal places in the answer is the same as in the original problem, that is $1.\underline{43} \times 3.\underline{4} = 4.\underline{862}$

Example 8.17 ▷

Work out the following.

a 76.8 ÷ 16

b 156 ÷ 2.4

a Firstly, estimate the answer, that is 80 ÷ 16 = 5.
Now consider the problem as 768 ÷ 16:

```
  768
- 640    (40 × 16)
  128
   64    (4 × 16)
   64
   64    (4 × 16)
    0    (48 × 16)
```

The position of the decimal point is shown by
the estimate, and so the answer is 4.8.

b Firstly, estimate the answer, that is 150 ÷ 3 = 50.
Now consider the problem as 1560 ÷ 24:

```
  1560
-  960    (40 × 24)
   600
-  480    (20 × 24)
   120
   120    (5 × 24)
     0    (65 × 24)
```

The position of the decimal point is shown by
the estimate, and so the answer is 65.

As you become used to this method of division, you can start to take away longer
'chunks' each time. For example, in **b** you could take away 60 × 24 instead of
40 × 24 and then 20 × 24. This will improve your mental multiplication too!

5

Exercise 8F

1 Without using a calculator, and using any other method you are happy with, work out
the following.

a	6.3 × 9.4	**b**	5.8 × 4.5
c	2.7 × 2.7	**d**	1.4 × 12.6
e	0.78 × 2.5	**f**	1.26 × 3.5
g	2.58 × 6.5	**h**	0.74 × 0.22

2 Without using a calculator, and using any other method you are happy with, work out
the following.

a	78.4 ÷ 14	**b**	7.92 ÷ 22
c	24 ÷ 3.2	**d**	12.6 ÷ 3.6
e	143 ÷ 5.5	**f**	289 ÷ 3.4
g	57 ÷ 3.8	**h**	10.8 ÷ 0.24

3 Roller ball pens cost £1.23 each. How much will 72 pens cost?

4 Number fans cost 65p each. How many can be bought for £78?

The box method can be used to do quite complicated decimal multiplications. For example, 2.56×4.862 can be worked out as follows:

×	4	0.8	0.06	0.002	Sum of row
2	8	1.6	0.12	0.004	9.724
0.5	2	0.4	0.03	0.001	2.431
0.06	0.24	0.048	0.0036	0.00012	0.29172
				Total	12.44672

Use the box method to calculate 1.47×2.429.

Check your answer with a calculator.

LEVEL BOOSTER

5
I can round numbers to one decimal place.
I can use bracket, square and square root keys on a calculator.
I can add and subtract decimals up to two decimal places.
I can multiply and divide decimals up to two decimal places.

6
I can round numbers to two decimal places.
I can multiply and divide by powers of 10.
I can approximate decimals when solving numerical problems.

5

1 *2003 5–7 Paper 1*

    a I pay **£16.20** to travel to work each week.

       I work for **45 weeks** each year.

       How much do I pay to travel to work each year?

       Show your working.

    b I could buy one season ticket that would let me travel for **45 weeks**.

       It would cost **£630**.

       How much is that per week?

2 *2007 5–7 Paper 2*

Kate buys **24 cans** of lemonade.

She buys the cans in **packs of 4**.

Each pack costs **£1.20**.

Pack of 4
Cost £1.20

Steve buys **24 cans** of lemonade.

He buys the cans in **packs of 6**.

Each pack costs **£1.60**.

Pack of 4
Cost £1.20

Kate pays more for her 24 cans than Steve pays for his 24 cans.

How much more?

6

3 *2002 Paper 1*

    a The number 6 is halfway between 4.5 and 7.5.

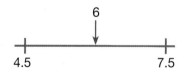

       What are the missing numbers below?

       The number 6 is halfway between 2.8 and …

       The number 6 is halfway between −12 and …

    b Work out the number that is halfway between 27×38 and 33×38.

FM 4 *2002 Paper 2*

A company sells and processes films of two different sizes.
The tables show how much the company charges:

Film size: 24 photos	
Cost of each film	£2.15
Postage	Free
Cost to print film	£0.99
Postage of each film	60p

Film size: 36 photos	
Cost of each film	£2.65
Postage	Free
Cost to print film	£2.89
Postage of each film	60p

I want to take 360 photos. I need to buy the film, pay for the film to be printed and pay for the postage.

a Is it cheaper to use all films of 24 photos or all films of 36 photos?

b How much cheaper is it?

Taxes

There are two types of taxes – direct tax and indirect tax.

Direct tax is tax taken directly from what you earn, for example Income tax.

Indirect tax is tax taken from what you spend, for example VAT.

Direct tax

Income tax
Each person has a tax allowance. This is the amount they are allowed to earn without paying income tax.

Tax rates
Basic rate: First £36 000 of taxable pay is taxed at the rate of 20%.

> **Example 1**
> Mr Gallagher's tax allowance is £5435.
> He earns £25 000.
> His taxable pay is £25 000 – £5435 = £19 565
>
> So his income tax is:
> **Basic rate: 20% of £19 565 = £3913**

Indirect tax

VAT
Value added tax is charged at three different rates on goods and services.

Standard rate (17.5%)
You pay VAT on most goods and services in the UK at the standard rate.

Reduced rate (5%)
In some cases, a reduced rate of VAT is charged, for example children's car seats and domestic fuel or power.

Zero rate (0%)
There are some goods on which you do not pay any VAT, for example:
- Food
- Books, newspapers and magazines
- Children's clothes
- Special exempt items, such as equipment for disabled people

> **Example 2**
> Work out the 17.5% VAT charged on a bicycle costing £180 excluding VAT.
>
> 10% of £180 = £18
> 5% of £180 = £9
> 2.5% of £180 = £4.50
> So 17.5% of £180 = £31.50

Use the information on taxes to answer these questions.

1 Sam earnt £20 000 last year. He spent £5000 of his earnings on a new car. What percentage of his earnings is this?

2 Hollie earnt £16 000 last year. This year she had a pay increase of 5%. How much does she earn now?

3 Miss Howe receives her gas bill. What is the rate of VAT that she will have to pay?

4 Mr Legg buys a wheelchair. What is the rate of VAT that he pays?

5 Bradley bought a new child seat. The cost was £90 excluding VAT.
   a What rate of VAT is charged?
   b Work out the total cost of the child seat including VAT.

6 Kerry bought a mobile phone. The cost was £260 excluding 17.5% VAT.
Work out the cost including VAT.

7 Mrs Pritchard earns £24 000. Her tax allowance is £6000. She pays tax on the rest at 20%.
   a How much does she pay tax on?
   b How much tax does she pay?

8 Miss France earns £14 000. Her tax allowance is £5600. She pays tax on the rest at 20%.
   a How much does she pay tax on?
   b How much does she earn after the tax is deducted?

9 Mr Ladds earns £5500. His tax allowance is £6200.
   a Explain why he does not pay any tax.
   b How much more can he earn before he has to pay tax?

2002	2003	2004	20
13,556.1	13,269.7	13,025.9	12,84
9,742.6	9,6?		
719.2	6?		
1,287.9	1,5		
1,022.7			
2,966.0			
1,168.			
2,338			
2			
1			

CHAPTER 9 Geometry and Measures 3

This chapter is going to show you

- How to recognise congruent shapes
- How to transform 2-D shapes by combinations of reflections, rotations and translations
- How to enlarge a shape by a scale factor

What you should already know

- How to reflect a 2-D shape in a mirror line
- How to rotate a 2-D shape about a point
- How to translate a 2-D shape
- How to use ratio

Congruent shapes

All the triangles on the grid below are reflections, rotations or translations of Triangle A. What do you notice about them?

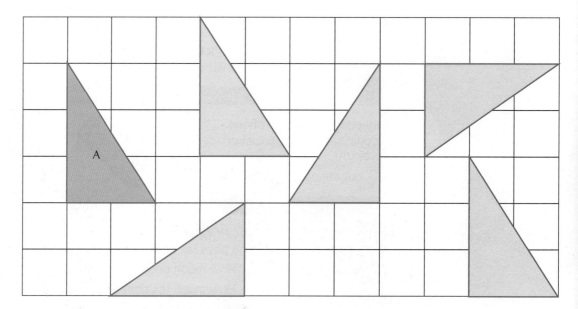

You should remember that the image triangles are exactly the same shape and size as the object Triangle A.

Two shapes are said to be **congruent** if they are exactly the same shape and size. Reflections, rotations and translations all produce images that are congruent to the original object. For shapes that are congruent, all the corresponding sides and angles are equal.

Example 9.1 ▶ Which two shapes below are congruent?

 a b c d

Shapes **b** and **d** are exactly the same shape and size, so **b** and **d** are congruent. Tracing paper can be used to check that two shapes are congruent.

Exercise 9A

① For each pair of shapes below, state whether they are congruent or not (use tracing paper to help if you are not sure).

a 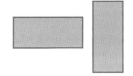   b 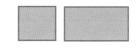   c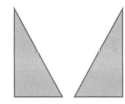

d 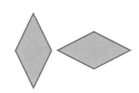   e 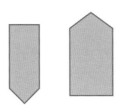   f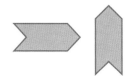

② Which pairs of shapes on the grid below are congruent?

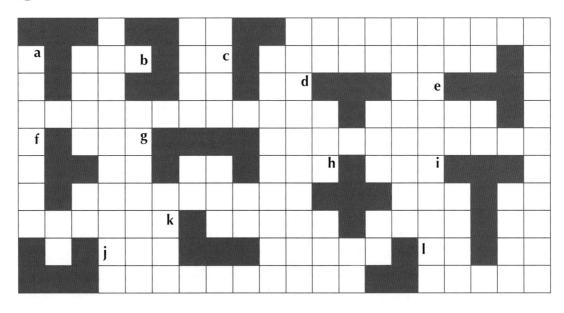

3 Which of the shapes below are congruent?

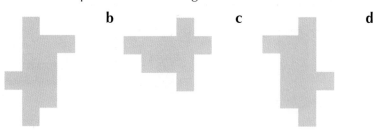

a   b   c   d

4 Two congruent right-angled triangles are placed together with two of their equal sides touching to make another shape, as shown on the diagram below:

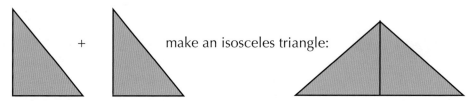

+   make an isosceles triangle:

a How many different shapes can you make? To help, you can cut out the triangles from a piece of card.

b Repeat the activity using two congruent isosceles triangles.

c Repeat the activity using two congruent equilateral triangles.

Extension Work

The 4-by-4 pinboard is divided into two congruent shapes.

1 Use square-dotted paper to show the number of different ways this can be done.

2 Can you divide the pinboard into four congruent shapes?

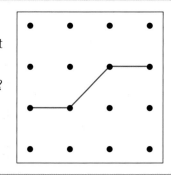

Combinations of transformations

The three single transformations you have met so far and the notation that we use to explain these transformations are shown below.

Reflections

Mirror line

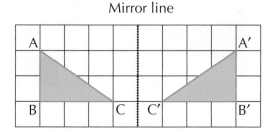

Triangle ABC is mapped onto triangle A'B'C' by a reflection in the mirror line. The object and the image are congruent.

Rotations

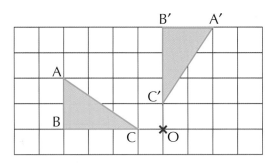

Triangle ABC is mapped onto triangle A'B'C' by a rotation of 90° clockwise about the centre of rotation O. The object and the image are congruent.

Translations

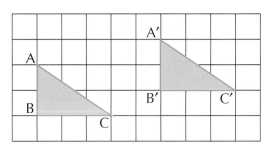

Triangle ABC is mapped onto triangle A'B'C' by a translation of five units to the right, followed by one unit up. The object and the image are congruent.

The example below shows how a shape can be transformed by a combination of two of the above transformations.

Example 9.2

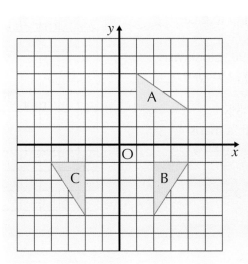

Triangle A is mapped onto triangle C after two combined transformations. Firstly, a rotation of 90° clockwise about the origin O maps A onto B, and secondly a reflection in the y-axis maps B onto C. So triangle A is mapped onto triangle C after a rotation of 90° clockwise about the origin O followed by a reflection in the y-axis.

Exercise 9B

Tracing paper and a mirror will be useful for this exercise.

1 Copy the diagram opposite onto squared paper.

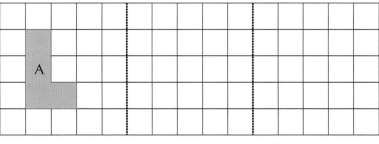

Mirror line 1   Mirror line 2

a Reflect shape A in mirror line 1 to give shape B.

b Reflect shape B in mirror line 2 to give shape C.

c Describe the single transformation that maps shape A onto shape C.

2 Copy the diagram opposite onto squared paper.

   a   Reflect shape A in the *x*-axis to give shape B.

   b   Reflect shape B in the *y*-axis to give shape C.

   c   Describe the single transformation that maps shape A onto shape C.

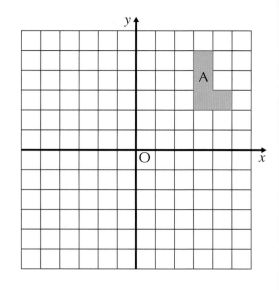

3 Copy the diagram opposite onto squared paper.

   a   Rotate shape A 90° clockwise about the origin O to give shape B.

   b   Rotate shape B 90° clockwise about the origin O to give shape C.

   c   Describe the single transformation that maps shape A onto shape C.

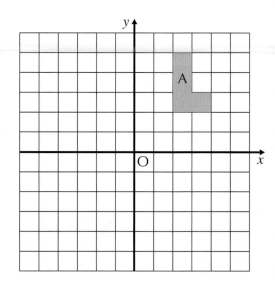

4 Copy the diagram onto squared paper.

   a   Translate shape A three units to the right, followed by two units up, to give shape B.

   b   Translate shape B four units to the right, followed by 1 unit down, to give shape C.

   c   Describe the single transformation that maps shape A onto shape C.

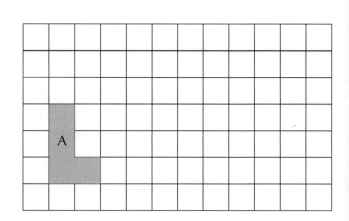

5 Copy the triangles A, B, C, D, E and F onto a square grid, as shown.

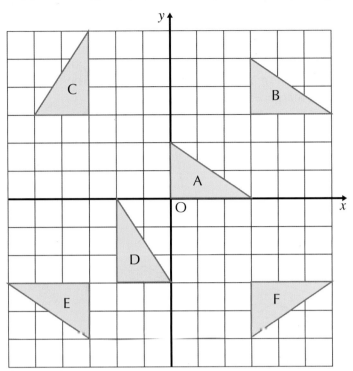

a Find a single transformation that will map:

    i A onto B   **ii** E onto F   **iii** B onto E   **iv** C onto B

b Find a combination of two transformations that will map:

    i A onto C   **ii** B onto F   **iii** F onto D   **iv** B onto E

c Find other examples of combined transformations for different pairs of triangles.

6 On squared paper, show how repeated reflections of a rectangle generate a tessellating pattern.

Extension Work

1 Copy the congruent 'T' shapes A, B, C and D onto a square grid, as shown.

Find a combination of two transformations that will map:

    a A onto B   **b** A onto C

    c A onto D   **d** B onto C

    e B onto D   **f** C onto D

2 Use ICT software, such as LOGO, to transform shapes by using various combinations of reflections, rotations and translations. Print out some examples and present them on a poster.

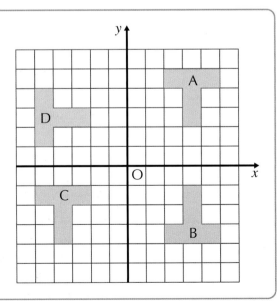

Enlargements

The three transformations you have met so far (reflections, rotations and translations) do not change the size of the object. You are now going to look at a transformation that does change the size of an object: **an enlargement**. The illustration shows a photograph that has been enlarged.

The diagram shows △ABC enlarged to give △A'B'C':

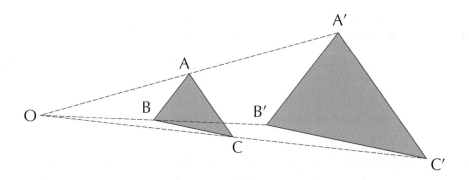

All the sides of △A'B'C' are twice as long as the sides of △ABC. Notice also that OA' = 2 × OA, OB' = 2 × OB and OC' = 2 × OC. We say that △ABC is enlarged by a scale factor of two about the centre of enlargement O to give the image △A'B'C'. The dotted lines are called the guidelines or rays for the enlargement.

To enlarge a shape we need a **centre of enlargement** and a **scale factor**.

Example 9.3 ▷ Enlarge the triangle XYZ by a scale factor of two about the centre of enlargement O:

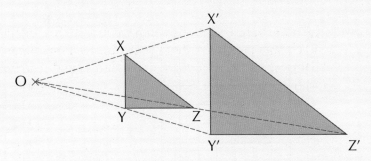

Draw rays OX, OY and OZ. Measure the length of the three rays and multiply each of these lengths by two. Then extend each of the rays to these new lengths measured from O and plot the points X', Y' and Z'. Join X', Y' and Z'.

ΔX'Y'Z' is the enlargement of ΔXYZ by a scale factor of two about the centre of enlargement O.

Example 9.4 ▷ The rectangle ABCD on the coordinate grid shown has been enlarged by a scale factor of 3 about the origin O to give the image rectangle A'B'C'D'.

The coordinates of the object are: A(0, 2), B(3, 2), C(3, 1) and D(0, 1). The coordinates of the image are: A'(0, 6), B'(9, 6), C'(9, 3) and D'(0, 3). Notice that if a shape is enlarged by a scale factor about the origin on a coordinate grid, the coordinates of the enlarged shape are multiplied by the scale factor.

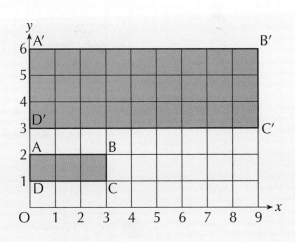

Exercise 9C

① Draw copies of (or trace) the shapes below and enlarge each one by the given scale factor about the centre of enlargement O.

a   Scale factor 2   b   Scale factor 3   c   Scale factor 2   d   Scale factor 3

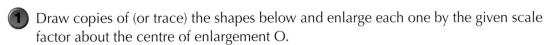

(**Note:** × is the centre of square)

2 Copy the diagrams below onto centimetre-squared paper and enlarge each one by the given scale factor about the origin O.

a

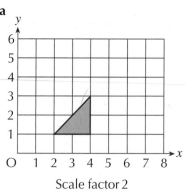

Scale factor 2

b

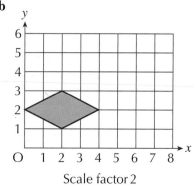

Scale factor 2

c

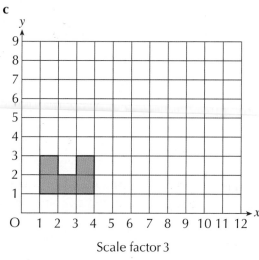

Scale factor 3

d

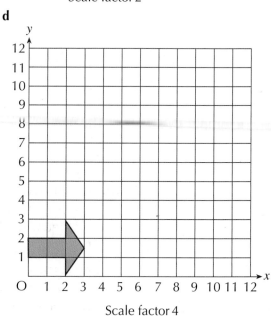

Scale factor 4

3 Draw axes for *x* and *y* from 0 to 10 on centimetre-squared paper. Plot the points A(4, 6), B(5, 4), C(4, 1) and D(3, 4) and join them together to form the kite ABCD. Enlarge the kite by a scale factor of 2 about the point (1, 2).

4 Copy the diagram shown onto centimetre-squared paper.

a Enlarge the square ABCD by a scale factor of two about the point (5, 5). Label the square A′B′C′D′. Write down the coordinates of A′, B′, C′ and D′.

b On the same grid, enlarge the square ABCD by a scale factor of three about the point (5, 5). Label the square A″B″C″D″. Write down the coordinates of A″, B″, C″ and D″.

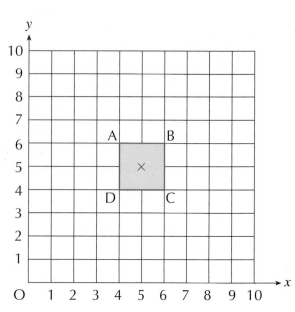

c On the same grid, enlarge the square ABCD by a scale factor of four about the point (5, 5). Label the square A'''B'''C'''D'''. Write down the coordinates of A''', B''', C''' and D'''.

d What do you notice about the coordinate points that you have written down?

5 Copy the diagram shown onto centimetre-squared paper.

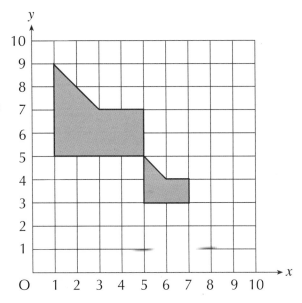

a What is the scale factor of the enlargement?

b By adding suitable rays to your diagram, find the coordinates of the centre of enlargement.

6 a Draw axes for *x* and *y* from 0 to 12 on centimetre-squared paper. Plot the points A(1, 3), B(3, 3), C(3, 1) and D(1, 1), and then join them together to form the square ABCD.

b Write down the area of the square.

c Enlarge the square ABCD by a scale factor of 2 about the origin. What is the area of the enlarged square?

d Enlarge the square ABCD by a scale factor of 3 about the origin. What is the area of the enlarged square?

e Enlarge the square ABCD by a scale factor of 4 about the origin. What is the area of the enlarged square?

f Write down anything you notice about the increase in area of the enlarged squares. Can you write down a rule to explain what is happening?

g Repeat the above using your own shapes. Does your rule still work?

Extension Work

1 Working in pairs or groups, design a poster to show how the 'stick-man' shown can be enlarged by different scale factors about any convenient centre of enlargement.

2 Use reference books or the Internet to explain how each of the following use enlargements.

    a Slide projectors   **b** Telescopes   **c** Microscopes

3 Use ICT software, such as LOGO, to enlarge shapes by different scale factors and with different centres of enlargement.

Shape and ratio

Ratio can be used to compare lengths, areas and volumes of 2-D and 3-D shapes, as the following examples show.

Example 9.5 ▷

A •————• B   C •————————————————• D
    12 mm   4.8 cm

To find the ratio of the length of the line segment AB to the length of the line segment CD, change the measurements to the smallest unit and then simplify the ratio. So the ratio is 12 mm : 4.8 cm = 12 mm : 48 mm = 1 : 4. Remember that ratios have no units in the final answer.

Example 9.6 ▷

Find the ratio of the area of rectangle A to the area of rectangle B, giving the answer in its simplest form.

The ratio is 12 cm^2 : 40 cm^2 = 3 : 10.

Example 9.7 ▷

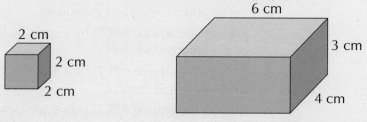

Find the ratio of the volume of the cube to the volume of the cuboid, giving the answer in its simplest form.

The ratio is 8 cm^3 : 72 cm^3 = 1 : 9.

Exercise 9D

1 Express each of the following ratios in its simplest form.

   a   10 mm : 25 mm   **b**   2 mm : 2 cm   **c**   36 cm : 45 cm
   d   40 cm : 2 m   **e**   500 m : 2 km

2 For the two squares shown, find each of the following ratios, giving your answers in their simplest form.

   a   The length of a side of square A to the length of a side of square B.

   b   The perimeter of square A to the perimeter of square B.

   c   The area of square A to the area of square B.

3 Three rectangles A, B and C are arranged as in the diagram. The ratio of the length of A to the length of B to the length of C is 3 cm : 6 cm : 9 cm = 1 : 2 : 3.

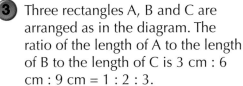
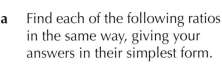
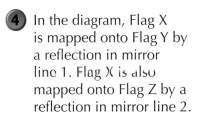

- **a** Find each of the following ratios in the same way, giving your answers in their simplest form.
  - **i** The width of A to the width of B to the width of C.
  - **ii** The perimeter of A to the perimeter of B to the perimeter of C.
  - **iii** The area of A to the area of B to the area of C.
- **b** Write down anything you notice about the three rectangles.

4 In the diagram, Flag X is mapped onto Flag Y by a reflection in mirror line 1. Flag X is also mapped onto Flag Z by a reflection in mirror line 2.

Find the ratio of each of the following lengths, giving your answers in their simplest form.

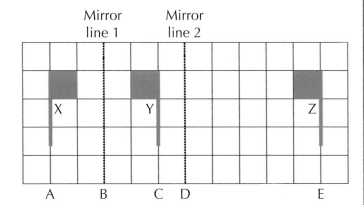

- **a** AB : BC
- **b** AB : AE
- **c** AC : AE
- **d** BD : CE

5 **a** Find the ratio of the area of the pink square to the area of the yellow surround, giving your answer in its simplest form.

- **b** Express the area of the pink square as a fraction of the area of the yellow surround.

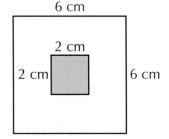

6 The dimensions of lawn A and lawn B are given on the diagrams.

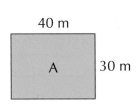
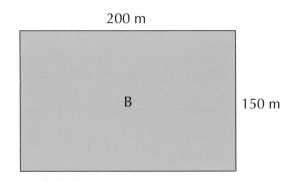

a Calculate the area of lawn A, giving your answer in square metres.

b Calculate the area of lawn B giving your answer in:

   i square meters.   **ii** hectares (1 hectare = 10 000 m²).

c Find the ratio of the length of lawn A to the length of lawn B, giving your answer in its simplest form.

d Find the ratio of the area of lawn A to the area of lawn B, giving your answer in its simplest form.

e Express the area of lawn A as a fraction of the area of lawn B.

7 The dimensions of a fish tank are given on this diagram.

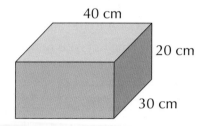

a Calculate the volume of the fish tank, giving your answer in litres (1 litre = 1000 cm³).

b The fish tank is filled with water to a depth of $\frac{3}{4}$ of the height. Calculate the volume of water in the fish tank, giving your answer in litres.

c Find the ratio of the volume of water in the fish tank to the total volume of the fish tank, giving your answer in its simplest form.

Extension Work

1

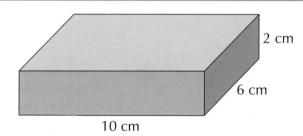

a Find the ratio of the sides of the two cuboids.

b Find the ratio of the total surface area of the two cuboids.

c Find the ratio of the volume of the two cuboids.

2 You will need a sheet each of A5, A4 and A3 paper for this activity. Measure the length and width of the sides of each sheet of paper to the nearest millimetre.

a What is the connection between the length and width of successive paper sizes?

b Find the ratio of the lengths for each successive paper size. Give your answer in the form 1 : *n*.

5
I can recognise congruent shapes.
I can recognise and visualise simple transformations of 2-D shapes.
I can solve problems using ratio.

6
I can transform 2-D shapes by a combination of reflections.
I can enlarge a 2-D shape by a scale factor.

National Test questions

1 *2002 Paper 1*

Four squares join together to make a bigger square.

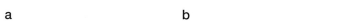

a   b   c

a **Four** congruent triangles join together to make a bigger triangle. On a copy of the diagram, draw **two more** triangles to complete the drawing of the bigger triangle.

b Four congruent trapezia join to make a bigger trapezium. On a copy of the diagram, draw **two more** trapezia to complete the drawing of the bigger trapezium.

c Four congruent trapezia join together to make a **parallelogram**.
On a copy of the diagram, draw **two more** trapeziums to complete the drawing of the parallelogram.

2 *2006 4–6 Paper 2*

Look at the square grids.

Each diagram shows an enlargement of scale factor 2.

The **centre** of this enlargement is marked with a cross.

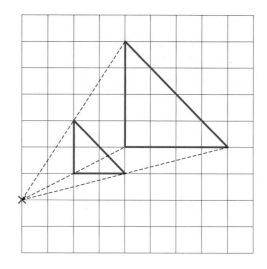

Where is the centre of enlargement in these diagrams?

Mark each one with a cross.

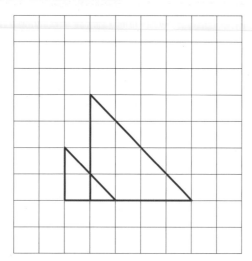 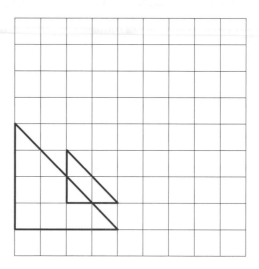

3 *2002 Paper 2*

On a copy of the grid, draw an **enlargement** of **scale factor 2** of the arrow.
Use **point C** as the centre of the enlargement.

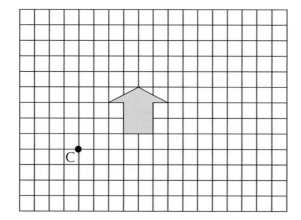

4   *2001 Paper 1*

Two parts of this square design are shaded black.
Two parts are shaded pink.

Show that the ratio of black to pink is 5 : 3.

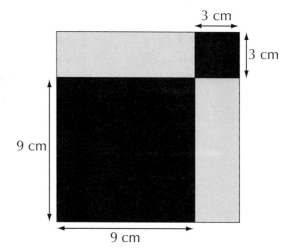

This chapter is going to show you	What you should already know
• How to solve more difficult equations • How to substitute into a formula • How to create your own expressions and formulae	• How to add, subtract and multiply negative numbers

Solving equations

The equations you are going to meet will contain an unknown value, often written as x. This is called the **unknown** of the equation. Solving the equation means finding the actual value of the x, which we can do in several different ways.

For example, there are many ways you could go about solving the equation $5x - 3 = 27$, but by carefully using the methods you will practise below, you can solve this sort of equation quickly and correctly every time.

Example 10.1 ▷

Solve the equation $5x - 3 = 27$.

Add 3 to both sides: $\quad 5x - 3 + 3 = 27 + 3$

$$5x = 30$$

Divide both sides by 5: $\quad \dfrac{5x}{5} = \dfrac{30}{5}$

$$x = 6$$

Example 10.2 ▷

Solve the equation $4(2z + 1) = 64$.

Expand the bracket: $\quad 8z + 4 = 64$

Subtract 4 from both sides: $8z + 4 - 4 = 64 - 4$

$$8z = 60$$

Divide both sides by 8: $\quad z = 7.5$

Exercise 10A ① Solve the following equations.

a	$2x + 3 = 17$	**b**	$4x - 1 = 19$	**c**	$5x + 3 = 18$
d	$2y - 3 = 13$	**e**	$4z + 5 = 17$	**f**	$6x - 5 = 13$
g	$10b + 9 = 29$	**h**	$2r - 3 = 9$	**i**	$3x - 11 = 1$
j	$7p + 5 = 82$	**k**	$5x + 7 = 52$	**l**	$9x - 8 = 55$

5

2 Solve the following equations.

a $3 + 2x = 11$ **b** $1 + 3w = 16$ **c** $5 + 4g = 17$

d $4 + 5x = 24$ **e** $7 + 4j = 23$ **f** $3 + 2x = 13$

g $2 + 3x = 38$ **h** $8 + 5x = 13$ **i** $3 + 4m = 11$

j $6 + 2n = 20$ **k** $4 + 3x = 31$ **l** $7 + 5x = 52$

3 Solve the following equations.

a $2x + 5 = 12$ **b** $2s - 3 = 10$ **c** $2t + 3 = 14$

d $2g - 5 = 12$ **e** $4x + 3 = 13$ **f** $4x - 5 = 13$

g $4v + 9 = 39$ **h** $4x - 3 = 11$ **i** $6x - 1 = 8$

j $6q + 5 = 26$ **k** $6x + 7 = 34$ **l** $6p - 8 = 37$

4 Each of the functions below has an expression involving x as its input, and a number as its output. By writing down an equation, find the value of x in each case. The first one has been done for you.

a $x - 11 \longrightarrow \boxed{\times 3} \longrightarrow 9$

Multiplying the input by 3 gives an output of 9, so we can write down the following equation and then solve it as normal.

$$3(x - 11) = 9$$
$$x - 11 = 3$$
$$x = 14$$

b $x + 5 \longrightarrow \boxed{\times 7} \longrightarrow 84$

c $x + 7 \longrightarrow \boxed{\times 5} \longrightarrow 55$

d $5x - 11 \longrightarrow \boxed{\times 3} \longrightarrow 12$

e $2x + 5 \longrightarrow \boxed{\times 7} \longrightarrow 77$

f $4x \longrightarrow \boxed{+ 7} \longrightarrow \boxed{\times 5} \longrightarrow 75$

5 Solve the following equations. Start by expanding the brackets.

a $2(x + 3) = 16$ **b** $4(x - 1) = 16$ **c** $5(x + 3) = 20$

d $4(x + 1) = 12$ **e** $6(x - 5) = 18$ **f** $30 = 2(x + 9)$

6 Solve the following equations. Start by expanding the brackets.

a $2(3x + 1) = 14$ **b** $4(2x - 1) = 36$ **c** $5(2x + 3) = 55$

d $4(3x + 5) = 32$ **e** $6(4x - 5) = 42$ **f** $110 = 10(2x + 9)$

An alternative method for solving the equation from Example 10.1 is to start off by dividing both sides by 4:

$$4(2z + 1) = 64$$

Divide both sides by 4: $\quad 2z + 1 = 16$

$$2z + 1 - 1 = 16 - 1$$
$$2z = 15$$
$$z = 7.5$$

Use this method, rather than expanding brackets, to solve the equations in questions 4 and 5 of Exercise 10A.

Equations involving negative numbers

The equations that you met in the last lesson all had solutions that were positive numbers. This is not always the case, and the exercise below will give you practice at solving equations involving negative numbers.

Example 10.3

Solve the equation $5x + 11 = 1$.

Subtract 11 from each side: $5x + 11 - 11 = 1 - 11$

$$5x = -10$$

Divide both sides by 5: $\quad \dfrac{5x}{5} = \dfrac{-10}{5}$

$$x = -2$$

Example 10.4

Solve the equation $-5x = 10$.

Divide both sides by -5: $\quad \dfrac{-5x}{-5} = \dfrac{10}{-5}$

$$x = -2$$

Example 10.5

Solve the equation $8 - 3x = 20$.

Subtract 8 from each side: $\quad 8 - 3x - 8 = 20 - 8$

$$-3x = 12$$

Divide both sides by -3: $\quad \dfrac{-3x}{-3} = \dfrac{12}{-3}$

$$x = -4$$

Exercise 10B

1 Solve the following equations.

a	$2x + 3 = 1$	**b**	$3x + 5 = 2$
d	$3h + 8 = 2$	**e**	$3d + 4 = 19$
g	$4x + 15 = 3$	**h**	$2x + 13 = 5$
j	$6n + 3 = 15$	**k**	$12 = 5r + 27$

c $2x + 9 = 5$
f $5x + 25 = 10$
i $2 = 3x + 11$
l $9x + 30 = 3$

2 Solve the following equations.

a $13 + 2x = 5$ **b** $21 + 3j = 6$ **c** $15 + 4x = 7$ **d** $24 + 5x = 4$

e $27 + 4x = 31$ **f** $15 + 2s = 9$ **g** $22 + 3x = 28$ **h** $18 + 5x = 3$

i $33 + 4p = 9$ **j** $17 + 2x = 1$ **k** $12 = 24 + 3x$ **l** $2 = 17 + 5y$

3 Solve the following equations.

a $3x + 6 = -12$ **b** $4x - 2 = -10$ **c** $3x + 1 = -14$ **d** $2x - 4 = -12$

e $4j + 3 = -13$ **f** $2k - 7 = -1$ **g** $2x + 9 = -39$ **h** $3x - 2 = -11$

i $6x - 2 = -8$ **j** $2m + 6 = -26$ **k** $-34 = 5x + 6$ **l** $3x - 10 = -37$

4 Solve the following equations.

a $-4x = 20$ **b** $-10x = 20$ **c** $-2x = 12$ **d** $-6x = 54$

e $-7x = 42$ **f** $9 = -3x$ **g** $-9x = 99$ **h** $8 = -2x$

i $-x = 13$ **j** $-5x = -20$

5 Solve the following equations.

a $15 - 2x = 19$ **b** $11 - 3x = 14$ **c** $15 - 4x = 27$ **d** $29 - 5x = 14$

e $15 - 4e = 3$ **f** $13 - 2x = 23$ **g** $20 - 3x = 29$ **h** $16 - 5x = 36$

i $20 = 40 - 4f$ **j** $10 = 16 - 2w$

6 Solve the following equations.

a $2(x + 3) = 4$ **b** $4(x - 1) = -16$ **c** $5(x + 3) = 5$

d $4(x + 5) = 8$ **e** $6(z - 5) = -36$ **f** $10(y + 9) = 20$

g $3(t - 11) = -15$ **h** $21 = 7(x + 5)$

7 Solve the following equations.

a $2(3x + 1) = -10$ **b** $4(2x - 1) = -28$ **c** $5(2x + 3) = 5$

d $4(3x + 5) = 8$ **e** $-26 = 2(4d - 5)$ **f** $10(2a + 9) = 230$

g $3(5v - 11) = 27$ **h** $7(2x + 5) = -7$

8 Victoria has made a mistake somewhere in her working for each of the equations shown opposite. Can you spot on which line the error occurs and work out the correct solution to each one?

a
$$18 - 3x = 30$$
$$18 - 3x + 3x = 30 + 3x$$
$$18 = 30 + 3x$$
$$18 + 30 = 30 + 3x - 30$$
$$48 = 3x$$
$$\frac{48}{3} = \frac{3x}{3}$$
$$x = 16 \quad ✗$$

b
$$4 - 5x = 24$$
$$4 + 5x - 4 = 24 - 4$$
$$5x = 20$$
$$\frac{5x}{5} = \frac{20}{5}$$
$$x = 4 \quad ✗$$

c
$$5(x + 10) = 5$$
$$5x + 10 = 5$$
$$5x + 10 - 10 = 5 - 10$$
$$5x = -5$$
$$\frac{5x}{5} = \frac{-5}{5}$$
$$x = -1 \quad ✗$$

d
$$5(4x + 7) = -5$$
$$\frac{5(4x + 7)}{5} = \frac{-5}{5}$$
$$4x + 7 = -1$$
$$4x + 7 - 7 = -1 - 7$$
$$4x = -8$$
$$\frac{4x}{4} = \frac{-8}{4}$$
$$x = 2 \quad ✗$$

139

1 The following equations each have two possible solutions, one where x is positive, and one where x is negative. Use a spreadsheet to help you find the solutions to each equation by trial and improvement.

   a $x(x + 5) = 24$

   b $x(x - 4) = 12$

2 Use a spreadsheet to help you solve $x(x + 8) = -12$ by trial and improvement. There are two answers, both negative, one greater than −4, the other less than −4.

Equations with unknowns on both sides

Sometimes there are unknown terms on both sides of an equation. You need to add or subtract terms in order to create an equation with the unknown term on one side only.

Example 10.8

Solve the equation $5x - 4 = 2x + 14$.

Subtract $2x$ from both sides: $\quad 5x - 4 - 2x = 2x + 14 - 2x$

$$3x - 4 = 14$$

Add 4 to both sides: $\quad\quad\quad\quad 3x - 4 + 4 = 14 + 4$

$$3x = 18$$

Divide both sides by 3: $\quad\quad\quad\quad \frac{3x}{3} = \frac{18}{3}$

$$x = 6$$

Example 10.7

Solve the equation $4x + 2 = 7 - x$.

Add x to each side: $\quad\quad\quad 4x + 2 + x = 7 - x + x$

$$5x + 2 = 7$$

Subtract 2 from both sides: $\quad 5x + 2 - 2 = 7 - 2$

$$5x = 5$$

Divide each side by 5: $\quad\quad\quad \frac{5x}{5} = \frac{5}{5}$

$$x = 1$$

Exercise 10C

1 Solve the following equations.

  a $2x = 4 + x$ **b** $3x = 12 + x$ **c** $4x = 15 + x$

  d $5x = 12 + x$ **e** $3x = 19 + 2x$ **f** $5x = 10 + 3x$

  g $4x = 14 + 2x$ **h** $5x = 15 + 2x$ **i** $7x = 12 + 4x$

  j $6x = 15 + 9x$ **k** $5x = 12 + 2x$ **l** $9x = 30 + 12x$

2 Solve the following equations.

a $5x + 3 = x + 15$ **b** $4x + 5 = x + 20$ **c** $6x + 4 = x + 14$

d $4x - 2 = 2x + 8$ **e** $5x - 3 = 2x + 9$ **f** $8x - 6 = 3x + 14$

g $2x - 5 = 6x - 9$ **h** $7x - 10 = 3x - 2$ **i** $4x - 6 = 9x - 21$

3 Solve the following equations.

a $4x + 3 = 9 + x$ **b** $8x + 5 = 19 + x$ **c** $5x + 4 = 12 + x$

d $6x - 4 = 12 - 2x$ **e** $7x - 3 = 17 + 2x$ **f** $4x - 5 = 7 + 2x$

g $7 - 5x = 2x - 14$ **h** $5 + 4x = 11 + 2x$ **i** $7 + 3x = 15 + 7x$

4 Solve the following equations. Begin by expanding the brackets.

a $2(x + 3) = 14 + x$ **b** $3(2x + 5) = 25 + x$

c $5(3x - 4) = 12 + 7x$ **d** $6x - 4 = 2(4 + 2x)$

e $9x + 3 = 3(8 + 2x)$ **f** $8x - 10 = 2(3 + 2x)$

g $2(5x + 7) = 3(7 + x)$ **h** $3(8 + 4x) = 4(9 + 2x)$

i $2(7x - 6) = 3(1 + 3x)$

Extension Work

Solve the following equations.

1 $3(x + 2) + 2(x - 1) = 4(x + 3)$

2 $5(x - 3) - 2(x + 2) = 2(x + 1)$

3 $6(x + 3) - 3(x + 4) = 4(x + 2) - 3(x - 1)$

4 $5(x - 2) + 2(x + 1) = 3(x + 5) + 2(x - 3)$

Substituting into expressions

Replacing the letters in an expression by numbers is called **substitution**. Substituting different numbers will give an expression different values. You need to be able to substitute negative numbers as well as positive numbers into expressions.

Example 10.8   What is the value of $5x + 7$ when: **i** $x = 3$ **ii** $x = -4$.

i   When $x = 3$, $5x + 7 = 5 \times 3 + 7 = 22$

ii   When $x = -4$, $5x + 7 = 5 \times (-4) + 7 = -20 + 7 = -13$

Exercise 10D

1 Write down the value of each expression for each value of x.

a $3x + 5$ **i** $x = 3$ **ii** $x = 7$ **iii** $x = -1$

b $4x - 2$ **i** $x = 4$ **ii** $x = 5$ **iii** $x = -3$

c $8 + 7x$ **i** $x = 2$ **ii** $x = 6$ **iii** $x = -2$

d $93 - 4x$ **i** $x = 10$ **ii** $x = 21$ **iii** $x = -3$

e $x^2 + 3$ **i** $x = 4$ **ii** $x = 5$ **iii** $x = -3$

		i		**ii**		**iii**	
f	$x^2 - 7$	**i**	$x = 6$	**ii**	$x = 2$	**iii**	$x = -10$
g	$21 + 3x^2$	**i**	$x = 7$	**ii**	$x = 3$	**iii**	$x = -5$
h	$54 - 2x^2$	**i**	$x = 3$	**ii**	$x = 5$	**iii**	$x = -1$
i	$5(3x + 4)$	**i**	$x = 5$	**ii**	$x = 4$	**iii**	$x = -2$
j	$3(5x - 1)$	**i**	$x = 3$	**ii**	$x = 2$	**iii**	$x = -6$

2 If $a = 2$ and $b = 3$ find the value of each of the following.

a $3a + b$ **b** $a - 3b$ **c** $3(b + 4a)$ **d** $5(3b - 2a)$

3 If $c = 5$ and $d = -2$ find the value of each of the following.

a $2c + d$ **b** $6c - 2d$ **c** $2(3d + 7c)$ **d** $4(3c - 5d)$

4 If $e = 4$ and $f = -3$ find the value of each of the following.

a $e^2 + f^2$ **b** $e^2 - f^2$
c $ef + 3e^2 - 2f^2$ **d** $e(4f^2 - e^2)$

5 If $g = 6$, $h = -4$ and $j = 7$ find the value of each of the following.

a $gh + j$ **b** $g - hj$
c ghj **d** $(g + h)(h + j)$

Extension **Work**

1 What values of n can be substituted into n^2 that give n^2 a value less than 1?

2 What values of n can be substituted into $(n - 4)^2$ that give $(n - 4)^2$ a value less than 1?

3 What values of n can be substituted into $1/n$ that give $1/n$ a value less than 1?

4 Find at least five different expressions that give the value 10 when $x = 2$ is substituted into them.

Substituting into formulae

Formulae occur in all sorts of situations, often when converting between two sorts of quantity. Some examples are converting between degrees Celsius and degrees Fahrenheit, or between different currencies, such as from pounds (£) to euros (€).

Example 10.9 ▷

The formula for converting degress Celsius (°C) to degress Fahrenheit (°F) is:

$$F = \frac{9C}{5} + 32$$

Convert 35 °C to °F.

Substituting $C = 35$ into the formula gives:

$$F = \frac{9 \times 35}{5} + 32 = 63 + 32 = 95$$

So, 35 °C = 95 °F.

Example 10.10 ▶ The formula for the area, A, of a triangle with base length b, and height h, is given by $A = \frac{1}{2}bh$.

Calculate the base length (b) of a triangle whose area is 14 cm^2 and whose height is 7 cm.

Substitute the values that you know into the formula:

$14 = \frac{1}{2} \times b \times 7$

Rearrange to get the unknown (b) by itself on one side:

$14 \div 7 = \frac{1}{2} \times b \times 7 \div 7$

$2 = \frac{1}{2} \times b$

$2 \times 2 = \frac{1}{2} \times b \times 2$

$4 = b$

So the base is 4 cm long.

Exercise 10E

1 If $A = LB$, find A when: **i** $L = 8$ and $B = 7$ **ii** $L = 6$ and $B = 1.5$

2 If $A = 6rh$, find A when: **i** $r = 6$ and $h = 17$ **ii** $r = 2.5$ and $h = 12$

3 If $A = 180(n - 2)$, find A when: **i** $n = 7$ **ii** $n = 12$

4 If $V = u + ft$

     a   find V when: **i** $u = 40$, $f = 32$ and $t = 5$ **ii** $u = 12$, $f = 13$ and $t = 10$

     b   find u when: $V = 5$, $f = 1$ and $t = 2$

5 If $D = \frac{M}{V}$

     a   find D when: **i** $M = 28$ and $V = 4$ **ii** $M = 8$ and $V = 5$

     b   find M when: $D = 7$ and $V = 3$

FM **6** A magician charges £25 for every show he performs, plus an extra £10 per hour spent on stage. The formula for calculating his charge is $C = 10t + 25$, where C is the charge in pounds and t is the length of the show in hours.

     a   How much does he charge for a show lasting:

         i   1 hour?   **ii**   3 hours?   **iii** $2\frac{1}{2}$ hours?

     b   The magician charges £30 for one of his shows. How long did the show last?

7 The area (A) of the trapezium shown is given by the formula $A = \frac{h(a + b)}{2}$.

     a   What is the area when:

         i $h = 12$ cm, $a = 7$ cm and $b = 5$ cm?

         ii $h = 9$ cm, $a = 1.5$ cm and $b = 8.5$ cm?

     b   If the area is 20 cm^2, $a = 4$ cm and $b = 6$ cm, then what is the height (h)?

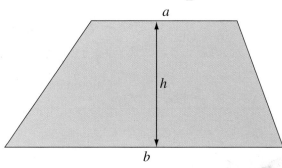

8 The following formula converts temperatures in degrees Celsius (*C*) to degrees Fahrenheit (*F*).

$$F = 1.8C + 32$$

a Convert each of these temperatures to degrees Fahrenheit.

    i   45 °C   **ii**   40 °C   **iii**   65 °C   **iv**   100 °C

b Convert each of these temperatures to degrees Celsius.

    i   50 °F   **ii**   59 °F   **iii**   41 °F   **iv**   23 °F

9 If $N = h(A^2 - B^2)$, find *N* when: **a** $h = 7$, $A = 5$ and $B = 3$ **b** $h = 15$, $A = 4$ and $B = 2$

10 If $V = hr^2$, find *V* when: **a** $h = 5$ and $r = 3$ **b** $h = 8$ and $r = 5$

11 The volume (*V*) of the cuboid shown is given by the formula:

$$V = abc$$

The surface area (*S*) of the cuboid is given by the formula:

$$S = 2ab + 2bc + 2ac$$

a Find: **i**   the volume.
           ii   the surface area,
              when $a = 3$ m, $b = 4$ m and $c = 5$ m.

b Find: **i**   the volume.
           ii   the surface area when $a = 3$ cm, and *a*, *b* and *c* are all the same length. What name is given to this cuboid?

12 The triangle numbers are given by the following formula:

$$T = \frac{n(n + 1)}{2}$$

The first triangle number is found by substituting in n = 1, which gives
$$T = 1 \times \frac{(1 + 1)}{2} = 1$$

a Find the first five triangle numbers.

b Find the 99th triangle number.

Extension Work

1 If $\dfrac{1}{F} = \dfrac{1}{U} - \dfrac{1}{V}$

Calculate: **a**   *F* when $U = 4$ and $V = 5$ **b**   *V* when $F = 2$ and $U = 3$

2 If $\dfrac{1}{T} = \dfrac{1}{A} + \dfrac{1}{B}$

Calculate: **a**   *T* when $A = 3$ and $B = 2$ **b**   *A* when $T = 2$, $B = 8$

Creating your own expressions and formulae

The last section showed you some formulae that could be used to solve problems. In this section you will be given problems and have to write down your own formulae to help solve them.

You will need to choose a letter to represent each variable in a problem, and use these when you write the formula. Usually these will be the first letters of the words they represent, for example, V often represents volume and A is often used for area.

Example 10.11

Find an expression for the sum, S, of any three consecutive whole numbers.

Let the smallest number be n.

The next number is $(n + 1)$ and the biggest number is $(n + 2)$.

So: $S = n + (n + 1) + (n + 2)$

$\quad\quad S = n + n + 1 + n + 2$

$\quad\quad S = 3n + 3$

Example 10.12

How many months are there in:
  i 5 years?
  ii t years?

There are 12 months in a year, so:
  i in 5 years there will be $12 \times 5 = 60$ months
  ii in t years there will be $12 \times t = 12t$ months

Exercise 10F

1 Using the letters suggested, construct a simple formula in each case.

  a The sum, S, of three numbers a, b and c.

  b The product, P, of two numbers x and y.

  c The difference, D, between the ages of two people; the eldest one being a years old and the other b years old.

  d The sum, S, of four consecutive integers. Let the first integer be n.

  e The number of days, D, in W weeks.

  f The average age, A, of three boys whose ages are m, n and p years.

2 How many days are there in:

  a 3 weeks?   **b** w weeks?

3 A girl is now 13 years old.

  a How many years old will she be in:

      i 5 years?   **ii** t years?

  b How many years old was she:

      i 3 years ago?   **ii** m years ago?

4 A car travels at a speed of 30 mph. How many miles will it travel in:

  a 2 hours?   **b** t hours?

5 How many grams are there in:

   a 5 kg?   **b** x kg?

6 How many minutes are there in m hours?

7 Write down the number that is half as big as b.

8 Write down the number that is twice as big as T.

9 If a boy runs at b miles per hour, how many miles does he run in k hours?

10 **a**   What is the cost, in pence, of 6 papers at 35 pence each?

      b   What is the cost, in pence, of k papers at 35 pence each?

      c   What is the cost, in pence, of k papers at q pence each?

11 A boy is b years old and his mother is 6 times as old.

      a   Find the mother's age in terms of b.

      b   Find the sum of their ages in y years time.

12 Mr Speed's age is equal to the sum of the ages of his three sons. The youngest son is aged x years, the eldest is 10 years older than the youngest and the middle son is 4 years younger than the eldest. How old is Mr Speed?

Extension Work

1 A man is now three times as old as his daughter. The sum of their ages is 76 years. How old was the man when his daughter was born?

2 Find three consecutive odd numbers for which the sum is 57. Let the first odd number be n.

3 A group of pupils had to choose between playing football and badminton. The number of pupils that chose football was three times the number that chose badminton. The number of players for each game would be equal if 12 pupils who chose football were asked to play badminton. Find the total number of pupils.

5 I can solve equations of the type $3x + 7 = 10$, for example, where the solution may be fractional or negative.

I can substitute positive and negative numbers into algebraic expressions, e.g. work out the value of $4a - 3b$, when $a = 3$ and $b = -2$.

I can substitute positive and negative numbers into formulae, for example work out the value of $A = 2b + 2w$ when $b = 5$ and $w = 3$.

I can devise algebraic formulae to represent simple ideas such as the distance travelled by a car doing 40mph in t hours.

6 I can solve equations of the type $2(3x - 8) = 14$, for example, where the solution may be fractional or negative.

I can solve equations of the type $4x + 9 = 3 + x$, for example, where the solution may be fractional or negative.

I can substitute positive and negative numbers into formulae, e.g. work out the value of $A = b^2 + c^2$, where $b = 3$ and $c = 4$.

National Test questions

1 *2002 Paper 1*

Look at this table:

	Age in years
Ann	a
Ben	b
Cindy	c

Copy the table below and write in words the meaning of each equation. The first one is done for you.

a	$b = 30$	Ben is 30 years old
b	$a + b = 69$	
c	$b = 2c$	
d	$\dfrac{a + b + c}{3} = 28$	

2 *2007 5–7 Paper 1*

a When $x = 8$, which of the following is the value of $5x$?

   5   13   40   58   None of these

b When $x = 8$, which of the following is the value of $3x - x$?

   0   3   16   30   None of these

c When $x = 8$, which of the following is the value of x^2?

   8   10   16   64   None of these

3 *2007 5–7 Paper 2*

Solve these equations:

$$32x + 53 = 501$$
$$375 = 37 + 26y$$

4 *2002 Paper 2*

Look at these equations:

$$3a + 6b = 24$$
$$2c - d = 3$$

a Use the equations above to work out the value of the expressions below.
The first one is done for you, (copy and complete the others).

$8c - 4d = \dots 12 \dots$

i $a + 2b = \dots\dots\dots$

ii $d - 2c = \dots\dots\dots$

b Use one or both of the equations above to write an expression that has a value of 21.

CHAPTER 11 Statistics 2

This chapter is going to show you

- How to construct statistical diagrams for discrete data
- When to use range, mean, median and mode
- How to construct stem and leaf diagrams
- How to use scatter graphs
- How to read pie charts

What you should already know

- How to interpret data from tables, graphs and charts
- How to find mode, median, mean and range for small data sets

Stem-and-leaf diagrams

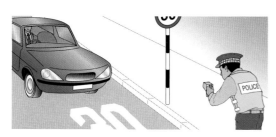

The speeds of vehicles in a 30 mile-per-hour limit are recorded. The speeds are sorted into order and put into a stem-and-leaf diagram. The slowest speed is 23 miles per hour. The fastest speed is 45 miles per hour. How can you tell this from the stem-and-leaf diagram?

```
2 | 3 7 7 8 9 9
3 | 1 2 3 5 5 5 5 7 9
4 | 2 2 5                    Key: 2 | 3 means 23 miles per hour
```

How many cars are breaking the speed limit?

Example 11.1 ▷ A teacher asked 25 pupils how many pieces of homework they were given in one week. The results are shown in the stem-and-leaf diagram:

```
0 | 1 1 2 2 2 2 3 5 7 7 7 8 9
1 | 0 0 1 1 1 2 4 4 5 6
2 | 1 3                       Key: 1 | 2 means 12 homeworks
```

Use the stem-and-leaf diagram to find:

a the median　　　**b** range　　　**c** mode

a As there are 25 pupils, the middle value is the thirteenth, so the median = 9.

b The most homeworks is the last value, 23, and the least homeworks is the first value, 1.

The range = biggest value – smallest value
$$= 23 - 1$$
$$= 22 \text{ homeworks}$$

c The mode occurs the most, so the mode = 2 homeworks because it occurs 4 times.

1 15 sales people have a competition to find out who sells the most items in one day. Below are the results.

```
1 | 2  2  3  7  7
2 | 1  4  4  4  5  5  6
3 | 0  2  5
```
Key: 1 | 2 means 12 items

a How many items did the winner sell? **b** What is the mode?
c Find the range. **d** Work out the median.

2 35 Year 8 pupils are asked to estimate how many text messages they send on their mobile phones each week. Their replies are put into a stem-and-leaf diagram.

```
0 | 5  5  6  7  8  8
1 | 0  0  0  0  0  1  1  4  4
1 | 8  9  9  9
2 | 0  0  1  3  3  3  4
2 | 5  6
3 | 0  0  4
3 | 5  6  6
```
Key: 0 | 5 means 5 text messages

Work out the following.

a The mode **b** The smallest estimate **c** The range **d** The median

3 A farmer records the number of animals of each type on his farm. His results are shown in the stem-and-leaf diagram below.

```
5 | 2  6  8
6 | 5  9
7 | 5
```
Key: 5 | 2 represents 52 animals of one type

a He has more sheep than any other type of animal. How many sheep does he have?

b How many animals has he altogether?

c Explain why a stem-and-leaf diagram may not be the best way to represent these data.

4 The ages of 30 people at a disco are as shown:

32	12	47	25	23	23	17	36	42	17
31	15	24	49	19	31	23	34	36	45
47	12	39	11	26	23	22	38	48	17

a Put the ages into a stem-and-leaf diagram (remember to show a key).

b State the mode.

c Work out the range.

Extension **Work**

Obtain your own data. This could be from the Internet or from a textbook from another subject. Alternatively, you could use some of the data collected for Exercise 11A.

Produce a brief summary of your data. Use a stem-and-leaf diagram to present the information.

Pie charts

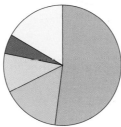

In the picture, which colour represents 'unfit adults'? How do you know? The pie chart is used because it shows the proportion of the whole amount and is quite easy to interpret.

Sometimes you will have to interpret pie charts that are already drawn and sometimes you will be asked to construct a pie chart.

In a pie chart, the information is represented by a whole circle (a pie) and each category is represented by a sector of the circle (a slice of the pie).

Example 11.2 ▷

This pie chart shows the proportion of British and foreign cars sold one weekend at a car salesroom. 40 cars were sold.

How many:

a British cars were sold?

b foreign cars were sold?

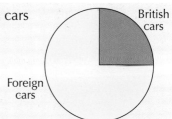

You can see from the pie chart that $\frac{1}{4}$ of the cars sold were British and $\frac{3}{4}$ were foreign. So:

a $\frac{1}{4}$ of 40 = 10: 10 British cars were sold.

b $\frac{3}{4}$ of 40 = 30: 30 foreign cars were sold.

Example 11.3 ▷

The pie chart shows how one country got rid of 3000 kg of dangerous waste in 2006.

How much waste was got rid of by:

a landfill?   **b** burning?

c dumping at sea?   **d** chemical treatment?

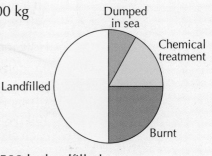

From the pie chart you can see that:

a $\frac{1}{2}$ of the waste was landfilled = $\frac{1}{2}$ of 3000 kg = 1500 kg landfilled

b $\frac{1}{4}$ of the waste was burnt = $\frac{1}{4}$ of 3000 kg = 750 kg burnt

c $\frac{30}{360} = \frac{1}{12}$ of the waste was dumped at sea, i.e. 3000 ÷ 12 = 250 kg dumped at sea

d $\frac{60}{360} = \frac{1}{6}$ of the waste was treated by chemicals, i.e. 3000 ÷ 6 = 500 kg treated by chemicals

Example 11.4 ▷ Draw a pie chart to represent the following set of data showing how a group of people travel to work.

Type of travel	Walk	Car	Bus	Train	Cycle
Frequency	24	84	52	48	32

It is easier to set out your workings in a table.

Type of travel	Frequency	Calculation	Angle
Walk	24	$\frac{24}{240} \times 360 = 36°$	36°
Car	84	$\frac{84}{240} \times 360 = 126°$	126°
Bus	52	$\frac{52}{240} \times 360 = 78°$	78°
Train	48	$\frac{48}{240} \times 360 = 72°$	72°
Cycle	32	$\frac{32}{240} \times 360 = 48°$	48°
TOTAL	240		360°

We work out the angle for each sector using.

$$\frac{\text{Frequency}}{\text{Total frequency}} \times 360°$$

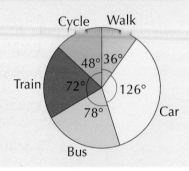

Example 11.5 ▷ The pie chart shows the types of housing on a new estate. Altogether there were 540 new houses built.

How many are:

a detached?   b semi-detached?

c bungalows?   d terraced?

You need to work out the fraction of 540 that each sector represents.

a $\frac{90}{360} \times 540 = 135$ detached

b $\frac{120}{360} \times 540 = 180$ semi-detached

c $\frac{40}{360} \times 540 = 60$ bungalows

d $\frac{110}{360} \times 540 = 165$ terraced

Exercise 11B

1 900 pupils in a school were asked to vote for their favourite subject.
The pie chart illustrates their responses.

How many voted for:

a   PE?   b   science?   c   maths?

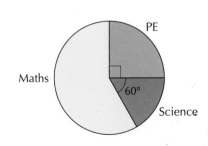

2 One weekend in Edale, a café sold 300 drinks. The pie chart illustrates the different drinks that were sold.

How many of the following drinks were sold that weekend?

a   Soft drinks   b   Tea

c   Hot chocolate   d   Coffee

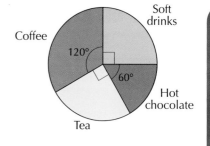

3 The pie chart illustrates how 450 kilograms of butter sold at a supermarket one week were sold on different days.

How many kilograms of butter were sold on each day of the week?

a   Monday   b   Tuesday   c   Wednesday

d   Thursday   e   Friday   f   Saturday

g   Sunday

4 Pat did a survey about fruit and nut chocolate. She asked 30 of her friends. The pie chart illustrates her results.

How many of these friends:

a   never ate fruit and nut chocolate?

b   sometimes ate fruit and nut chocolate?

c   called fruit and nut their favourite chocolate?

5 The pie chart shows the daily activities of Joe one Wednesday. It covers a 24-hour time period.

How long did Joe spend:

a   at school?   b   at leisure?

c   travelling?   d   asleep?

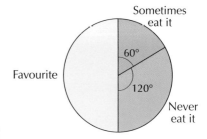

6 On a train one morning, the guard inspected all the tickets in order to report how many of each sort there were. The pie chart illustrates his results for the 240 tickets he saw that morning.

How many of the following tickets did he see that morning?

a   Open return   b   Season ticket

c   Day return   d   Travel pass

e   Super saver

More about pie charts

1 Draw pie charts to represent the following data.

a The favourite subject of 36 pupils:

Subject	Maths	English	Science	Languages	Other
Frequency	12	7	8	4	5

b The type of food that 40 people usually eat for breakfast:

Food	Cereal	Toast	Fruit	Cooked	Other	None
Frequency	11	8	6	9	2	4

c The number of goals scored by an ice-hockey team in 24 matches:

Goals	0	1	2	3	4	5 or more
Frequency	3	4	7	5	4	1

d The favourite colour of 60 Year 8 pupils:

Colour	Red	Green	Blue	Yellow	Other
Frequency	17	8	21	3	11

2 The pie chart shows the results of a survey of 216 children about their favourite foods.

How many chose:

a chips? **b** pizza?

c pasta? **d** curry?

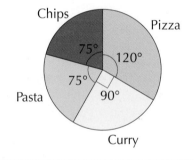

Extension Work

Design a poster to show some information about the pupils in your class. Choose hair colour, eye colour or colour of their top. Either include pie charts that you have drawn yourself or use a spreadsheet to produce the pie charts. Make sure that any pie chart you produce has labels and is easy to understand.

Scatter graphs

A doctor records the size of the pupils of people's eyes and the brightness of the sunlight.

He then plots the results on a graph. What can you tell about the connection between the brightness and the pupil size of the people?

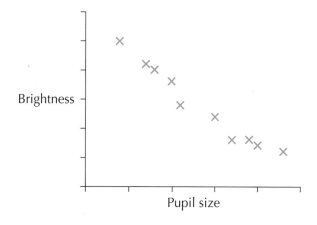

Example 11.6 Below are three scatter graphs. Describe the relationships in each graph.

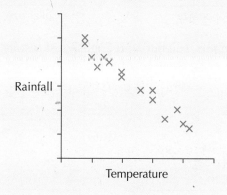

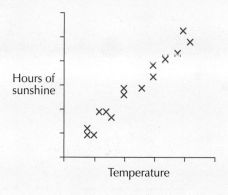

The first graph shows a **negative correlation**. Here, this means that the higher the temperature, the less rainfall there is.

The second graph shows a **positive correlation**. Here, this means that the higher the temperature, the more hours of sunshine there are.

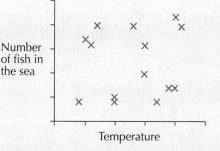

The third graph shows **no correlation**. Here, this means that there is no connection between the temperature and the number of fish in the sea.

Exercise 11D

1. After a study into temperature, rainfall and the sales of ice creams, umbrellas and the hire of deckchairs, the following scatter diagrams were created. Describe the type of correlation and what each graph tells you.

a

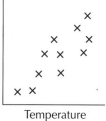

b

c

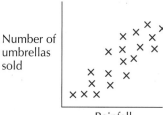

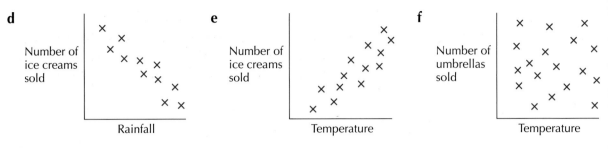

2 After a study into heights, weights and shoe size, the following scatter diagrams were created. Describe the type of correlation and what each graph tells you.

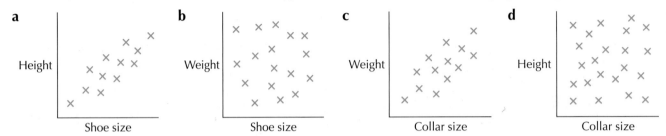

3 After a series of maths, science and English test results, the following scatter diagrams were created. Describe the type of correlation and what each graph tells you.

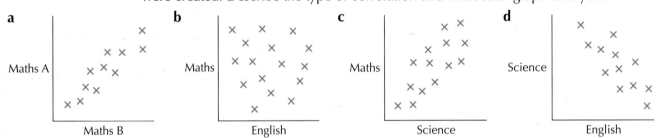

4 A study was made into the transfer price and age of some goalkeepers as well as how many goals they let in their first full season. The following scatter diagrams were created. Describe the type of correlation and what each graph tells you.

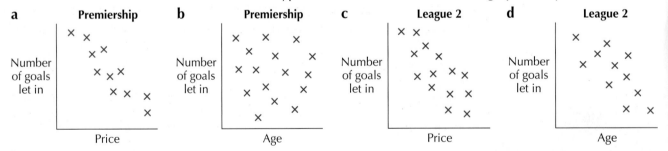

5 A study was made into the weight distance to travel, price and how long it took for parcels to be delivered by a private delivery service. The following scatter diagrams were created. Describe the type of correlation and what each graph tells you.

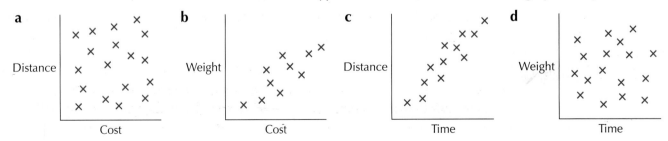

More about scatter graphs

Exercise 11E

① A survey is carried out to compare pupils' ages with the amount of money that they spend each week.

Age (year)	11	16	14	13	13	18	10	12	14	15
Amount spent	£3	£3.50	£6	£5	£6.50	£12	£2.50	£4	£8	£7.50

a Plot the data on a scatter graph.

Use the x-axis for Age from 10 to 20 years.

Use the y-axis for Amount spent from £0 to £15.

b Describe in words what the graph tells you and what sort of correlation there is.

② The table shows how much time pupils spend watching television and how long they spend on homework per week.

Time watching TV (hours)	12	8	5	7	9	3	5	6	10	14
Time spent on homework (hours)	4	7	10	6	5	11	9	6	6	3

a Plot the data on a scatter graph (take each axis as Time from 0 to 15 hours).

b Describe in words what the graph tells you and what sort of correlation there is.

③ The table shows the value of a car and the age of the car.

Age (years)	1	2	3	4	5	6	7
Amount spent	£10 000	£8300	£7500	£6000	£5300	£4200	£3400

a Plot the data on a scatter graph.

Use the x-axis for Age from 1 to 10 years.

Use the y-axis for Amount spent from £1000 to £11 000.

b Describe in words what the graph tells you about what happens to a car's value as it gets older.

LEVEL BOOSTER

5 I can interpret a pie chart.

6 I can interpret stem and leaf diagrams.
I can construct a pie chart.
I can understand a scatter diagram and can describe the correlation, if any is shown.

National Test questions

1 *2001 Paper 1*

There are 60 pupils in a school. 6 of these pupils wear glasses.

a The pie chart is not drawn accurately.

What should the angles be? Show your working.

b Exactly half of the 60 pupils in the school are boys.

From this information, is the percentage of boys in this school that wear glasses 5%, 6%, 10%, 20%, 50% or not possible to tell?

2 *2001 Paper 2*

A teacher asked two different classes: 'What type of book is your favourite?'

a Results from class A (total 20 pupils):

Type of book	Frequency
Crime	3
Non-fiction	13
Fantasy	4

Draw a pie chart to show this information. Show your working and draw your angles accurately.

b The pie chart on the right shows the results from all of class B.

Each pupil had only one vote.

The sector for non-fiction represents 11 pupils.

How many pupils are in class B?

Show your working.

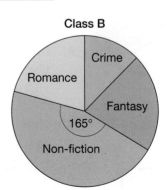

3 *2005 4–6 Paper 1*

Bumps are built on a road to slow cars down.

The stem-and-leaf diagrams show the speeds of 15 cars before and after the bumps were built.

Before					
2					
2	7	8			
3	0	2	4		
3	5	6	8	9	
4	1	3	4	4	4
4	6				

After					
2	3	4	4		
2	6	6	7	8	8	9
3	0	0	0	1	2
3	5				
4					
4					

Key:

2 | 3 means 23 miles per hour

Use the diagrams to write the numbers missing from these sentences:

Before the bumps:

The maximum speed was …… mph, and …… cars went at more than 30 mph.

After the bumps:

The maximum speed was …… mph, and …… cars went at more than 30 mph.

4 *2006 4–6 Paper 1*

The scatter graph shows 15 pupils' coursework and test marks.

To find a pupil's **total mark**, you add the coursework mark to the test mark.

a Which pupil had the highest **total** mark?

b Is the statement below **true** or **false**?

"The range of coursework marks was greater than the range of test marks."

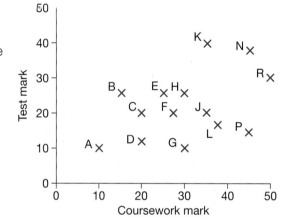

c Pupils with total marks in the shaded region on the graph below win a prize.

What is the **smallest total mark** needed to win a prize?

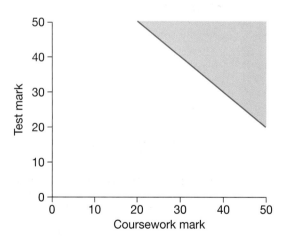

Football attendances

The Sheffield football teams have had various support over the years as they have moved in and out of the divisions. Below is a table comparing their attendances over the years 1989 to 2007.

Year	Sheffield Wednesday			Sheffield United		
	Level	Place	Attendance	Level	Place	Attendance
1989	1	15	20 035	3	2	12 279
1990	1	18	20 928	2	2	17 008
1991	2	3	26 190	1	10	21 600
1992	1	3	29 578	1	9	21 805
1993	1	7	27 264	1	14	18 985
1994	1	7	27 187	1	20	19 562
1995	1	13	26 596	2	8	14 408
1996	1	15	24 877	2	9	12 904
1997	1	7	25 714	2	5	16 675
1998	1	13	28 706	2	6	17 936
1999	1	12	26 745	2	8	16 258
2000	1	19	24 855	2	16	13 700
2001	2	17	19 268	2	10	17 211
2002	2	20	20 882	2	13	18 031
2003	2	21	20 327	2	3	18 073
2004	3	16	22 336	2	8	21 646
2005	3	5	23 100	2	8	19 594
2006	2	19	24 853	2	2	23 650
2007	2	9	23 638	1	18	30 512

Use the information to answer the questions.

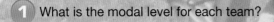

1 What is the modal level for each team?

2 What is the range of levels played at for each team?

3 What is the median average attendance of each team?

4 What is the range of the average attendances for each club?

5 What is the mean level played at by each team during these years?

6 What is the mean average attendance for each team during the years shown?

7 Find the total of the average attendances for both Sheffield teams for every year and make a suitable comment.

8 Put the data into a grouped bar chart showing the number of times the average attendances were in the bands 10000–15000, 15001–20000, 20001–25000, 25001–30000, 30001–35000.

9 Illustrate the data in the tables in pie charts to show the differences between the two clubs in regards to levels played and average attendances.

This chapter is going to show you	What you should already know
● How to add and subtract fractions with any denominators ● How to use BODMAS or BIDMAS with more complex problems ● How to solve problems using decimals, fractions, percentages and units of measurement	● How to add and subtract fractions with the same denominator ● How to find equivalent fractions ● How to use the four operations with decimals

Fractions

This section recalls some of the rules you have already met about fractions.

Example 12.1 ▷ Work out the following.

a How many sevenths are in 4 whole ones?

b How many fifths are in $3\frac{3}{5}$?

a There are 7 sevenths in one whole, so there are $4 \times 7 = 28$ sevenths in 4 whole ones.

b There are $3 \times 5 = 15$ fifths in 3 whole ones, so there are $15 + 3 = 18$ fifths in $3\frac{3}{5}$.

Example 12.2 ▷ Write the following as mixed numbers.

a $\frac{48}{15}$　　　　**b** The fraction of a kilometre given by 3150 metres

a $48 \div 15 = 3$ remainder 3, so $\frac{48}{15} = 3\frac{3}{15}$, which can cancel to $3\frac{1}{5}$. (*Note:* It is usually easier to cancel after the fraction has been written as a mixed number rather than before.)

b 1 kilometre is 1000 metres, so the fraction is $\frac{3150}{1000} = 3\frac{150}{1000} = 3\frac{3}{20}$.

Exercise 12A　**1** Find the missing number in each of these fractions.

a $\frac{5}{3} = \frac{\square}{9}$　　　　　**b** $\frac{9}{8} = \frac{\square}{16}$　　　　　**c** $\frac{25}{9} = \frac{\square}{27}$

d $\frac{8}{5} = \frac{\square}{15}$　　　　　**e** $\frac{12}{7} = \frac{48}{\square}$　　　　　**f** $\frac{20}{9} = \frac{80}{\square}$

g $\frac{8}{5} = \frac{\square}{15}$　　　　　**h** $\frac{7}{2} = \frac{\square}{6}$　　　　　**i** $\frac{13}{3} = \frac{52}{\square}$

5

2 a How many sixths are in $3\frac{5}{6}$?   **b** How many eighths are in $4\frac{1}{2}$?

c How many tenths are in $2\frac{2}{5}$?   **d** How many ninths are in $5\frac{7}{9}$?

3 Write each mixed number in Question 2 as a top-heavy fraction in its simplest form.

4 Write each of the following as a mixed number in its simplest form.

a $\frac{14}{12}$ **b** $\frac{15}{9}$ **c** $\frac{24}{21}$ **d** $\frac{35}{20}$ **e** $\frac{28}{20}$ **f** $\frac{70}{50}$

g $\frac{28}{24}$ **h** $\frac{26}{12}$ **i** $\frac{44}{24}$ **j** $\frac{32}{10}$ **k** $\frac{36}{24}$ **l** $\frac{75}{35}$

5 Write these fractions as mixed numbers (cancel down if necessary).

a Seven thirds   **b** Sixteen sevenths   **c** Twelve fifths   **d** Nine halves

e $\frac{20}{7}$ **f** $\frac{24}{5}$ **g** $\frac{13}{3}$ **h** $\frac{19}{8}$ **i** $\frac{146}{12}$ **j** $\frac{78}{10}$ **k** $\frac{52}{12}$ **l** $\frac{102}{9}$

6 Write the following as fractions.

a The turn of the minute hand round a clock as it goes from:
   i 7:15 to 9:45   **ii** 8:25 to 10:10   **iii** 6:12 to 7:24
   iv 8:55 to 10:45   **v** 7:05 to 10:20   **vi** 9:36 to 11:24

b The fraction of a metre given by:
   i 715 cm   **ii** 2300 mm   **iii** 405 cm
   iv 580 cm   **v** 1550 mm   **vi** 225 cm

c The fraction of a kilogram given by:
   i 2300 g   **ii** 4050 g   **iii** 7500 g
   iv 5600 g   **v** 1225 g   **vi** 6580 g

Extension Work

A gallon is an imperial unit of capacity still in common use. There are 8 pints in a gallon. A litre is about $1\frac{3}{4}$ pints and a gallon is about $4\frac{1}{2}$ litres. Write the missing mixed numbers to make these statements true.

a 2 litres = ... pints   **b** 10 pints = ... gallons   **c** 5 gallons = ... litres

d 3 litres = ... pints   **e** 3 gallons = ... litres   **f** 20 pints = ... gallons

Adding and subtracting fractions

This section will give you more practice with adding and subtracting fractions.

Example 12.3

Work out:

a $\frac{3}{8} + 1\frac{1}{4}$ **b** $1\frac{7}{8} - \frac{3}{4}$

Previously, we used a fraction chart or line to do these. A fraction line is drawn below.

a Start at 0 and count on $\frac{3}{8}$, then 1 and then $\frac{1}{4}$ to give $\frac{3}{8} + 1\frac{1}{4} = 1\frac{5}{8}$.

b Start at $1\frac{7}{8}$ and count back $\frac{3}{4}$ to give $1\frac{7}{8} - \frac{3}{4} = 1\frac{1}{8}$.

When denominators are not the same, they must be made the same before the numerators are added or subtracted. To do this, we need to find the Lowest Common Multiple (LCM) of the denominators.

Example 12.4 ▶

Work out:

a $\frac{2}{3} + \frac{1}{4}$ **b** $\frac{8}{9} - \frac{5}{6}$

a   The LCM of 3 and 4 is 12, so the two fractions need to be written as twelfths:
$\frac{2}{3} + \frac{1}{4} = \frac{8}{12} + \frac{3}{12} = \frac{11}{12}$

b   The LCM of 9 and 6 is 18, so the two fractions need to be written as eighteenths:
$\frac{8}{9} - \frac{5}{6} = \frac{16}{18} - \frac{15}{18} = \frac{1}{18}$

Exercise 12B

1   Work out the following (the number line on page 163 may help).

   a $\frac{5}{8} + \frac{1}{2}$ **b** $1\frac{1}{8} + \frac{3}{8}$ **c** $2\frac{3}{8} + 1\frac{5}{8}$ **d** $\frac{3}{8} + 1\frac{1}{2} + 1\frac{3}{4}$

   e $\frac{5}{8} - \frac{1}{2}$ **f** $2\frac{1}{8} - \frac{5}{8}$ **g** $2\frac{3}{8} - 1\frac{5}{8}$ **h** $1\frac{3}{4} + 1\frac{1}{2} - 1\frac{7}{8}$

2   Work out the following. Cancel down answers to lowest terms and convert top-heavy fractions to mixed numbers.

   a $\frac{1}{5} + \frac{1}{5}$ **b** $\frac{5}{8} + \frac{5}{8}$ **c** $\frac{3}{10} + \frac{3}{10}$ **d** $\frac{3}{7} + \frac{5}{7} + \frac{2}{7}$

   e $\frac{14}{15} - \frac{2}{15}$ **f** $\frac{7}{9} - \frac{4}{9}$ **g** $\frac{11}{12} - \frac{5}{12}$ **h** $\frac{3}{10} + \frac{9}{10} - \frac{5}{10}$

3   Firstly, convert the following fractions to equivalent fractions with a common denominator, and then work out the answer, cancelling down or writing as a mixed number as appropriate.

   a $\frac{1}{3} + \frac{1}{4}$ **b** $\frac{1}{6} + \frac{1}{3}$ **c** $\frac{3}{10} + \frac{1}{4}$ **d** $\frac{1}{9} + \frac{5}{6}$

   e $\frac{4}{15} + \frac{3}{10}$ **f** $\frac{7}{8} + \frac{5}{6}$ **g** $\frac{7}{12} + \frac{1}{4}$ **h** $\frac{3}{4} + \frac{1}{3} + \frac{1}{2}$

   i $\frac{1}{3} - \frac{1}{4}$ **j** $\frac{5}{6} - \frac{1}{3}$ **k** $\frac{3}{10} - \frac{1}{4}$ **l** $\frac{8}{9} - \frac{1}{6}$

   m $\frac{4}{15} - \frac{1}{10}$ **n** $\frac{7}{8} - \frac{5}{6}$ **o** $\frac{7}{12} - \frac{1}{4}$ **p** $\frac{3}{4} + \frac{1}{3} - \frac{1}{2}$

4   A magazine has $\frac{1}{3}$ of its pages for advertising, $\frac{1}{12}$ for letters and the rest is for articles.
   a   What fraction of the pages is for articles?
   b   If the magazine has 120 pages, how many are used for articles?

5   A survey of pupils showed that $\frac{1}{5}$ of them walked to school, $\frac{2}{3}$ came by bus and the rest came by car.
   a   What fraction came by car?
   b   If there were 900 pupils in the school, how many came by car?

6   A farmer plants $\frac{2}{7}$ of his land with wheat and $\frac{3}{8}$ with maize; the rest is used for cattle.
   a   What fraction of the land is used to grow crops?
   b   What fraction is used for cattle?

Extension **Work**

Consider the series $\frac{1}{2} + \frac{1}{4} + \frac{1}{8} + \frac{1}{16} + \frac{1}{32} + \frac{1}{64} + \frac{1}{128} \ldots$ If we write down the first term, then add the first two terms, then add the first three terms, we obtain the series $\frac{1}{2}, \frac{3}{4}, \frac{7}{8}, \ldots$

1   Continue this sequence for another four terms.

2   What total will the series reach if it continues for an infinite number of terms?

3   Repeat with the series $\frac{1}{3} + \frac{1}{9} + \frac{1}{27} + \frac{1}{81} + \frac{1}{243} + \frac{1}{729} + \frac{1}{2187} \ldots$

Order of operations

B	– Brackets		B	– Brackets
O	– pOwers		I	– Indices
DM	– Division and Multiplication		DM	– Division and Multiplication
AS	– Addition and Subtraction		AS	– Addition and Subtraction

BODMAS and BIDMAS are ways of remembering the order in which mathematical operations are carried out.

Example 12.5 ▷

Evaluate:

a $2 \times 3^2 + 6 \div 2$ **b** $(2 + 3)^2 \times 8 - 6$

Show each step of the calculation.

a Firstly, work out the power, which gives: $2 \times 9 + 6 \div 2$
Secondly, the division, which gives: $2 \times 9 + 3$
Thirdly, the multiplication, which gives: $18 + 3$
Finally, the addition to give: 21

b Firstly, work out the bracket, which gives: $5^2 \times 8 - 6$
Secondly, the power, which gives: $25 \times 8 - 6$
Thirdly, the multiplication, which gives: $200 - 6$
Finally, the subtraction to give: 194

Note: If we have a calculation that is a string of additions and subtractions, or a string of multiplications and divisions, then we do the calculation from left to right.

Example 12.6 ▷

Calculate:

a $\dfrac{(2 + 6)^2}{2 \times 4^2}$ **b** $3.1 + [4.2 - (1.7 + 1.5) \div 1.6]$

a $\dfrac{(2 + 6)^2}{2 \times 4^2} = \dfrac{8^2}{2 \times 16} = \dfrac{64}{32} = 2$

b $3.1 + [4.2 - (1.7 + 1.5) \div 1.6] = 3.1 + (4.2 - 3.2 \div 1.6) = 3.1 + (4.2 - 2) = 3.1 + 2.2 = 5.3$

Note: If there are 'nested brackets', then the inside ones are calculated first.

Exercise 12C

1 Write the operation that you do first in each of these calculations, and then work out each one.

a	$5 + 4 \times 7$	**b**	$18 - 6 \times 3$	**c**	$7 \times 7 + 2$	**d**	$16 \div 4 - 2$
e	$(5 + 4) \times 7$	**f**	$(18 - 6) \div 3$	**g**	$7 \times (7 + 2)$	**h**	$16 \div (4 - 2)$
i	$5 + 9 - 7 - 2$	**j**	$2 \times 6 \div 3 \times 4$	**k**	$12 - 15 + 7$	**l**	$12 \div 3 \times 6 \div 2$

2 Work out the following, showing each step of the calculation.

a	$3 + 4 + 4^2$	**b**	$3 + (4 + 4)^2$	**c**	$3 \times 4 + 4^2$	**d**	$3 \times (4 + 4)^2$
e	$5 + 3^2 - 7$	**f**	$(5 + 3)^2 - 7$	**g**	$2 \times 6^2 + 2$	**h**	$2 \times (6^2 + 2)$
i	$\dfrac{200}{4 \times 5}$	**j**	$\dfrac{80 + 20}{4 \times 5}$	**k**	$\sqrt{(4^2 + 3^2)}$	**l**	$\dfrac{(2 + 3)^2}{6 - 1}$
m	$3.2 - (5.4 + 6.1) + (5.7 - 2.1)$			**n**	$8 \times (12 \div 4) \div (2 \times 2)$		

3 Write out each of the following and insert brackets to make the calculation true.

a $3 \times 7 + 1 = 24$ **b** $3 + 7 \times 2 = 20$ **c** $2 \times 3 + 1 \times 4 = 32$
d $2 + 3^2 = 25$ **e** $5 \times 5 + 5 \div 5 = 26$ **f** $5 \times 5 + 5 \div 5 = 10$
g $5 \times 5 + 5 \div 5 = 30$ **h** $5 \times 5 + 5 \div 5 = 6$ **i** $15 - 3^2 = 144$

4 Work out the following (calculate the inside bracket first).

a $120 \div [25 - (3 - 2)]$ **b** $120 \div (25 - 3 - 2)$ **c** $5 + [8 \times (6 - 3)]$
d $5 + (8 \times 6 - 3)$ **e** $[120 \div (60 - 20)] + 20$ **f** $(120 \div 60 - 20) + 20$
g $[120 \div (20 \div 4)] + 3$ **h** $(120 \div 20 \div 4) + 3$ **i** $[(3 + 4)^2 - 5] \times 2$

Extension Work

By putting brackets in different places, one calculation can be made to give many different answers. For example:

$4 \times 6 + 4 - 3 \times 8 + 1 = 24 + 4 - 24 + 1 = 5$

without brackets or with brackets, it could be:

$4 \times (6 + 4) - 3 \times (8 + 1) = 4 \times 10 - 3 \times 9 = 40 - 27 = 13$

1 By putting brackets into the appropriate places in the calculation above, obtain answers of:
a 33 **b** 17 **c** 252

2 Similarly, put brackets into $12 \div 6 - 2 \times 1 + 5 \times 3$ to make:
a 54 **b** 15 **c** 0

Multiplying decimals

This section will give you more practice on multiplying integers and decimals.

Example 12.7 Find:

a 0.02×0.03 **b** 400×0.008 **c** $20 \times 0.06 \times 0.009$

a $2 \times 3 = 6$. There are four decimal places in the multiplication, so there are four in the answer. So, $0.02 \times 0.03 = 0.0006$.

a $2 \times 3 = 6$. There are four decimal places in the multiplication, so there are four in the answer. So, $0.02 \times 0.03 = 0.0006$.

b Rewrite the problem as equivalent products, that is $400 \times 0.008 = 40 \times 0.08 = 4 \times 0.8 = 3.2$.

c Calculate this in two parts. Firstly, $20 \times 0.06 = 2 \times 0.6 = 1.2$.

Secondly, rewrite 1.2×0.009 as $9 \times 12 = 108$, but with four decimal places in the answer. So:

$20 \times 0.06 \times 0.009 = 0.0108$

Example 12.8 A sheet of paper is 0.005 cm thick. How thick is a pack of paper containing 3000 sheets?

This is a multiplication problem:

$0.005 \times 3000 = 0.05 \times 300 = 0.5 \times 30 = 15$ cm

1 Without using a calculator, write down the answers to the following.

a	0.2×0.3	**b**	0.4×0.2	**c**	0.6×0.6	**d**	0.7×0.2
e	0.02×0.4	**f**	0.8×0.04	**g**	0.06×0.1	**h**	0.3×0.03
i	0.7×0.8	**j**	0.07×0.08	**k**	0.9×0.3	**l**	0.006×0.9
m	0.5×0.09	**n**	0.5×0.5	**o**	0.8×0.005	**p**	0.06×0.03

2 Without using a calculator, work out the following.

a	300×0.8	**b**	0.06×200	**c**	0.6×500	**d**	0.02×600
e	0.03×400	**f**	0.004×500	**g**	0.007×200	**h**	0.002×9000
i	0.005×8000	**j**	200×0.006	**k**	300×0.01	**l**	800×0.06
m	500×0.5	**n**	400×0.05	**o**	300×0.005	**p**	200×0.0005

(FM) 3 Screws cost £0.06. An engineering company orders 20 000 screws. How much will this cost?

4 A grain of sand weighs 0.006 g. How much would 500 000 grains weigh?

5 Without using a calculator, work out the following.

a	$0.006 \times 400 \times 200$	**b**	$0.04 \times 0.06 \times 50\,000$	**c**	$0.2 \times 0.04 \times 300$
d	$300 \times 200 \times 0.08$	**e**	$20 \times 0.008 \times 40$	**f**	$0.1 \times 0.07 \times 2000$

6 A kilogram of uranium ore contains 0.000 002 kg of plutonium.

a How much plutonium is in a tonne of ore?

b In a year, 2 million tonnes of ore are mined. How much plutonium will this give?

Extension Work

1 Work out the following.

a	0.1×0.1	**b**	$0.1 \times 0.1 \times 0.1$	**c**	$0.1 \times 0.1 \times 0.1 \times 0.1$

2 Using your answers, write down the answers to the following.

a	0.1^5	**b**	0.1^6	**c**	0.1^7	**d**	0.1^{10}

3 Write down the answers to the following.

a	0.2^2	**b**	0.3^2	**c**	0.4^2	**d**	0.5^2	**e**	0.8^2
f	0.2^3	**g**	0.3^3	**h**	0.4^3	**i**	0.5^3	**j**	0.8^3

Dividing decimals

This section gives more practice on dividing integers and decimals.

Example 12.9 ▶

Work out:

a $0.08 \div 0.2$ **b** $20 \div 0.05$

a Rewrite the sum as equivalent divisions, $0.08 \div 0.2 = 0.8 \div 2 = 0.4$. You must multiply both numbers by 10 at a time, to keep the calculation equivalent.

b Rewriting this as equivalent divisions gives:

$$20 \div 0.05 = 200 \div 0.5 = 2000 \div 5 = 400$$

Example 12.10 ▶ Work out:

a   4.8 ÷ 80   **b**   24 ÷ 3000

a   Divide both numbers by 10 to make the calculation easier:
     4.8 ÷ 80 = 0.48 ÷ 8 = 0.06

It may be easier to set this out as a short-division problem: $\dfrac{0.06}{8\overline{)0.48}}$

b   24 ÷ 3000 = 2.4 ÷ 300 = 0.24 ÷ 30 = 0.024 ÷ 3 = 0.008
Both numbers are divided by 1000 overall, then the
equivalent calculation is done as a short-division problem: $\dfrac{0.008}{3\overline{)0.024}}$

Exercise 12E

1   Without using a calculator, work out the following.

a 0.4 ÷ 0.02	**b** 0.8 ÷ 0.5	**c** 0.06 ÷ 0.1	**d** 0.9 ÷ 0.03
e 0.2 ÷ 0.01	**f** 0.06 ÷ 0.02	**g** 0.09 ÷ 0.3	**h** 0.12 ÷ 0.3
i 0.16 ÷ 0.2	**j** 0.8 ÷ 0.02	**k** 0.8 ÷ 0.1	**l** 0.24 ÷ 0.08
m 0.2 ÷ 0.2	**n** 0.08 ÷ 0.8	**o** 0.9 ÷ 0.09	**p** 0.4 ÷ 0.001

2   Without using a calculator, work out each of these.

a 200 ÷ 0.4	**b** 300 ÷ 0.2	**c** 40 ÷ 0.08	**d** 200 ÷ 0.02
e 90 ÷ 0.3	**f** 40 ÷ 0.04	**g** 50 ÷ 0.1	**h** 400 ÷ 0.2
i 300 ÷ 0.5	**j** 400 ÷ 0.05	**k** 400 ÷ 0.1	**l** 200 ÷ 0.01
m 30 ÷ 0.5	**n** 50 ÷ 0.5	**o** 60 ÷ 0.5	**p** 400 ÷ 0.5

3   Without using a calculator, work out each of these.

a 3.2 ÷ 20	**b** 2.4 ÷ 400	**c** 12 ÷ 400	**d** 3.6 ÷ 90
e 24 ÷ 800	**f** 2.4 ÷ 2000	**g** 1.4 ÷ 70	**h** 1.6 ÷ 40
i 32 ÷ 2000	**j** 0.18 ÷ 300	**k** 0.24 ÷ 0.2	**l** 0.032 ÷ 4000

(FM) **4**   Bolts cost £0.03. How many can I buy with £6000?

5   Grains of salt weigh 0.002 g. How many grains are in a
kilogram of salt?

6   How many gallons of sea water will produce 3 kg of gold if
each gallon contains 0.000 002 g of gold?

Extension Work

1   Given that 46 × 34 = 1564, write down the answers to the following.
    a   4.6 × 34   **b**   4.6 × 3.4   **c**   1564 ÷ 3.4   **d**   15.64 ÷ 0.034

2   Given that 57 × 32 = 1824, write down the answers to the following.
    a   5.7 × 0.032   **b**   0.57 × 32 000   **c**   5700 × 0.32   **d**   0.0057 × 32

3   Given that 2.8 × 0.55 = 1.540, write down the answers to the following.
    a   28 × 55   **b**   154 ÷ 55   **c**   15.4 ÷ 0.028   **d**   0.028 × 5500

5
I can simplify fractions by cancelling common factors.
I can add and subtract simple fractions.
I know the correct order of operations, including using brackets.
I can multiply simple decimals without using a calculator.

6
I can add and subtract fractions by writing them with a common denominator.
I can multiply and divide decimals.

National Test questions

1 *2004 5–7 Paper 1*

Look at this diagram:

The diagram can help you work out some fraction calculations.

Calculate:

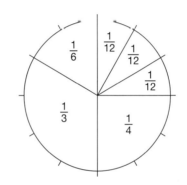

$\frac{1}{2} + \frac{1}{4} =$

$\frac{1}{3} + \frac{1}{4} =$

$\frac{1}{3} - \frac{1}{6} =$

2 *2005 5–7 Paper 2*

Use your calculator to work out the answers to:

$(48 + 57) \times (61 - 19) =$

$\frac{48 + 57}{61 - 19} =$

3 *2005 5–7 Paper 1*

How many eighths are there in one quarter? Now work out $\frac{3}{4} + \frac{1}{8}$.

4 *2007 5–7 Paper 1*

Copy the following fraction sums and write in the missing numbers:

$\frac{1}{4} + \frac{\boxed{}}{8} = 1$ $\frac{1}{3} + \frac{8}{\boxed{}} = 1$

FM Shopping for bargains

The more you buy, the more you save

Collect 15 points for every litre

When you have 5000 points you receive a £5 voucher to spend in store

Petrol £1.20 per litre

Diesel £1.30 per litre

1
a How many litres would you need to buy to collect a voucher?

b Petrol is £1.20 a litre.

How much would you spend on petrol before you receive a voucher?

c Estimate the number of weeks it would take to receive a voucher if you use an average of 30 litres of petrol each week.

d The saving is equivalent to 1.5p per litre.

Work out the percentage saving per litre.

2 Nina uses an average of 40 litres of diesel each week. Diesel is £1.30 per litre.

a How much does she spend on diesel each week?

b Her car uses 1 litre of diesel for every 14 miles travelled. If Nina drives 140 fewer miles each week, how much will she save each week?

c If the price of diesel goes up by 10p a litre, how much more would she spend on diesel in a year (52 weeks)?

d Work out the percentage increase.

3 Here is some information about three business people and their company cars.

	Car fuel	Annual distance travelled (km)	CO_2 emissions (grams per km)
Managing director	Diesel	14 000	140
Secretary	Petrol	8 000	200
Delivery driver	Diesel	22 000	110

The company wants to encourage each person to reduce the CO_2 emissions.

a Work out the annual amount of CO_2 emissions for each car.
Give your answer in kilograms.

b The company wants each person to reduce the CO_2 emissions by reducing each person's travelling by 20%.
Work out the reduction in CO_2 emissions for each car.
Give your answer in kilograms.

Chocolate
Only £1 Was £1.19

Mint sauce
3 for £2 Normally 85p each

Almost Butter
Buy one get one free £1.38

Milk
2 for £2 or £1.25 each

Cheese
Save £1 was £3.25

Scotch eggs
Were £1.15 Save 20% Now 92p

Grillsteaks
520g Half price
Was £2.99 Now £1.49

Baby shampoo
Save $\frac{1}{3}$ Was £2.47 Now £1.64

Luxury Crisps
2 for £2.50 £1.49 each

Yoghurts
48p each Buy 3 get 3 free

Bread 95p

Coffee £3.90

Baked beans 45p

Orange juice £1.30

5 You decide to take up all the offers shown.

a How much will you save on each offer compared with the full price?

b How much will you save altogether?

4 You have £20 to spend but you have to buy, bread, coffee, baked beans and orange juice.

a How much do these four items cost altogether?

b How much does this leave you to spend on other items?

c Using the offers, make **two** different shopping lists of items you could now afford to buy. Try to spend as close to £20 altogether as possible. (*Hint:* You can buy single items but then you would not get the offer price.)

6 The shopping can be ordered on the Internet and delivered to your home.

The delivery charge is £4.50.

The journey to the supermarket and back is 8 miles altogether.

It costs 60p per mile to run your car.

Explain the advantages and disadvantages of having the shopping delivered.

This chapter is going to show you

- How to expand and then simplify expressions
- How to solve a range of linear equations
- How to construct equations and solve them
- How to work with negative gradients
- How to change the subject of a formula

What you should already know

- How to solve simple equations
- The arithmetic of negative numbers
- How to find the gradient of a line

Expand and simplify

In algebra we often have to rearrange expressions and formulae. You have met two methods for doing this before, *expansion* and *simplification*.

Expansion means removing the brackets from an expression by multiplying each term inside the brackets by the term outside the brackets.

Example 13.1

Expand:

   a $2(x + 3y)$ **b** $m(5p - 2)$

   a $2(x + 3y) = 2x + 6y$

   b $m(5p - 2) = 5mp - 2m$

We need to be careful if there is a negative term in front of the bracket because, in effect, that will then change the sign of the term in the expansion.

Example 13.2

Expand:

   a $4 - (a + b)$ **b** $10 - (2x - 3y)$ **c** $T - 3(2m + 4n)$

   a $4 - (a + b) = 4 - a - b$

   b $10 - (2x - 3y) = 10 - 2x + 3y$

   c $T - 3(2m + 4n) = T - 6m - 12n$

Simplification means gathering together all the like terms in an expression to write it as simply as possible.

Example 13.3

Simplify:

a $5a + b + 2a + 5b$ **b** $4c + 3d - c - 2d$ **c** $4x - 2y + 2x - 3y$

a $5a + b + 2a + 5b = 7a + 6b$

b $4c + 3d - c - 2d = 3c + d$

c $4x - 2y + 2x - 3y = 6x - 5y$

You can sometimes simplify an expression after you have expanded the brackets.

Example 13.4

Expand and simplify:

a $3a + c + 2(a + 3c)$ **b** $10t - 3(2t - 4m)$

a $3a + c + 2(a + 3c) = 3a + c + 2a + 6c = 5a + 7c$

b $10t - 3(2t - 4m) = 10t - 6t + 12m = 4t + 12m$

Exercise 13A

1 Simplify the following.

a	$2a + 3a$	**b**	$5b - 3b$	**c**	$4c + 3c - 2c$
d	$8d - 3d + 5d$	**e**	$4x + x$	**f**	$6t - t$
g	$m + 3m - 2m$	**h**	$3d - 5d$	**i**	$t - 4t$
j	$2n - 5n + 4n$	**k**	$3a - 5a - 7a$	**l**	$a - a - a + a$

2 Simplify the following.

a	$3m + 2k + m$	**b**	$2p + 3q + 5p$	**c**	$4t + 3d - t$
d	$5k + g - 2k$	**e**	$5p + 2p + 3m$	**f**	$2w + 5w + k$
g	$m + 3m - 2k$	**h**	$3x + 5x - 4t$	**i**	$3k + 4m + 2m$
j	$2t + 3w + w$	**k**	$5x + 6m - 2m$	**l**	$4y - 2p + 5p$

3 Expand the following.

a	$3(2a + 3b)$	**b**	$2(4t - 3k)$	**c**	$5(n + 3p)$
d	$4(2q - p)$	**e**	$a(3 + t)$	**f**	$b(4 + 3m)$
g	$x(5y - t)$	**h**	$y(3x - 2n)$	**i**	$a(m + n)$
j	$a(3p - t)$	**k**	$x(6 + 3y)$	**l**	$t(2k - p)$

4 Expand and simplify the following.

a	$3x + 2(4x + 5)$	**b**	$8a - 3(2a + 5)$	**c**	$12t - 2(3t - 4)$
d	$4x + 2(3x - 4)$	**e**	$5t - 4(2t - 3)$	**f**	$12m - 2(4m - 5)$
g	$6(2k + 3) - 5k$	**h**	$5(3n - 2) - 4n$	**i**	$2(6x + 5) - 7x$

5 Expand and simplify the following.

a	$2(3k + 4) + 3(4k + 2)$	**b**	$5(2x + 1) + 2(3x + 5)$
c	$3(5m + 2) + 4(3m + 1)$	**d**	$5(2k + 3) - 2(k + 3)$
e	$4(3t + 4) - 3(5t + 4)$	**f**	$2(6k + 7) - 3(2k + 3)$
g	$4(3 + 2m) - 2(5 + m)$	**h**	$5(4 + 3d) - 3(4 + 2d)$
i	$3(5 + 4k) - 2(3 + 5k)$		

In a magic square, each row and each column add up to the same amount.

Show that the square below is a magic square.

$x + m$	$x + y - m$	$x - y$
$x - y - m$	x	$x + y + m$
$x + y$	$x - y + m$	$x - m$

Solving equations

You have met a number of different types of linear equation so far. We solve them by adding, subtracting, multiplying or dividing both sides of the equation by the same thing, to leave the variable on its own on one side of the equation.

Example 13.5 ▷

Solve each of the equations below.

a $3x = 15$ **b** $2 = \dfrac{12}{n}$ **c** $4t - 3 = 17$ **d** $3(2x + 4) = 54$

a $3x = 15$

Divide both sides by 3, to give:

$x = 5$

b $2 = \dfrac{12}{n}$

Multiply both sides by n to give:

$2n = 12$

Now divide both sides by 2, to give:

$n = 6$

c $4t - 3 = 17$

Add 3 to both sides, to give:

$4t = 20$

Now divide both sides by 4, to give:

$t = 5$

d $3(2x + 4) = 54$

Divide both sides by 3, to give:

$2x + 4 = 18$

Now subtract 4 from both sides, to give:

$2x = 14$

Now divide both sides by 2, to give:

$x = 7$

1 Solve the following equations.

a $4x = 12$ **b** $5x = 30$ **c** $2m = 14$

d $3n = 15$ **e** $2x = 7$ **f** $2x = 11$

g $10x = 8$ **h** $10x = 13$ **i** $5x = 3$

j $5x = 8$ **k** $5x = 21$ **l** $4x = 15$

2 Solve the following equations.

a $4 = \dfrac{12}{n}$ **b** $5 = \dfrac{15}{x}$ **c** $3 = \dfrac{18}{m}$

d $7 = \dfrac{21}{x}$ **e** $2 = \dfrac{10}{x}$ **f** $4 = \dfrac{20}{m}$

g $5 = \dfrac{45}{x}$ **h** $2 = \dfrac{7}{n}$ **i** $2 = \dfrac{25}{k}$

j $10 = \dfrac{17}{x}$ **k** $5 = \dfrac{13}{x}$ **l** $4 = \dfrac{17}{n}$

3 Solve the following equations.

a $1.5x + 3.6 = 5.4$ **b** $2.4x + 7.1 = 13.1$ **c** $3.4m - 4.3 = 7.6$

d $5.6k - 2.9 = 5.5$ **e** $4.5n - 3.7 = 12.5$ **f** $1.8t + 7.1 = 18.8$

g $28 - 3.6x = 11.8$ **h** $31.3 - 2.8x = 27.1$ **i** $2.4 - 1.8m = 8.7$

4 Solve the following equations.

a $3(2t + 5) = 33$ **b** $2(5m + 3) = 36$ **c** $5(2m + 1) = 45$

d $4(3k + 2) = 56$ **e** $2(2t - 3) = 18$ **f** $4(3x - 2) = 28$

g $3(5t - 4) = 18$ **h** $5(9 - 2x) = 15$ **i** $3(2k + 7) = 9$

j $4(2m + 9) = 8$ **k** $5(3 - 2x) = 55$ **l** $3(5 - 4k) = 45$

5 Solve the following equations.

a $3(x + 1) + 2(x - 1) = 21$ **b** $4(x + 3) + 3(x - 2) = 41$

c $4(2x + 1) + 5(3x + 2) = 83$ **d** $5(2x + 3) - 2(3x + 1) = 29$

e $4(6x + 5) - 2(4x + 3) = 54$ **f** $3(4x + 5) - 5(2x - 3) = 37$

Extension Work

Solve the following equations.

1 $2(x - 2) - 3(x + 2) = 3(x + 2)$

2 $4(x + 1) - 3(x - 2) = 6(x + 1)$

3 $2(x - 3) - 5(x - 1) = 2(x - 1) - 3(x + 2)$

4 $4(x + 1) - 2(x - 1) = 2(x + 3) + 2(x + 1)$

Constructing equations to solve

The first step of solving a problem with algebra is to write down an equation. This is called **constructing** an equation.

You need to choose a letter to stand for each variable in the problem. This might be x or the first letter of a suitable word. For example, t is often used to stand for time.

Example 13.6 ▷ I think of a number, add 7 to it, multiply it by 5 and get the answer 60. What is the number I first thought of?

Let my number be x.

'Add 7 to it' gives $x + 7$.

'Multiply it by 5' gives $5(x + 7)$.

'I get the answer 60' allows us to form the equation $5(x + 7) = 60$.

We can solve this now:

$$5(x + 7) = 60$$

Divide both sides by 5: $\qquad x + 7 = 12$

Subtract 7 from both sides: $\qquad x = 5$

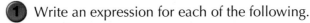

Exercise 13C

1 Write an expression for each of the following.

a Two numbers add up to 100. If one of the numbers is x, write an expression for the other.

b The difference between two numbers is 8. If the smaller of the two numbers is y, write down an expression for the larger number.

c Jim and Ann have 18 marbles between them. If Jim has p marbles, how many marbles has Ann?

d Lenny rides a bike at an average speed of 8 km/h. Write down an expression for the distance he travels in t hours.

e If n is an even number, find an expression for the next consecutive even number.

2 Solve each of the following problems by creating an equation and then solving it.

a A mother is four times as old as her son now. If the mother is 48 years old, find the son's age now. Let the son's age be n.

b If n is an odd number:

    i Write an expression for the next three consecutive odd numbers.

    ii If the sum of these four numbers is 32, find n.

c The sum of two consecutive even numbers is 54. Find the numbers. Let the smaller number be n.

d If the sum of two consecutive odd numbers is 208, what are the numbers? Let the smaller number be n.

e John weighs 3 kg more than his brother. Their total weight is 185 kg. How much does John weigh? Let John's weight be w.

f Joy's Auntie Mary is four times as old as Joy. If the sum of their ages is 70, find their ages. Let Joy be x years old.

g A teacher bought 20 books in a sale. Some cost £8 each and the others cost £3 each. She spent £110 in all. How many of the £3 books did she buy? Let x be the number of £3 books she bought.

h The sum of six consecutive even numbers is 174. What is the smallest of the numbers? Let the smallest number be n.

i The sum of seven consecutive odd numbers is 133. What is the largest of the numbers? Let the largest number be n.

1   The sum of two numbers is 56, and their difference is 14. What is their product?

2   The sum of two numbers is 43, and their product is 450. What is their difference?

3   The difference of two numbers is 12, and their product is 448. What is their sum?

4   The sum of two numbers is 11, and twice the first plus half the second
    is 10. Find the product of the two numbers.

Problems with graphs

In Chapter 7 it was found that the graph of any linear equation is a straight line, and the equation written in the form $y = mx + c$ tells us the *gradient* of the line (*m*) and the *y-axis intercept* (*c*).

The gradient of a straight line is found by dividing the vertical rise of the line by its corresponding horizontal run.

The gradient is positive if it runs from the bottom left to the top right and negative if it runs from top left to bottom right.

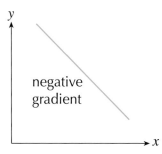
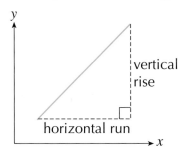

Exercise 13D

1   Each diagram shows the horizontal run and the vertical rise of a straight line. Find the gradient of each line.

a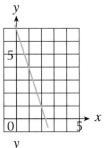

b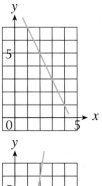

c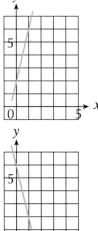

d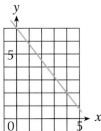

e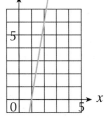

f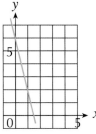

2 Find the gradient and the *y*-axis intercept of each of the following equations.

   a $y = 4x + 1$ **b** $y = 3x - 1$ **c** $y = 5x$ **d** $y = -2x + 3$

3 Write the equation of the line in the form $y = mx + c$, where:

   a $m = 3$ and $c = 2$ **b** $m = 4$ and $c = -3$ **c** $m = -2$ and $c = 5$

   d $m = -4$ and $c = -1$ **e** $m = 4$ and $c = 0$ **f** $m = 0$ and $c = 8$

4 Find the gradient, the *y*-intercept and the equation of each linear graph shown.

   a 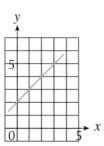   **b** 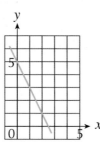   **c**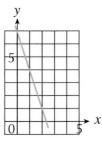

   d    **e** 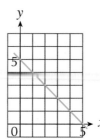   **f**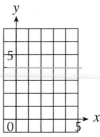

5 Look at the following equations.

   i $y = 2x + 5$ **ii** $y = 3x + 2$ **iii** $y = 2x - 3$

   iv $y = 2 - x$ **v** $y + 5 = 3x$ **vi** $y = x$

   Which of the graphs described by these equations satisfy the following conditions?

   a   Passes through the origin   **b**   Has a gradient of 2

   c   Passes through the point (0, 2)   **d**   Has a gradient of 1

   e   Are parallel to each other

Extension Work

1 Draw the following points on a coordinate grid.

   a   (0, 3) and (2, 9)   **b**   (2, 5) and (6, 17)   **c**   (2, 10) and (3, 4)

   d   (3, 9) and (5, 3)   **e**   (–1, 2) and (1, 8)   **f**   (–3, 8) and (–1, –2)

      i   Find the gradient of the line joining the points.

      ii   Extend the line through the points to cross the *y*-axis if necessary.

      iii   Write down the equation of the line that passes through the points.

2 For the following equations:

   a $y = 2x + 3$ **b** $y = 3x - 2$ **c** $y = -2x + 6$

      i   Plot a point where the graph crosses the *y*–axis.

      ii   Draw a line from that point with the appropriate gradient.

      iii   Label the graph you have drawn.

Real-life graphs

Graphs are used to show a relationship that exists between two variables.

Example 13.7 Draw a sketch graph to illustrate that a hot cup of tea will take about 20 minutes to go cold.

The graph is as shown. The two axes needed are temperature and time, with time on the horizontal axis.

The temperature starts hot at 0 minutes, and is at cold after 20 minutes.

The graph needs a negative gradient.

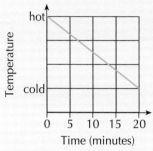

Exercise 13E

1 Sketch graphs to illustrate the following comments, clearly labelling each axis.

    a   The more sunshine we have, the hotter it becomes.

    b   The longer the distance, the longer it takes to travel.

    c   In 2 hours all the water in a saucer had evaporated.

    d   My petrol tank starts a journey full, with 40 litres of petrol in. When my journey has finished, 300 miles later, my tank is nearly empty. It just has 5 litres of petrol left in it.

2 The graph shows a car park's charges.

    a   How much are the car park charges for the following durations?

       i   30 minutes

       ii less than 1 hour

      iii 2 hours

      iv 2 hours 59 minutes

       v 3 hours 30 minutes

      vi 6 hours

    b   How long can I park for:

       i   £1?

       ii £2?

      iii £5?

    c   This type of graph is called a step graph. Explain why it is called this.

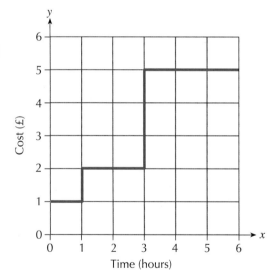

FM 3 A country's parcel post costs are given in the table shown.

Draw step graphs to show charges against weight for:

 a The home country

b Abroad

Weight	Home country	Abroad
0 grams to 500 grams	£1.40	£3.50
Above 500 grams and up to 1 kg	£2.50	£4.60
Above 1 kg and up to 2 kg	£3.20	£5.90
Above 2 kg and up to 3 kg	£4.60	£7.00
Above 3 kg and up to 5 kg	£5.50	£9.50
Above 5 kg and up to 10 kg	£6.00	£12.00
Above 10 kg and up to 20 kg	£8.00	£15.00

FM **④** A taxi's meter reads £2 at the start of every journey. Once two miles has been travelled, an extra £3 is added to the fare. The reading then increases in steps of £3 for each whole mile covered up to five miles. For journeys over five miles, an extra £1 is added per mile over the five.

a How much is charged for the following journeys?

    i Half a mile   **ii** 1 mile   **iii** 3 miles

    iv 5 miles   **v** 6 miles   **vi** 10 miles

b Draw a step graph to show the charges for journeys up to 10 miles.

⑤ Match the four graphs shown here to the situations given below.

a The amount John gets paid against the number of hours he works.

b The temperature of an oven against the time it is switched on.

c The amount of tea in a cup as it is drunk.

d The cost of posting a letter compared to the weight.

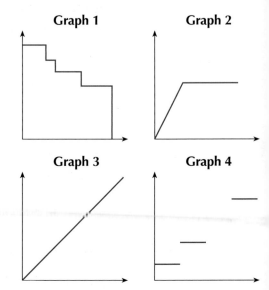

Graph 1   Graph 2

Graph 3   Graph 4

Extension Work

1 Harry decides to take a bath.
The graph shows the depth of water in the bath.

Match each section of the graph to the events below. 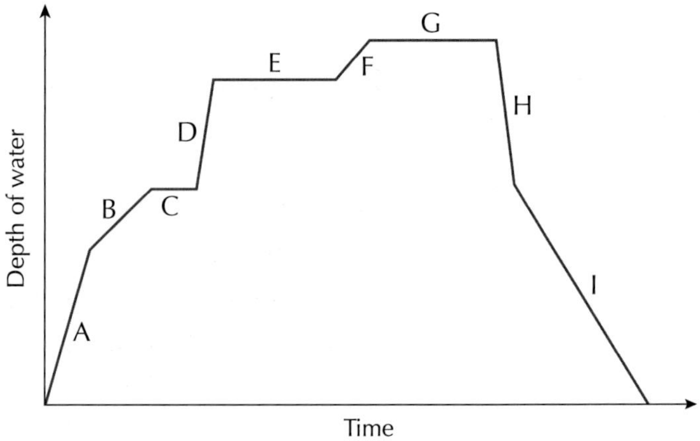
i The bath gets topped up with hot water
ii Harry lays back for a soak
iii Harry gets in the bath
iv The hot and cold taps are turned on
v The cold tap is turned off and only the hot tap is left on
vi Harry washes himself
vii The plug is pulled and the bath empties
viii Harry gets out of the bath
ix The hot tap is turned off.

2 Draw graphs to show these other bath stories.

a Jade turns the taps on, then starts talking to her friend on the phone. The bath overflows. Jade rushed back in and pulls the plug.

b Jane decides to wash her dog. She fills the bath with a few inches of water then puts the dog in. The dog jumps around and whilst being washed splashes most of the water out of the bath. The plug is then pulled and the small amount of water left empties out.

c Jake fills the bath then gets in. Then the phone rings and Jake gets out dripping a lot of water on the floor. He gets back in the bath, finishes his bath, gets out and pulls the plug.

Change of subject

Look at the following formula:

$P = a + 2$

The formula states the value of the variable P, in terms of a.

We say P is the **subject** of the formula. Often we need to rearrange a formula to make another variable into the subject.

This is done in a very similar way to how we solve equations, by adding, subtracting, multiplying or dividing both sides of the equation by the same amount.

Example 13.8

Change the formula $E = 5t + 3$, to make t the subject.

The formula needs altering so that t is on its own on the left-hand side of the formula.

Subtract 3 from both sides: $\qquad\qquad\qquad\qquad E - 3 = 5t$

Divide both sides by 5: $\qquad\qquad\qquad\qquad \dfrac{E - 3}{5} = t$

Turn it round so that t is on the left-hand side: $\qquad t = \dfrac{E - 3}{5}$

Example 13.9

Rewrite the formula $N = \frac{m}{2}$ to express m in terms of N.

Multiply both sides by 2: $\qquad\qquad\qquad 2N = m$

Turn it round to get m on the left-hand side: $\quad m = 2N$

Exercise 13F

1　**a**　$A = 2k$; express k in terms of A. 　　　　**b**　$A = \frac{h}{2}$; express h in terms of A.

　　c　$C = r - 5$; express r in terms of C. 　　　**d**　$A = x + 2$; express x in terms of A.

2　**a**　$C = \pi d$; make d the subject of the formula.

　　b　$P = a + 1$; make a the subject of the formula.

　　c　$S = h - 2$; make h the subject of the formula.

　　d　$A = \frac{h}{3}$; make h the subject of the formula.

　　e　$S = 5t$; make t the subject of the formula.

3　$E = 5n + 8$

　　a　Find E when $n = 15$. 　　**b**　Make n the subject of the formula.

　　c　Find n when $E = 23$.

4　$S = a + 3$

　　a　Find S when $a = 7$. 　　　**b**　Make a the subject of the formula.

　　c　Find a when $S = 24$.

5　$y = x - 2$

　　a　Find y when $x = 2$. 　　　**b**　Make x the subject of the formula.

　　c　Find x when $y = 5$.

6 $T = \frac{R}{4}$

    a   Find T when $R = 20$.   **b**   Make R the subject of the formula.

    c   Find R when $T = 16$.

7 $V = 12r$

    a   Find V when $r = 5$.   **b**   Make r the subject of the formula.

    c   Find r when $V = 36$.

8 Use the formula $S = m + 8$ to find the value of m when $S = 36$.

Extension Work

1 The area of a circle is given by $A = \pi r^2$. Make r the subject of the formula.

2 The volume of a cone is given by $V = \frac{4}{3}\pi r^3$. Make r the subject of the formula.

3 The surface area of a sphere is given by the formula $A = 4\pi r^2$. Make r the subject of the formula.

LEVEL BOOSTER

4 I can simplify algebraic expressions by collecting like terms, for example $3a + 5m + 2a - 3m = 5a + 2m$.

I can solve simple equations of the form $4x = 32$.

5 I can solve equations of the form $6 = \frac{21}{x}$.

I can solve equations of the type $3x + 7 = 10$, for example, where the solution may be fractional or negative.

I can expand brackets such as $4(2a - 1) = 8a - 4$.

I can use algebra to represent a practical situation.

6 I can expand and simplify expressions such as $2(3x + 5) + 2(x - 1) = 8x + 8$.

I can solve equations of the type $2(3x - 8) = 14$, for example, where the solution may be fractional or negative.

I can solve equations of the type $4x + 9 = 3 + x$, for example, where the solution may be fractional or negative.

I can use algebra to set up an equation to represent a practical situation.

I can calculate the gradient of a straight line drawn on a coordinate grid and can distinguish between a positive and a negative gradient.

I can plot the graph of $y = 2x + 1$, for example, using the gradient intercept method.

I can draw and interpret graphs that describe real-life situations.

7 I can solve equations of the type $\frac{4x + 3}{x + 2}$, for example.

I can find the equation of a line using the gradient intercept method.

I can change the subject of a formula with at most two variables, for example making a the subject of the formula $b = a + 2$.

1 *2005 4–6 Paper 1*

Solve these equations:

$3y + 1 = 16$

$18 = 4k + 6$

2 *2006 4–6 Paper 2*

Multiply out this expression.

$5(x + 2) + 3(7 + x)$

Write your answer as simply as possible.

3 *2007 4–6 Paper 1*

Solve this equation.

$2(2n + 5) = 12$

4 *2007 4–6 Paper 2*

Jenny wants to multiply out the brackets in the expression $3(2a + 1)$.

She writes: **$3(2a + 1) = 6a + 1$**

Show why Jenny is **wrong**.

5 *2004 5–7 Paper 1*

Rearrange these equations:

$b + 4 = a$ $b = \ldots$

$4d = c$ $d = \ldots$

$m - 3 = 4k$ $m = \ldots$

6 *2007 5–7 Paper 1*

Look at the cube.

The area of a **face** of the cube is $9x^2$.

Write an expression for the **total surface area** of the cube.

Write your answer as simply as possible.

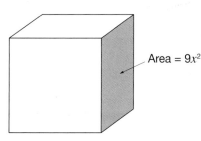

Area = $9x^2$

FM Train timetable

Use the timetable to answer the questions.

Sheffield - Barnsley - Huddersfield/Leeds

Mondays to Fridays

										G												
Sheffield	0516	0536	0550	0614	0636	0649	0704	0725	0736	0751	0808	0836	0851	0908	0936	0951	1008	1036	1051	1108	1136	1151
Meadowhall	0522	0542	0556	0620	0642	0655	0710	0731	0742	0757	0814	0842	0857	0914	0942	0957	1014	1042	1057	1114	1142	1157
Chapeltown	0528	0548	—	0626	0648	—	0716	—	0748	—	0820	0848	—	0920	0948	—	1020	1048	—	1120	1148	—
Elsecar	0533	—		0631	—	—	0721	—	—	—	0825	—	—	0925	—	—	1025	—	—	1125	—	—
Wombwell	0537	0555	—	0635	0655	—	0725	—	0755	—	0829	0855	—	0929	0955	—	1029	1055	—	1129	1155	—
Barnsley	0542	0601	0611	0641	0701	0710	0731	0748	0801	0812	0835	0901	0912k	0935	1001	1012	1035	1101	1112	1135	1201	1212
Dodworth	—	0607	—	—	0707	—	—	—	0807	—	—	0907	—	—	1007	—	—	1107	—	—	1207	—
Silkstone Common	—	0611	—	—	0711	—	—	—	0811	—	—	0911	—	—	1011	—	—	1111	—	—	1211	—
Penistone	—	0618	—	—	0718	—	—	—	0825n	—	—	0918	—	—	1018	—	—	1118	—	—	1218	—
Denby Dale	—	0625	—	—	0724	—	—	—	0831	—	—	0924	—	—	1024	—	—	1124	—	—	1224	—
Shepley	—	0630	—	—	0729	—	—	—	0836	—	—	0929	—	—	1029	—	—	1129	—	—	1229	—
Stocksmoor	—	0632	—	—	0732	—	—	—	0839	—	—	0932	—	—	1032	—	—	1132	—	—	1232	—
Brockholes	—	06360	—	—	0736	—	—	—	0843	—	—	0936	—	—	1036	—	—	1136	—	—	1236	—
Honley	—	639	—	—	0738	—	—	—	0845	—	—	0938	—	—	1038	—	—	1138	—	—	1238	—
Berry Brow	—	0642	—	—	0741	—	—	—	0848	—	—	0941	—	—	1041	—	—	1141	—	—	1241	—
Lockwood	—	0644	—	—	0744	—	—	—	0851	—	—	0944	—	—	1044	—	—	1144	—	—	1244	—
Huddersfield	—	0650	—	—	0749	—	—	—	0856	—	—	0949	—	—	1049	—	—	1149	—	—	1249	—
Darton	—	—	0646	—	—	0736	—	—	—	0840	—	—	0940	—	—	1040	—	—	1140	—	—	
Wakefield Kirkgate	—	—	0629	0658	—	0729	0747	—	—	0829	0852	—	0929	0952	—	1029	1052	—	1129	1152	—	1229
Normanton	—	—	0633	0702	—	0733	0752	—	—		0856	—		0956	—		1056	—		1156	—	
Castleford	—	—	0710	—	—	0800	—	—	—	0904	—	—	1004	—	—	1104	—	—	1204	—	—	
Woodlesford	—	—	—	0719	—	—	0809	—	—	—	0913	—	—	1013	—	—	1113	—	—	1213	—	—
Leeds	—	—	0650	0733	—	0750	0823	—	—	0851	0927	—	0950	1027	—	1050	1127	—	1150	1227	—	1250

Notes: G Through train from Retford   k Arrives 7 minutes earlier   n Arrives 1818

1 How long does the 0536 from Sheffield take to get to Huddersfield?

2 How long does the 1008 from Sheffield take to get to Leeds?

3 How long does the 0635 from Wombwell take to get to Normanton?

4 What is the last station before Huddersfield?

5 If you arrive at Sheffield station at 0730, how long will you have to wait for the next train to Leeds?

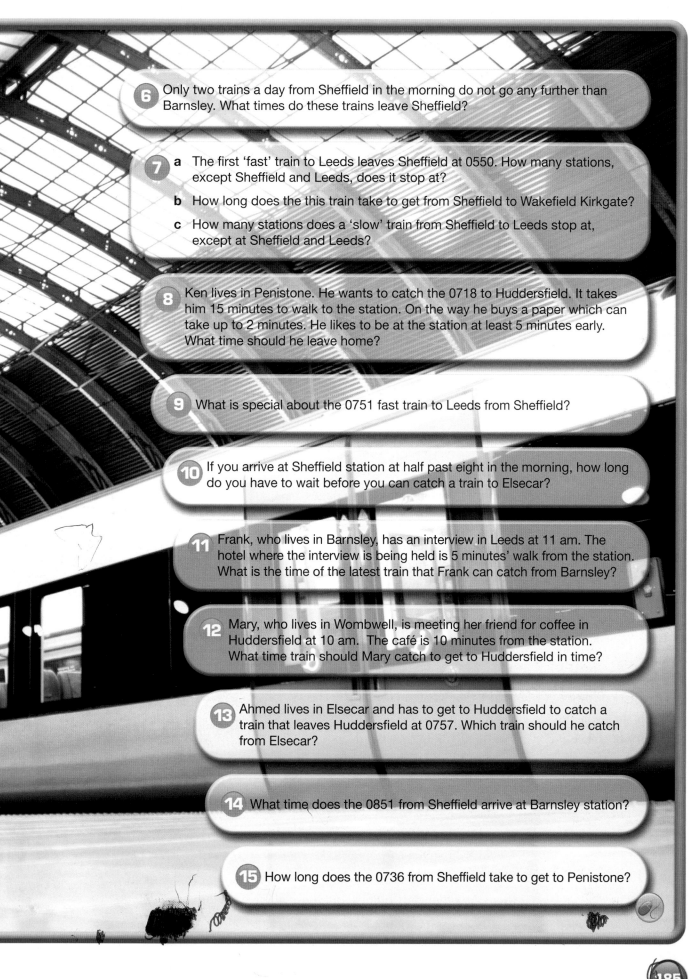

6 Only two trains a day from Sheffield in the morning do not go any further than Barnsley. What times do these trains leave Sheffield?

7 **a** The first 'fast' train to Leeds leaves Sheffield at 0550. How many stations, except Sheffield and Leeds, does it stop at?

b How long does the this train take to get from Sheffield to Wakefield Kirkgate?

c How many stations does a 'slow' train from Sheffield to Leeds stop at, except at Sheffield and Leeds?

8 Ken lives in Penistone. He wants to catch the 0718 to Huddersfield. It takes him 15 minutes to walk to the station. On the way he buys a paper which can take up to 2 minutes. He likes to be at the station at least 5 minutes early. What time should he leave home?

9 What is special about the 0751 fast train to Leeds from Sheffield?

10 If you arrive at Sheffield station at half past eight in the morning, how long do you have to wait before you can catch a train to Elsecar?

11 Frank, who lives in Barnsley, has an interview in Leeds at 11 am. The hotel where the interview is being held is 5 minutes' walk from the station. What is the time of the latest train that Frank can catch from Barnsley?

12 Mary, who lives in Wombwell, is meeting her friend for coffee in Huddersfield at 10 am. The café is 10 minutes from the station. What time train should Mary catch to get to Huddersfield in time?

13 Ahmed lives in Elsecar and has to get to Huddersfield to catch a train that leaves Huddersfield at 0757. Which train should he catch from Elsecar?

14 What time does the 0851 from Sheffield arrive at Barnsley station?

15 How long does the 0736 from Sheffield take to get to Penistone?

CHAPTER 14

Solving Problems

This chapter is going to show you	**What you should already know**
● How to investigate problems involving numbers and measures	● When to use symbols, words or algebra to describe a problem
● How to identify important information in a question	● When to use tables, diagrams and graphs
● How to interpret information from graphs	● How to break down a calculation into simpler steps
● How to use examples to prove a statement is true or false	● How to solve simple problems using ratio and proportion
● How to divide a quantity using proportion or ratio	

Number and measures

A newspaper has 48 pages. The pages have stories, adverts or both on them. 50% of the pages have both. Twice as many pages have adverts only as have stories only. How many pages have stories only?

Example 14.1 ▷ Use the digits 1, 2, 3 and 4 once only to make the largest possible product.

To make large numbers, the larger digits need to have the greatest value.

So try a few examples:

$$41 \times 32 = 1312$$
$$42 \times 31 = 1302$$
$$43 \times 21 = 903$$
$$431 \times 2 = 862$$

There are other possibilities, but these all give smaller answers.

The biggest product is $41 \times 32 = 1312$.

1 Three consecutive numbers add up to 75. What are the numbers?

2 a Find two consecutive odd numbers with a product of 1763.

b Use the digits 1, 3, 6 and 7 once each to form the largest possible product of two numbers.

For example, $13 \times 67 = 871$

$137 \times 6 = 822$

3 Here is a magic square in which each row, column and diagonal add up to 15:

8	1	6
3	5	7
4	9	2

Complete the magic squares on the right so that each row, column and diagonal adds up to 15.

4		8
	7	

2		4
	7	

6		7
	6	

4 A dog and a cat run round a track, 48 m long, in the same direction. They set off together. The dog runs at 6 m per second, the cat at 4 m per second.

a How long does it take each animal to run once round the track?

b After how many laps for each animal will they both pass the starting point together?

5 a Copy and complete the table.

Powers of 3	Answer	Units digit
3^1	3	3
3^2	9	9
3^3	27	7
3^4	81	1
3^5	243	
3^6		
3^7		

b What is the units digit of 3^{44}?

6 Amy is 6 years older than Bill. Two years ago Amy was three times as old as Bill. How old will Amy be in 4 years' time?

7 A map has a scale of 1 cm to $2\frac{1}{2}$ km. The road between two towns is 5 cm on the map, to the nearest centimetre.

a Calculate the shortest possible actual distance between the two towns.

b Calculate the difference between the shortest and longest possible distances between the two towns.

8 Which is the greater mass, 3 kg or 7 pounds (lb)? Explain your answer.

9 Which is the greater length, 10 miles or 15 kilometres? Explain your answer.

10 Which is the greater area, 1 square mile or 1 square kilometre? Explain your answer.

Extension **Work**

Make up a recipe in imperial units (for example, 6 ounces of flour, 2 pints of water, etc). Use metric conversions and rewrite the recipe in metric units. If you need to find out the conversions, use a textbook or the internet.

Using algebra, graphs and diagrams to solve problems

Of three chickens (A, B and C), A and B have a total mass of 4.1 kg, A and C have a total mass of 5.8 kg, and B and C have a total mass of 6.5 kg. What is the mass of each chicken?

Example 14.2 ▷

A gardener has a fixed charge of £5 and an hourly rate of £3 per hour. Write down an equation for the total charge £C when the gardener is hired for n hours. State the cost of hiring the gardener for 6 hours.

The formula is:

C = 5 (for the fixed charge) plus 3 × n (for the hours worked)

$C = 5 + 3n$

If $n = 6$ then the total charge $C = 5 + (3 × 6)$

$$C = 23$$

So the charge is £23.

Example 14.3 ▷

I think of a number, add 3 and then double it. The answer is 16. What is the number?

| ? | → | + 3 | → | × 2 | → | 16 |

Working this flowchart backwards:

| 5 | ← | − 3 | ← | ÷ 2 | ← | 16 |

The answer is 5.

1 A man and his suitcase weigh 84 kg, to the nearest kilogram. The suitcase weighs 12 kg to the nearest kilogram. What is the heaviest that the man could weigh?

2 The sum of two numbers is 43 and the difference is 5. What are the two numbers?

FM **3 a** A tool-hire company has a fixed charge of £12 plus £5 per day to hire a tool. Write the total hire charge, £C, as a formula in terms of n, the number of days.

b Work out the cost for 10 days.

c A different company represents its charges on the graph:

Use the graph to work out the fixed charge and the daily rate.

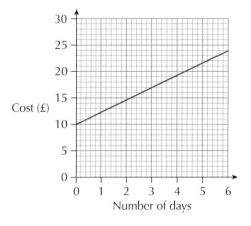

4 Look at the following sequences.

a Draw the next pattern in the sequence.

b How many squares will the fifth pattern have?

5 I think of a number, double it and add one. The answer is 33.

a Write down an equation to represent this information.

b What is the number?

6 I think of a number, square it and subtract five. The answer is 31.

a Write down an equation to represent this information.

b What is the number?

7 I think of a number, double it and add five. The answer is the same as the number plus twelve.

a Write down an equation to represent this information.

b What is the number?

FM **8** Each year a man invests £50 more than the year before. In the first year he invested £100.

a How much does he invest in the tenth year?

b Write down a formula for the amount he invests in the nth year.

9 A grid has 100 squares. If the squares are labelled 1p, 2p, 4p, 8p, 16p, ... , what is the label on the 100th square? Write your answer as a power of 2.

Hint: 1st square = 1p
2nd square = 2p (2)
3rd square = 4p (2 × 2)

10 There are 32 teams in a knockout tournament. In the first round there will be 16 matches. How many matches will there be altogether?

Extension Work

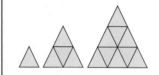

Equilateral triangles are pieced together to make a pattern of triangles as shown. The first diagram has only one small triangle. How many small triangles are in the next two patterns? Extend the patterns to see if you can work out a formula for the number of small triangles in the tenth pattern. What is the special name given to this pattern?

Logic and proof

Look at the recipe, which is for four people. How much of each ingredient is needed to make a chocolate cake for six people?

Chocolate cake
500g flour
100g sugar
35g cocoa powder
60g butter

Example 14.4

Take any three consecutive numbers. Multiply the first number by the third number and square the middle number. Work out the difference between the two answers. Example:

7, 8, 9

$7 \times 9 = 63$

$8^2 = 8 \times 8 = 64$

Difference = 1

Note: Whichever numbers you choose, you will always get an answer of 1.

Example 14.5

Prove that the sum of three odd numbers is always odd.

Call the three odd numbers x, y and z.

$x + y$ is an even number because odd + odd = even.

$(x + y) + z$ is odd, because even + odd = odd.

This is true whatever odd numbers x, y and z actually are.

Exercise 14C

1 Copy and complete the following number problems, filling in the missing digits.

a
```
    □ 5 □
  +  □ 7
  ───────
    5 4 9
```

b
```
    □ 1 6
  -   5 □
  ───────
    7 □ 9
```

c
```
      □ 3
  ×   1 □
  ───────
    5 1 6
```

2 Give an example to show that the sum of three odd numbers is always odd.

3 Explain why the only even prime number is 2.

4 Show that the product of two consecutive numbers is always even.

5 **a** Find the three numbers below 30 that have exactly three factors.
   b What do you notice about these numbers?

6 Find the six factors of 18.

7 Find the twelve factors of 60.

FM **8** Which bottle, among the three shown, is the best value for money?

FM **9** Which is the better value for money?

   a 6 litres for £7.50 or 3 litres for £3.80.
   b 4.5 kg for £1.80 or 8 kg for £4.00.
   c 200 g for £1.60 or 300 g for £2.10.
   d Six chocolate bars for £1.50 or four chocolate bars for 90p.

10 Prove that the sum of two consecutive whole numbers is always odd.

11 Prove that the product of three consecutive numbers is divisible by 6.

FM **12** A recipe uses 750 g of meat and makes a meal for five people. How many grams of meat would be needed if the meal was for eight people?

13 **a** $1\square\square^2 = \square 2\,3\,2\,\square$

   b $4\square^2 = 1\square\square 1$

   c $\sqrt{1\square\square 2\square} = \square\square 3$

Extension **Work**

Invent your own recipes for two people. Rewrite them for four people and then for five people. Remember that you cannot have half an egg!

Proportion

Look at the picture. Can you work out how many pints are in 3 litres?

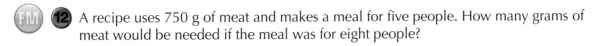

A litre of water is a pint and three-quarters

Example 14.6 ▷ A café sells 200 cups of tea, 150 cups of coffee and 250 other drinks in a day.

What proportion of the drinks sold are:

a cups of tea?   **b** cups of coffee?

a There are 200 cups of tea out of 600 cups altogether, so the proportion of cups of tea is $\frac{200}{600} = \frac{1}{3}$.

b There are 150 cups of coffee out of 600 cups altogether, so the proportion of cups of coffee is $\frac{150}{600} = \frac{1}{4}$.

Exercise 14D

1 A green paint is made by mixing blue and yellow paint in the ratio 3 : 7. How many litres of blue and yellow paint are needed to make:

     a 20 litres of green paint?   **b** 5 litres of green paint?

2 5 miles is approximately 8 km.

     a How many miles are equal to 24 km?

     b How many kilometres are equal to 25 miles?

3 30 cm is approximately 1 foot.

     a How many feet is 75 cm?

     b How many feet is 45 cm?

4 Four cakes cost £10. What will six cakes cost?

5 Six towels cost £18. What will four towels cost?

6 10 candles cost £12. What will 15 candles cost?

7 A lorry travels at 60 miles per hour on the motorway.

     a How far will it travel in 15 minutes?

     b How far will it travel in 1 hour and 15 minutes?

8 In 15 minutes a car travelled 12 km. If it continues at the same speed, how far will it travel in:

     a 30 minutes?   **b** 45 minutes?   **c** 20 minutes?

9 Roast ham costs 80p for 100 grams. How much will 250 grams cost?

10 In 30 minutes, 40 litres of water runs through a pipe. How much water will run through the pipe in 12 minutes?

11 An orange drink is made using one part juice to four parts water. What proportion of the drink is juice? Give your answer as a fraction, decimal or percentage.

12 A woman spends £75 on food and £25 on clothing. What proportion of her spending is on food?

13 A supermarket uses $\frac{3}{4}$ of its space for food and the rest for non-food items. What is the ratio of food to non-food items?

Extension Work

Design a spreadsheet that a shopkeeper could use to increase the price of items by 20%.

Ratio

John and Mary are sharing out the sweets. John wants twice as many sweets as Mary, and there are 21 sweets altogether. Can you work out how many sweets they each get?

Example 14.7

Alice and Michael have 128 CDs altogether. Alice has three times as many as Michael. How many CDs do they each have?

If Alice has three times as many as Michael, then the ratio is 3:1. This means that, altogether, there are 4 (3 + 1) parts to share out.

4 parts is all 128 CDs, so 1 part = 128 ÷ 4 CDs
$$= 32 \text{ CDs}$$

So Michael has 32 CDs and Alice has 32 × 3 = 96 CDs.

You can check your answer by adding 32 and 96. The answer should be 128.

Example 14.8

James and Briony are two goalkeepers. James has let in twice as many goals as Briony. Altogether they have let in 27 goals. How many goals has James let in?

James has let in twice as many goals as Briony, so we can say that if Briony has let in x goals then James has let in $2x$.

Altogether, this means that $3x = 27$, so $x = 9$ and $2x = 18$.

So James has let in 18 goals.

Exercise 14E

1 Simplify the following ratios.

a	6 : 4	**b**	10 : 25	**c**	21 : 7
d	6 : 9	**e**	5 : 20	**f**	8 : 2
g	12 : 3	**h**	20 cm : 15 cm	**i**	4 km : 12 km
j	£7.50 : £3.50	**k**	15p : 3p	**l**	1 m : 25 cm
m	400 g : 1 kg	**n**	500 mm : 1 m	**o**	£1 : 70p
p	1 tonne : 750 kg	**q**	2 hours : 30 minutes	**r**	1 day : 6 hours
s	20 mm : 3 cm	**t**	50p : £2.50		

2 **a** Divide 32 cm in the ratio 3 : 1   **b** Divide 20 kg in the ratio 1 : 4

    c Divide £30 in the ratio 3 : 2   **d** Divide 120 g in the ratio 7 : 5

    e Divide £250 in the ratio 3 : 7   **f** Divide 40 litres in the ratio 2 : 3

    g Divide 49p in the ratio 4 : 2 : 1   **h** Divide 20 million in the ratio 2 : 2 : 1

3 Harriet and Richard go shopping and buy 66 items altogether. Harriet buys twice as many items as Richard. How many items does Harriet buy?

4 At a concert the numbers of males to females are in the ratio 3 : 2. There are 350 people altogether. How many females are at the concert?

5 180 people see a film at the cinema. The numbers of children to adults are in the ratio 5 : 4. How many children see the film?

6 In a fishing contest the number of trout caught to the number of carp caught is in the ratio 1 : 2. The total number of trout and carp is 72. How many carp were caught?

7 A bakery makes 1400 loaves. The ratio of white to brown is 4 : 3. How many brown loaves did the bakery make?

8 A do-it-yourself shop sells paints. The ratio of gloss paint to emulsion paint sold on one day is 2 : 3. If they sell 85 litres of paint, how much gloss paint do they sell?

Extension   Work

1   Draw a cube of side 1cm. Double the length of the sides and find the volume of the new cube. Work out the ratio of the new volume to the previous volume. Double the side length several more times, working out the new : previous volume ratio each time.

2   Repeat this exercise, but triple or quadruple the side length each time instead.

3   Can you find a connection between the new : previous volume ratio and the new : previous side ratio?

LEVEL BOOSTER

5
I can identify the information needed to solve a problem.
I can check a result to see if it is sensible.
I can explain my reasoning.

6
I can solve a complex problem by breaking it down into smaller tasks.
I can justify answers by testing for particular cases.
I can calculate using ratios in appropriate situations.

5

1 *2006 3–5 Paper 1*

a I am thinking of a number.
My number is a **multiple of 4.**

Which of the statements below is true?

My number must be even   My number must be odd   My number could be odd or even

Explain how you know.

b I am thinking of a **different** number.
My number is a **factor of 20**.

Which of the statements below is true?

My number must be even   My number must be odd   My number could be odd or even

Explain how you know.

2 *2006 3–5 Paper 2*

Work out the number of boys and girls in each class below.

a In class 8M, there are **27 pupils**.

There are **twice as many boys** as girls.

b In class 8K, there are **28 pupils**.

There are **two more boys** than girls.

c In class 8T, there are **9 boys**.

The ratio of boys to girls is **1 : 2.**

 3 *2007 3–5 Paper 2*

Kate buys **24 cans** of lemonade.
She buys the cans in **packs of 4**.
Each pack costs **£1.20**.

Steve buys **24 cans** of lemonade.
He buys the cans in **packs of 6**.
Each pack costs **£1.60**.

Kate pays more for her 24 cans than Steve pays for his 24 cans.

How much more?

Pack of 4
Cost £1.20

Pack of 6
Cost £1.60

4 You can work out the cost of an advert in a newspaper by using this formula:

$$C = 15n + 75$$

C is the cost in £
n is the number of words in the advert

a An advert has 18 words. Work out the cost of the advert (show your working).

b The cost of an advert is £615. How many words are in the advert? Show your working.

5 *2005 4–6 Paper 1*

a Look at this information:

> Two numbers **multiply** to make zero.

One of the statements below is true.

Write it down.

> Both numbers must be zero.
> At least one number must be zero.
> Exactly one number must be zero.
> Neither number can be zero.

b Now look at this information:

> Two numbers **add** to make zero.

If **one** number is **zero**, what is the other number?

If **neither** number is **zero**, give an example of what the numbers could be.

6 *2006 4–6 Paper 1*

a Give an example to show the statement below is **not correct**:

> When you multiply a number by 2, the answer is always greater than 2.

b Now give an example to show the statement below is **not correct**:

> When you subtract a number from 2, the answer is always less than 2.

7 *2007 4–6 Paper 2*

Look at this information:

$$x = 4 \qquad y = 13$$

Complete the rules below to show **different** ways to get y using x.

The first one is done for you.

To get y, **multiply** x by ..2.. and **add** ..5...   This can be written as $y = \underline{2x + 5}$.

To get y, **multiply** x by ...... and add ....   This can be written as $y = ...$

To get y, **multiply** x by ...... and **subtract** ....   This can be written as $y = ...$

To get y, **divide** x by ...... and **add** ....   This can be written as $y = ...$

8 *2005 4–6 Paper 2*

I think of a number.
I multiply this number by **8**, then subtract **66**.
The result is twice the number that I was thinking of.

What is the number I was thinking of?

This chapter is going to show you

- How to draw plans, elevations and scale drawings
- How to solve problems using coordinates
- How to construct a triangle given three sides
- How to find the circumference and area of a circle
- How to use bearings
- How to solve problems with cuboids

What you should already know

- How to draw nets of 3-D shapes
- How to plot coordinates in all four quadrants
- How to construct triangles from given data
- How to measure and draw angles
- How to calculate the surface area and volume of cuboids

Plans and elevations

A **plan** is the view of a 3-D shape when it is looked at from above. An **elevation** is the view of a 3-D shape when it is looked at from the front or from the side.

Example 15.1

The 3-D shape shown is drawn on centimetre isometric dotted paper. Notice that the paper must be used the correct way round, so always check that the dots form vertical columns.

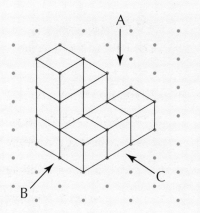

The plan, front elevation and side elevation can be drawn on centimetre-squared paper:

Plan from **A**

Front elevation from **B**

Side elevation from **C**

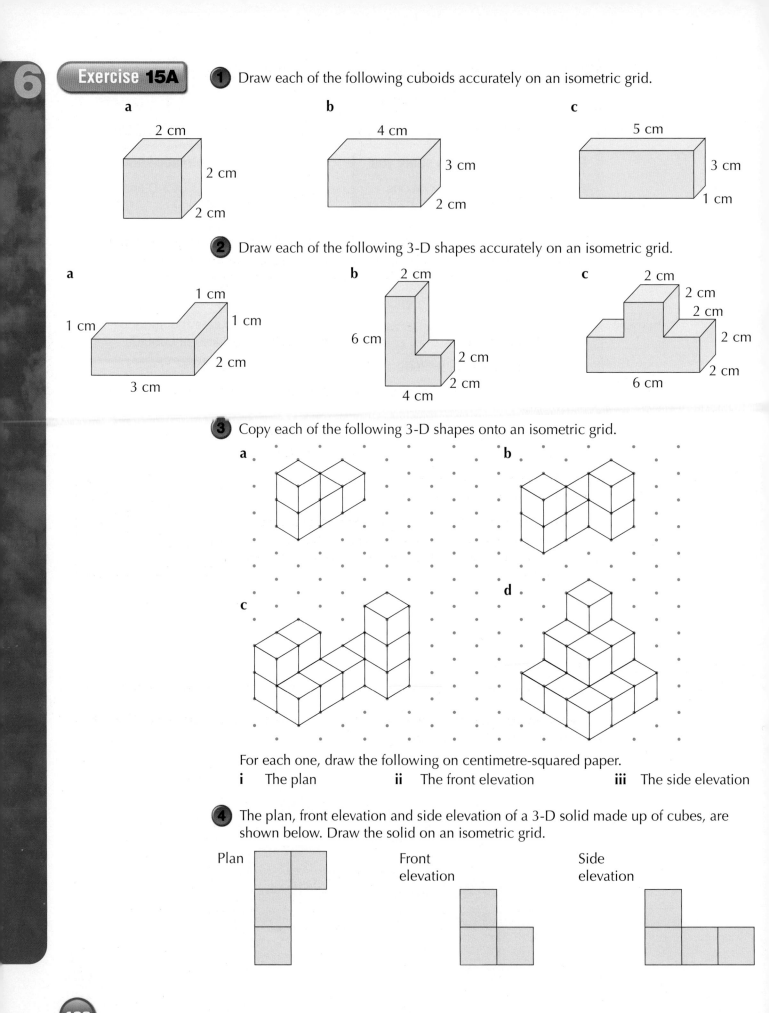

Exercise 15A

1. Draw each of the following cuboids accurately on an isometric grid.

   a
   2 cm
   2 cm
   2 cm

   b
   4 cm
   3 cm
   2 cm

   c
   5 cm
   3 cm
   1 cm

2. Draw each of the following 3-D shapes accurately on an isometric grid.

   a
   1 cm
   1 cm
   1 cm
   2 cm
   3 cm

   b
   2 cm
   6 cm
   2 cm
   2 cm
   4 cm

   c
   2 cm
   2 cm
   2 cm
   2 cm
   2 cm
   6 cm

3. Copy each of the following 3-D shapes onto an isometric grid.

   a

   b

   c

   d

   For each one, draw the following on centimetre-squared paper.
   i The plan   **ii** The front elevation   **iii** The side elevation

4. The plan, front elevation and side elevation of a 3-D solid made up of cubes, are shown below. Draw the solid on an isometric grid.

   Plan

   Front elevation

   Side elevation

5 The diagrams below are the views of various 3-D shapes from directly above.

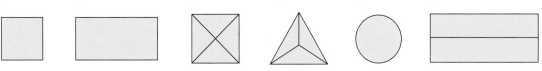

a   b   c   d   e   f

For each one, write down the name of a 3-D shape that could have this plan.

6 Make a 3-D solid from multi-link cubes. On centimetre-squared paper draw its plan, front elevation and side elevation and show these to a partner. Ask your partner to construct the solid using multi-link cubes. Compare the two solids made.

Extension Work

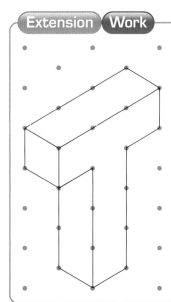

1 The letter 'T' is drawn on an isometric grid, as shown on the left.

  a Draw other capital letters that can be drawn on an isometric grid.

  b Explain why only certain capital letters can be drawn easily on the grid.

  c Design a poster, using any of these letters, to make a logo for a person who has these letters as their initials.

2 The diagram on the right is another way of representing a cube in 2-D.

This representation is known as a **Schlegel diagram**, named after a famous German mathematician. Investigate Schlegel diagrams, using reference books or the Internet.

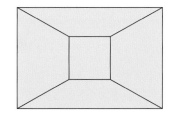

Scale drawings

A **scale drawing** is a smaller drawing of an actual object. A scale must always be clearly given by the side of the scale drawing.

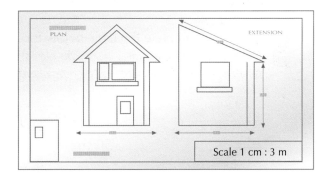

Scale 1 cm : 3 m

Example 15.2 ▷

Shown is a scale drawing of Rebecca's room.

- On the scale drawing, the length of the room is 5 cm, so the actual length of the room is 5 m.

- On the scale drawing, the width of the room is 3.5 cm, so the actual width of the room is 3.5 m.

- On the scale drawing, the width of the window is 2 cm, so the actual width of the window is 2 m.

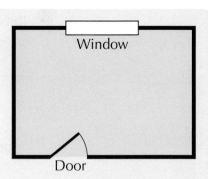

Scale: 1 cm to 1 m

Exercise 15B

1 The lines shown are drawn using a scale of 1 cm to 10 m. Write down the length each line represents.

a ▬▬▬▬▬▬

b ▬▬▬▬▬▬▬▬▬▬▬▬

c ▬▬▬▬▬▬▬▬

d ▬▬▬▬▬▬▬▬▬▬▬▬▬▬

e ▬▬▬▬▬▬▬▬▬▬▬▬▬

FM 2 The diagram shows a scale drawing for a school hall.

a Find the actual length of the hall.

b Find the actual width of the hall.

c Find the actual distance between the opposite corners of the hall.

Scale: 1 cm to 5 m

FM 3 The diagram shown is Ryan's scale drawing for his Mathematics classroom. Nathan notices that Ryan has not put a scale on the drawing, but he knows that the length of the classroom is 8 m.

a What scale has Ryan used?

b What is the actual width of the classroom?

c What is the actual area of the classroom?

4 Copy and complete the table below for a scale drawing in which the scale is 4 cm to 1 m.

	Actual length	Length on scale drawing
a	4 m	
b	1.5 m	
c	50 cm	
d		12 cm
e		10 cm
f		4.8 cm

5 The plan shown is for a bungalow.

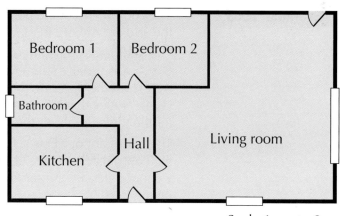

Scale 1 cm to 2 m

a Find the actual dimensions of each of the following rooms.
  i   The kitchen
  ii The bathroom
  iii Bedroom 1
  iv Bedroom 2

b Calculate the actual area of the living room.

6 The diagram shows the plan of a football pitch. It is not drawn to scale. Use the measurements on the diagram to make a scale drawing of the pitch (choose your own scale).

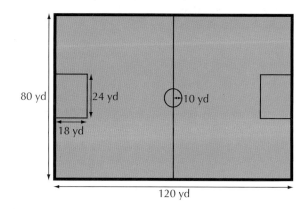

Extension Work

1 On centimetre-squared paper, design a layout for a bedroom. Make cut-outs for any furniture you wish to have in the room (use a scale of 2 cm to 1 m).

2 (You will need a metre rule or a tape measure for this activity.) Draw a plan of your classroom, including the desks and any other furniture in the room (choose your own scale).

3 *Scales as ratios*. A plan has a scale that is given as 1 cm to 2 m. When the scale is changed to the same units it becomes 1 cm to 200 cm. This can be written as the ratio 1 : 200. So a scale of 1 cm to 2 m can also be written as a scale of 1 : 200. Scales on maps are sometimes written in this way. Write each of the scales below as a ratio.

  a 1 cm to 1 m   **b** 1 cm to 4 m   **c** 4 cm to 1 m
  d 1 cm to 1 km   **e** 2 cm to 1 km

Finding the mid-point of a line segment

The next example will remind you how to plot points in all four quadrants using *x*- and *y*-coordinates.

It will also show you how to find the mid-point of a line that joins two points.

Example 15.3 ▷ The coordinates of the points of A, B, C and D on the grid are A(4, 4), B(–2, 4), C(2, 1) and D(2, –3).

The mid-point of the line segment that joins A and B is X (X is usually referred to as the mid-point of AB). From the diagram, the coordinates of X are (1, 4). Notice that the y-coordinates are the same for the three points on the line.

The mid-point of CD is Y. From the diagram, the coordinates of Y are (2, –1). Notice that the x-coordinates are the same for the three points on the line.

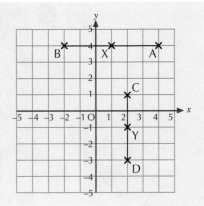

Exercise 15C

5

1 Copy the grid on the right and plot the points A, B, C, D, E and F.

a Write down the coordinates of the points A, B, C, D, E and F.

b Using the grid to help, write down the coordinates of the mid-point of each of the following line segments.

    i AB

    ii CD

    iii BE

    iv EF

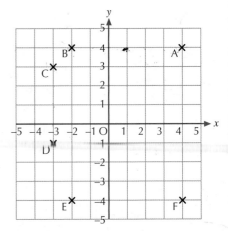

2 Copy the grid on the right and plot the points P, Q, R and S.

a Write down the coordinates of the points P, Q, R and S.

b Join the points to form the rectangle PQRS. Using the grid to help, write down the coordinates of the mid-point of each of the following lines.

    i PQ   **ii** QR

    iii PS   **iv** SR

c Write down the coordinates of the mid-point of the diagonal PR.

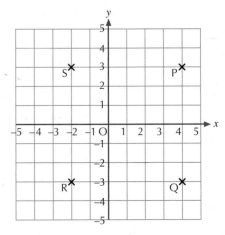

3 a Copy and complete the table on the next page, using the points on the grid to the right. The first row of the table has been completed for you.

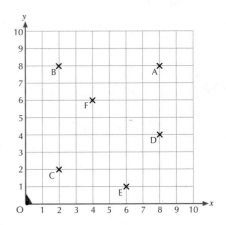

Line segment	Coordinates of the first point on the line segment	Coordinates of the second point on the line segment	Coordinates of the mid-point of the line segment
AB	A(8, 8)	B(2, 8)	(5, 8)
AD			
BC			
BF			
AF			
CE			

b Can you spot a connection between the coordinates of the first and second points and the coordinates of the mid-point? Write down a rule in your own words.

4 By using the rule you found in Question 3 or by plotting the points on a coordinate grid, find the mid-points of the line that joins each of the following pairs of coordinate points.

a A(3, 2) and B(3, 6)   **b** C(4, 6) and D(6, 10)

c E(3, 2) and F(5, 4)   **d** G(8, 6) and H(2, 3)

e I(5, 6) and J(−3 , −2)

To find a formula for the mid-point of a line segment AB:

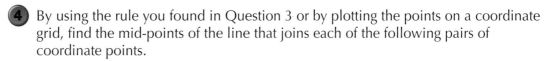

On the x-axis above, what number lies half way between 4 and 8? Can you see a way of getting the answer without using the number line? The answer of 6 can be found by finding the mean of 4 and 8 or $\frac{4+8}{2}$.

Test this rule by trying other numbers.

x_1 and x_2 lie on the x-axis, as shown below. What number lies half way between x_1 and x_2? The answer is the mean of x_1 and x_2, which is $\frac{x_1+x_2}{2}$.

The same rule will work for numbers on the y-axis:

On the y-axis shown, what number lies half way between y_1 and y_2? The answer is the mean of y_1 and y_2, which is $\frac{y_1+y_2}{2}$.

This rule can now be applied to find the coordinates of the mid-point of the line AB on the grid to the right.

Point A has coordinates (x_1, y_1) and point B has coordinates (x_2, y_2). Using the above rule for both axes, we find that the coordinates of the mid-point of AB is given by the formula:

$$\left(\frac{x_1 + x_2}{2}, \frac{y_1 + y_2}{2}\right)$$

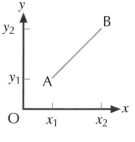

Points A, B, C, D and E are plotted on the grid shown. Use the formula above to find the mid-point for each of the following line segments.

a AB

b BC

c CD

d DE

e AE

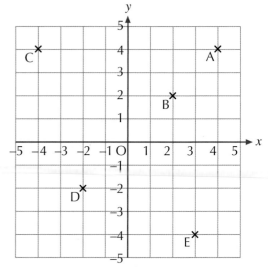

To construct a triangle given three sides

In Year 7, Book 2 showed you how to construct triangles, using a ruler and a protractor, from given data. You were able to construct the following:

● A triangle given two sides and the included angle (SAS):

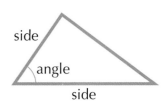

● A triangle given two angles and the included side (ASA):

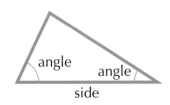

The example below shows you how to construct a triangle given three sides (SSS). You need a ruler and compasses for this construction.

Example 15.4 ▷

To construct the triangle PQR.

Draw line QR 6 cm long. Set compasses to a radius of 4 cm and, with centre at Q, draw a large arc above QR. Set compasses to a radius of 5 cm and, with the centre at R, draw a large arc to intersect the first arc. The intersection of the two arcs is P. Join QP and RP to complete the triangle. Leave your construction lines on the diagram.

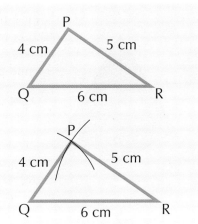

Exercise 15D

1 Construct each of the following triangles (remember to label all the lines).

a
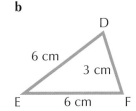

b
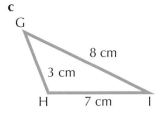

c

d
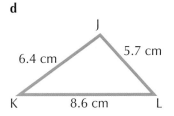

2 Construct the ΔXYZ with XY = 6.5 cm, XZ = 4.3 cm and YZ = 5.8 cm.

3 Construct the ΔPQR with PQ = 5 cm, QR = 12 cm and PR = 13 cm. What type of triangle have you drawn?

4 Construct equilateral triangles with sides of length:

   a 3 cm   **b** 5 cm   **c** 4.5 cm

5 Paul thinks that he can construct a triangle with sides of length 3 cm, 4 cm and 8 cm, but finds that he cannot draw it.

   a Try to construct Paul's triangle.

   b Explain why it is not possible to draw Paul's triangle.

Extension Work

1 Construct the quadrilaterals shown using only a ruler and compasses.

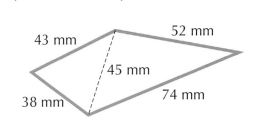

5

2 **a** Draw the net below accurately on card. Cut out the net to make a square-based pyramid. Make the square 4 cm × 4 cm, and each equilateral triangle 4 cm × 4 cm × 4 cm.

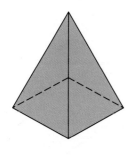

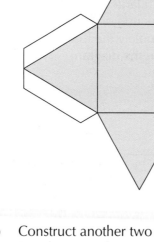

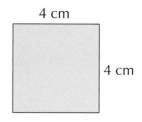

4 cm

4 cm

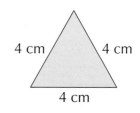

4 cm   4 cm

4 cm

b Construct another two square-based pyramids and paste their bases together to make an octahedron, like the one in the diagram.

3 If you have access to ICT facilities, find out how to construct triangles using programs such as LOGO.

Circumference and area of a circle

The perimeter of a circle is known as the circumference.

r is the radius of the circle and *d* is the diameter.

The formula for the circumference, *C*, of a circle is given by:

$$C = \pi d$$

π (pronounced *pi*) is a special number in mathematics and cannot be written down exactly.

The value of π is usually taken to be 3.14, but on a calculator a more accurate version is 3.141592654.

Look for the π key on your calculator (SHIFT ×10^x).

It can also be shown that the area, *A*, of a circle is given by:

$$A = \pi r^2$$

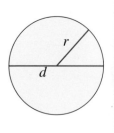

Example 15.5 Calculate the circumference of each of the following circles. Give each answer to one decimal place.

a   5 cm

b   3 cm

a   The diameter, $d = 5$ cm, which gives:

$C = \pi d = \pi \times 5 = 15.7$ cm (to 1 dp)

b   The radius, $r = 3$ cm, so $d = 6$ cm, which gives:

$C = \pi d = \pi \times 6 = 18.8$ cm (to 1 dp)

Example 15.6 Calculate the area of each of the following circles. Give each answer to one decimal place.

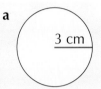

a   3 cm

b   7 cm

a   The radius, $r = 3$ cm, which gives:

$A = \pi r^2 = \pi \times 9 = 28.3$ cm² (to 1 dp)

b   The diameter, $d = 7$ cm, so $r = 3.5$ cm, which gives:

$A = \pi r^2 = \pi \times 3.5 \times 3.5 = 38.5$ cm² (to 1 dp)

Exercise 15E   In this exercise, take $\pi = 3.14$ or use SHIFT ×10^x on your calculator.

1 Calculate the circumference of each of the following circles. Give each answer to one decimal place.

a 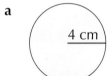 4 cm   **b** 5 cm   **c** 8 cm

d 6 cm   **e** 4 cm   **f** 9 cm

2 Calculate the area of each of the following circles. Give each answer to one decimal place.

a 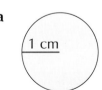 1 cm   **b** 5 cm   **c** 4 cm

d 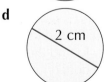 2 cm   **e** 5 cm   **f** 6.2 cm

3 A circular coaster has a radius of 4.8 cm. Calculate its circumference.

Give your answer to one decimal place.

6

④ The diameter of a 2p coin is 26 mm. Calculate its area.
Give your answer to the nearest square millimetre.

Calculate the perimeter and area of the following shapes. Give your answers to one decimal place.

1

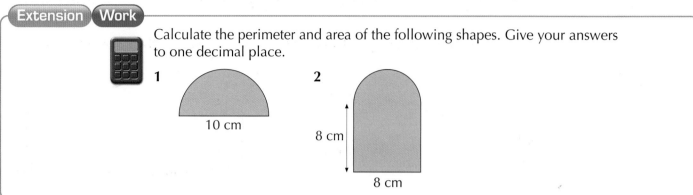

10 cm

2

8 cm

8 cm

Bearings

There are four main directions on a compass – north (N), south (S), east (E) and west (W). These directions are examples of **compass bearings**. A **bearing** is a specified direction in relation to a fixed line. The line that is usually taken is due north. The symbol for due north is: N

↑

You have probably seen this symbol on maps in Geography.

Bearings are mainly used for navigation purposes at sea, in the air and in sports such as orienteering. A bearing is measured in degrees (°) and the angle is always measured **clockwise** from the **north line**. A bearing is always given using three digits and is referred to as a **three-figure bearing**. For example, the bearing for the direction east is 090°.

Example 15.7 ▶

On the diagram, the three-figure bearing of B from A is 035° and the three-figure bearing of A from B is 215°.

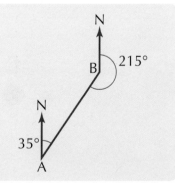

Example 15.8 ▶

The diagram shows the positions of Manchester and Leeds on a map.

The bearing of Leeds from Manchester is 050° and the bearing of Manchester from Leeds is 230°. To find the bearing of Manchester from Leeds, use the dotted line to find the alternate angle of 50° and then add 180°. Notice that the two bearings have a difference of 180°. Such bearings are often referred to as 'back bearings'.

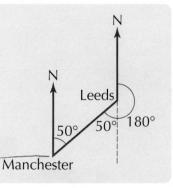

Exercise 15F

1 Write down each of the following compass bearings as three-figure bearings.

    a South   **b** West   **c** North-east   **d** South-west

2 Write down the three-figure bearing of B from A for each of the following.

a 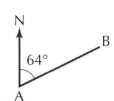   **b**    **c** 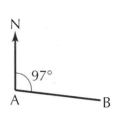   **d**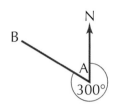

3 Find the three-figure bearing of X from Y for each of the following.

a 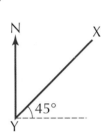   **b**    **c** 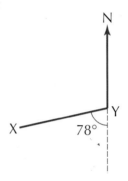   **d**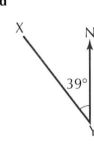

4 Draw a rough sketch to show each of the bearings below (mark the angle on each sketch).

    a From a ship A, the bearing of a light-house B is 030°.

    b From a town C, the bearing of town D is 138°.

    c From a gate E, the bearing of a trigonometric point F is 220°.

    d From a control tower G, the bearing of an aircraft H is 333°.

5 The two diagrams show the positions of towns and cities in England.
Find the bearing of each of the following:

    a **i**   Nottingham from Birmingham

         ii Birmingham from Nottingham

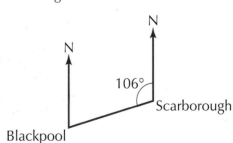

    b **i**   Scarborough from Blackpool

         ii Blackpool from Scarborough

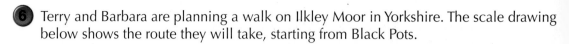

6 Terry and Barbara are planning a walk on Ilkley Moor in Yorkshire. The scale drawing below shows the route they will take, starting from Black Pots.

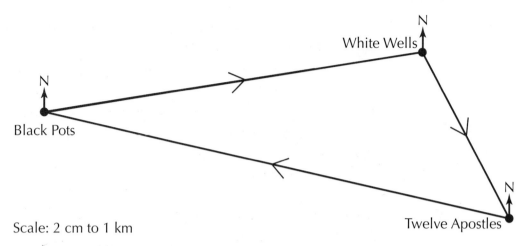

Scale: 2 cm to 1 km

a What is the total distance of their walk if they keep to a direct route between the land marks?

b They have to take three figure bearings between each land mark because of poor visibility. Use a protractor to find the bearing of:

i White Wells from Black Pots

ii Twelve Apostles from White Wells

iii Black Pots from the Twelve Apostles

Extension Work

1 A liner travels from a port X on a bearing of 140° for 120 nautical miles to a port Y. It then travels from port Y on a bearing of 250° for a further 160 nautical miles to a port Z.

a Make a scale drawing to show the journey of the liner (use a scale of 1 cm to 20 nautical miles).

b Use your scale drawing to find:

i the direct distance the liner travels from port Z to return to port X.

ii the bearing of port X from port Z.

2 The diagram shows the approximate direct distances between three international airports.

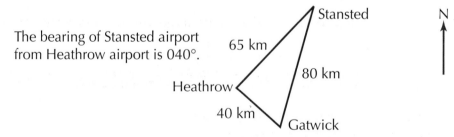

The bearing of Stansted airport from Heathrow airport is 040°.

a Use this information to make a scale drawing to show the positions of the airports (use a scale of 1 cm to 10 km).

b Use your scale drawing to find:

i the bearing of Gatwick airport from Heathrow airport.

ii the bearing of Gatwick airport from Stansted airport.

A cube investigation

For this investigation you will need a collection of cubes and centimetre isometric dotted paper.

Two cubes can only be arranged in one way to make a solid shape, as shown.

Copy the diagram onto centimetre-isometric dotted paper. The surface area of the solid is 10 cm².

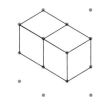

Three cubes can be arranged in two different ways, as shown.

Copy the diagrams onto centimetre isometric dotted paper. The surface area of both solids is 14 cm².

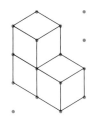

OR

Exercise 15G

Here is an arrangement of four cubes:
The surface area of the solid is 18 cm².

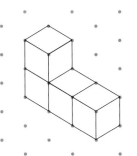

1 How many different arrangements can you make using four cubes?

2 Draw all the different arrangements on centimetre-isometric dotted paper.

3 What is the greatest surface area for the different solids you have made?

4 What is the least surface area for the different solids you have made?

5 Draw a table to show your results and write down anything you notice.

6 What do you think are the greatest and least surface areas of a solid made from five cubes?

LEVEL BOOSTER

5
I can use coordinates in all four quadrants.
I know how to make a scale drawing.
I know how to use three-figure bearings.
I can construct a triangle given three sides.

6
I know how to draw plans and elevations.
I can calculate the volume and surface area of shapes made from cubes and cuboids.
I can find the circumference and area of a circle.

5

1 *2003 4–6 Paper 1*

Use compasses to construct a triangle that has sides **8 cm**, **6 cm** and **7 cm**.
Leave in your construction lines.

2 *2005 4–6 Paper 2*

A newspaper printed this information about London and Madrid:

Show this information on a scale drawing.

Use the scale **1 cm represents 200 km**.

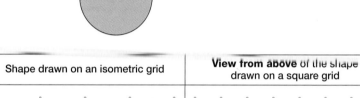

From London to Madrid, the angle
from north is **195° clockwise**.

Madrid is **1300 km** from London.

6

3 *2003 4–6 Paper 1*

Kevin is working out the **area** of a circle with **radius 4**.
He writes: Area = π × 8

Explain why Kevin's working is **wrong**.

4 *2006 4–6 Paper 2*

Each shape below is made from
five cubes that are joined together.

Copy and complete the missing
diagrams shown right.

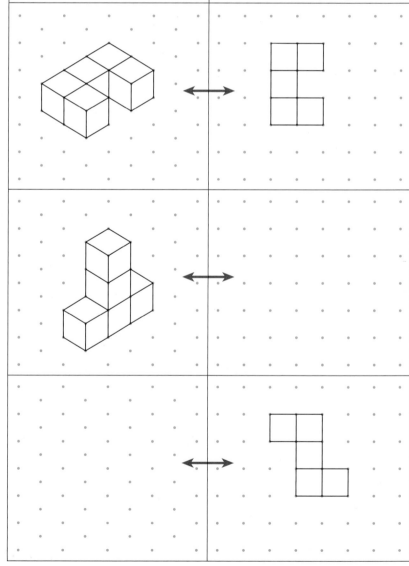

5   *2005 4–6 Paper 1*

a   P is the **midpoint** of line AB.

What are the coordinates of point **P**?

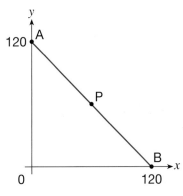

b   Q is the **midpoint** of line MN.

The coordinates of Q are (30, 50).

What are the coordinates of points **M** and **N**?

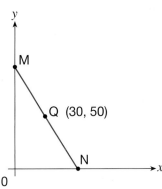

FM Photographs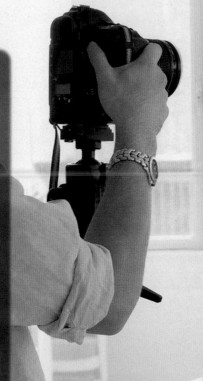

FastPrint advertises the cost of photograph prints in their shop.

Print size	Price each	
3" × 2" (4)	£0.99	
	Quantity	**Price**
13 cm × 9 cm	1–99	£0.10 each
	100–249	£0.09 each
	250+	£0.08 each
	Quantity	**Price**
	1–49	£0.15 each
	50–99	£0.12 each
6" × 4"	100–249	£0.09 each
	250–499	£0.08 each
	500–750	£0.06 each
	751+	£0.05 each
7" × 5"	£0.29	
8" × 6"	£0.45	
10" × 8"	£1.20	
12" × 8"	£1.20	
45 cm × 30 cm	£6.99	

1 A school decides to use FastPrint to buy prints of a year group photograph. Pupils can choose the size of the prints they want. They can also choose to buy more than one size.

The school's order is as follows:

	128	13 cm × 9 cm prints
	87	6" × 4" prints
	75	10" × 8" prints
and	60	12" × 8" prints

What is the total cost of buying these prints?

2 The print sizes are given in both imperial units (" means inches) and metric units.

a Use the conversion factor 1 cm = 0.394 inches to change the 13 cm × 9 cm and the 45 cm × 30 cm print sizes into imperial sizes. Give your answers to one decimal place.

b Find the area of each of the imperial sized prints. (The units are square inches or sq in.)

c Which pairs of prints are twice the size in area?

3 Here are the sizes of three picture frames A, B and C.

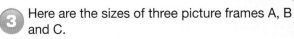

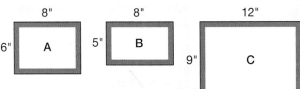

a The 7" × 5" print will fit inside frame A. What will be the area of the outside border?

b Which of the prints will best fit inside the other two frames if a suitable border is to be left around the print?

5 EasyPrint also advertises the cost of photograph prints in their shop.

3" × 2" print	£0.25 each
6" × 4" print	£0.12 each
7" × 5" print	£0.20 each
8" × 6" print	£0.42 each
10" × 8" print	£1.20 each
12" × 8" print	£1.32 each

a If you order one of each print size from EasyPrint, which prints are cheaper than FastPrint?

b If you wanted to order 120 4" × 6" prints, which shop would you choose? How much would you save?

c How much more do you pay for a 10" × 8" print at FastPrint?

d What is the percentage increase in the price if you ordered 8" × 12" prints from EasyPrint rather than from FastPrint?

4 Some of the prints are actual mathematical enlargements of each other.

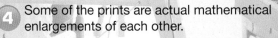

Write down the sizes of the prints that are exact enlargements of each other and state the scale factor of the enlargement.

6 Any rectangle whose length and width are in the ratio 1.618 : 1 is known as a Golden Rectangle.

The Golden Rectangle is said to be one of the most visually pleasing rectangular shapes. Many artists and architects have used the shape within their work.

a Work out the ratio of the length to the width in the form $n : 1$ for each print size at EasyPrint.

For example, for the 3" × 2" print, 3 : 2 = 1.5 : 1.

b Which of the prints are close to being golden rectangles?

This chapter is going to show you	What you should already know
● How to calculate statistics from given data ● How to calculate a mean using an assumed mean ● How to construct frequency diagrams for continuous data ● How to construct simple line graphs for time series ● How to compare two distributions by using an average and the range ● How to compare theoretical probabilities with experimental probabilities	● How to construct frequency tables for discrete data ● How to find the mode, median, range and modal class for grouped data ● How to calculate the mean from a simple frequency table ● How to construct graphs and diagrams to represent data

Frequency tables

There are three equal periods in an ice hockey game. Use the picture to work out the time on the clock at the end of each period.

Example 16.1 ▶ The journey times, in minutes, for a group of 16 railway travellers are shown below:

25, 47, 12, 32, 28, 17, 20, 43, 15, 34, 45, 22, 19, 36, 44, 17

Construct a frequency table to represent the data.

Looking at the data, 10 minutes is a sensible class interval size.

The class intervals are written in the form $10 < T \le 20$.

$10 < T \le 20$ is a way of writing the time interval 10 minutes to 20 minutes, including 20 minutes but not 10 minutes.

There are six times in this group: 12, 17, 15, 19, 20 and 17.
There are three times in the group $20 < T \le 30$: 25, 28, and 22.
There are three times in the group $30 < T \le 40$: 32, 34 and 36.
There are four times in the group $40 < T \le 50$: 47, 43, 45 and 44.

Putting all this information into the table gives:

Time, T (minutes)	Frequency
$10 < T \le 20$	6
$20 < T \le 30$	3
$30 < T \le 40$	3
$40 < T \le 50$	4

Exercise 16A

1. The length of time 25 customers spend in a shop is recorded in the table given.

   One of the customers was in the shop for exactly 20 minutes. In which class was the customer recorded?

Time, T (minutes)	Frequency
$0 < T \le 10$	12
$10 < T \le 20$	7
$20 < T \le 30$	6

2. The heights (in metres) of 20 people are given below:

   1.65, 1.53, 1.71, 1.62, 1.48, 1.74, 1.56, 1.55, 1.80, 1.85, 1.58, 1.61, 1.82, 1.67, 1.47, 1.76, 1.79, 1.66, 1.68, 1.73

   Copy and complete the frequency table on the right.

Height, h (metres)	Frequency
$1.40 < h \le 1.50$	
$1.50 < h \le 1.60$	
$1.60 < h \le 1.70$	
$1.70 < h \le 1.80$	
$1.80 < h \le 1.90$	

3. The masses (in kilograms) of fish caught in one day by a fisherman are shown below:

   0.3, 5.6, 3.2, 0.4, 0.6, 1.1, 2.4, 4.8, 0.5, 1.6, 5.1, 4.3, 3.7, 3.5

   Copy and complete the frequency table on the right.

Mass, M (kilograms)	Frequency
$0 < M \le 1$	
$1 < M \le 2$	
. . .	
. . .	
. . .	
. . .	

4 The temperature (in °C) of 16 towns in Britain is recorded on one day:

12, 10, 9, 13, 12, 14, 17, 16, 18, 10, 12, 11, 15, 15, 12, 13

Copy and complete the frequency table on the right.

Temperature, T (°C)	Frequency
$8 < T \leq 10$	
$10 < T \leq 12$	
. . .	
. . .	
. . .	

Extension Work

Record the number of pages in a large number of school textbooks. Decide on suitable class intervals for the data to be collected together into a frequency table and complete the table. Comment on your results.

Assumed mean and working with statistics

The father's age is double the combined age of his children. Two years ago the children had an average age of 7 years. The difference in the children's ages is 2 years. How old is the father?

Example 16.2 ▷ Find the mean of the four numbers 26.8, 27.2, 34.1, 36.4. Use 30 as the assumed mean.

Subtracting 30 from each number gives: –3.2, –2.8, 4.1, 6.4

Adding these numbers up gives: –3.2 + –2.8 + 4.1 + 6.4 = 4.5

So the mean of these numbers is: 4.5 ÷ 4 = 1.125

Adding the 30 back on gives a mean for the original numbers of:

30 + 1.125 = 31.125

Example 16.3 ▷ A set of numbers has a mean of 6 and a range of 7.

What happens to the mean and range when the numbers are:

a multiplied by 2?   **b** increased by 5?

a As each number has doubled, the mean will also double. For example, if the numbers were 3, 5 and 10, then the new numbers would be 6, 10 and 20.

The old mean is $\frac{3 + 5 + 10}{3} = 6$ and the new mean is $\frac{6 + 10 + 20}{3} = 12$.

The old range is 7 and the new range is 20 – 6 = 14, which is also double.

b As each number has increased by 5, then the mean will also increase by 5. For example, if the numbers were 3, 5 and 10, then the new numbers would be 8, 10 and 15.

The old mean is $\frac{3 + 5 + 10}{3} = 6$ and the new mean is $\frac{8 + 10 + 15}{3} = 11$.

The old range is 6 and the new range is 15 − 8 = 6, which is still the same.

Exercise 16B

1 Find the mean of 34, 35, 37, 39, 42. Use 37 as the assumed mean.

2 Find the mean of 18, 19, 20, 21, 27. Use 20 as the assumed mean.

3 The heights, in centimetres, of five brothers are 110, 112, 115, 119 and 124. Find their mean height using an assumed mean of 110 cm.

4 Four students each use a trundle wheel to measure the length of their school field in metres. Their results are 161.0, 164.5, 162.5 and 165.0. Find the mean of their results using an assumed mean of 160 m.

5 A box of matches has 'Average contents 600' written on it. Sunil counts the matches in 10 boxes and obtains the following results: 588, 592, 600, 601, 603, 603, 604, 605, 605, 607. Calculate the mean number of matches using an assumed mean of 600. Comment on your answer.

6 The mean of five numbers 5, 9, 10, 20 and x is 10. Find the value of x.

7 Write down three numbers with a mean of 7 and a range of 4.

8 Write down three numbers with a median of 6 and a range of 3.

9 The mean of five numbers is 7, the mode is 10 and the range is 7. What are the five numbers?

10 The mean of a set of numbers is 5 and the range is 6. The numbers are now doubled.

    a What is the new mean?   **b** What is the new range?

11 The mean of a set of numbers is 11 and the range is 8. The numbers are now increased by 5.

    a What is the new mean?   **b** What is the new range?

12 The mode of a set of numbers is 15 and the range is 6. The numbers are now halved.

    a What is the new mode?   **b** What is the new range?

Extension Work

Draw two straight lines of different lengths. Ask other pupils to estimate the lengths of the lines. Record the results and calculate the mean and range for each line. Compare the accuracy of the estimates for the two lines. You could then extend this by repeating for two curved lines and compare the accuracy of the estimates for straight and curved lines.

Drawing frequency diagrams

Look at the picture. How could the organisers record the finishing times to find out when most of the runners finish?

Example 16.4

Construct a frequency diagram for the following data about journey times:

Journey times, t (minutes)	Frequency
$0 < t \leq 15$	4
$15 < t \leq 30$	5
$30 < t \leq 45$	10
$45 < t \leq 60$	6

It is important that the diagram has a title and labels, as shown right:

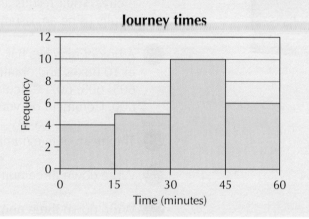

Example 16.5

Look at the graph for ice cream sales. In which month were sales at their highest? Give a reason why you think this happened.

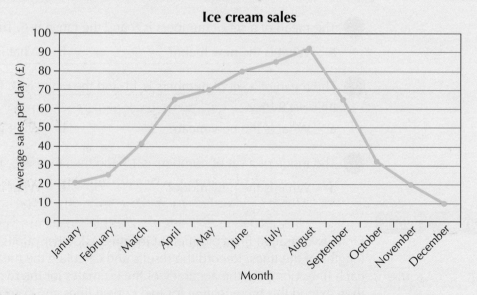

The highest sales were in August (£92 per day). This was probably because the weather was warmer, as people tend to buy ice creams in warm weather.

1 For each frequency table, construct a frequency diagram.

a Aircraft flight times:

Time, T (hours)	Frequency
$0 < T \le 1$	3
$1 < T \le 2$	6
$2 < T \le 3$	8
$3 < T \le 4$	7
$4 < T \le 5$	4

b Temperatures of capital cities:

Temperature, T (°C)	Frequency
$0 < T \le 5$	2
$5 < T \le 10$	6
$10 < T \le 15$	11
$15 < T \le 20$	12
$20 < T \le 25$	7

c Length of metal rods:

Length, l (centimetres)	Frequency
$0 < l \le 10$	9
$10 < l \le 20$	12
$20 < l \le 30$	6
$30 < l \le 40$	3

d Mass of animals on a farm:

Mass, M (kg)	Frequency
$0 < M \le 20$	15
$20 < M \le 40$	23
$40 < M \le 60$	32
$60 < M \le 80$	12
$80 < M \le 100$	6

FM 2 The graph below shows the mean monthly temperature for two cities:

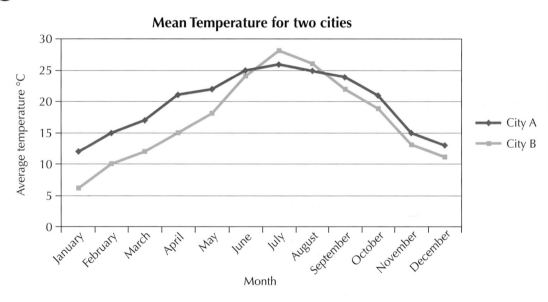

Mean Temperature for two cities

a Which city has the hottest mean monthly temperature?
b Which city has the coldest mean monthly temperature?
c How many months of the year is the temperature higher in City A than City B?
d What is the difference in average temperature between the two cities in February?

Extension Work

Use a travel brochure to compare the temperatures of two European destinations.
Make a poster to advertise one destination as being better than the other.

Comparing data

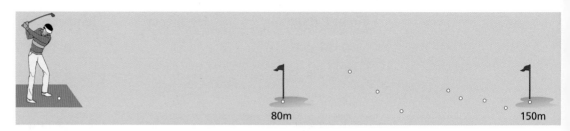

Look at the picture. What is the range of the golfer's shots?

Example 16.6

The table shows the mean and range of basketball scores for two teams:

	Team A	Team B
Mean	75	84
Range	20	10

Compare the mean and range and explain what they tell you.

The means tell you that the average score for Team B is higher than that for Team A, so they have higher scores generally.

The range compares the difference in their lowest and highest scores. As this is higher for team A, there is more variation in their scores. You could say that they are less consistent.

Exercise 16D

1 A factory worker records the start and finish times of a series of jobs:

Job Number	1	2	3	4	5
Start time	9.00 am	9.20 am	9.50 am	10.10 am	10.20 am
Finish time	9.15 am	9.45 am	10.06 am	10.18 am	10.37 am

a Work out the range of the times taken for each job.

b Calculate the mean value of the ranges.

2 The minimum and maximum temperatures are recorded for four counties in England in April.

County	Northumberland	Leicestershire	Oxfordshire	Surrey
Minimum	2°C	4°C	4°C	4.5°C
Maximum	12°C	15°C	16.5°C	17.5°C

a Find the range of the temperatures for each county.

b Comment on any differences you notice.

3 The table shows the mean and range of a set of test scores for Jon and Matt.

Compare the mean and range and explain what they tell you.

	Jon	Matt
Mean	64	71
Range	35	23

Fiona recorded how long, to the nearest hour, Everlast, Powercell and Electro batteries lasted in her CD player. She did 5 trials of each make of battery. Her results are given below.

Everlast (£1.00 each)	Powercell (50p each)	Electro (£1.50 each)
6	4	9
5	6	8
6	3	9
6	3	9
7	4	9

a Find the mean and range of the lifetime for each make of battery.

b Which type of battery would you buy and why?

Extension **Work**

Use an atlas or another data source (the Internet or a software program) to compare the populations of the 4 largest cities in China and the United States of America, using the mean and the range.

Which average to use?

Look at the queue of people. Why is it impossible to find the most common height?

This table will help you decide which type of average to use for a set of data.

	Advantages	Disadvantages	Example
Mean	Uses every piece of data. Probably the most used average.	May not be representative if the data contains extreme values.	1, 1, 1, 2, 4, 15 Mean $= \dfrac{1 + 1 + 1 + 2 + 4 + 15}{6} = 4$ which is a higher value than most of the data.
Median	Only looks at the middle values, so it is a better average to use if the data contains extreme values.	Not all values are considered so could be misleading.	1, 1, 3, 5, 10, 15, 20 Median = 4th value = 5. Note that above the median the numbers are a long way from the median but below the median they are very close.
Mode	It is the most common value.	If the mode is an extreme value it is misleading to use it as an average.	Weekly wages of a boss and his 4 staff: £150, £150, £150, £150, £1000. Mode is £150 but mean is £320.
Modal class for continuous data	This is the class with the greatest frequency.	The actual values may not be centrally placed in the class.	<table><tr><td>Time (T) minutes</td><td>Frequency</td></tr><tr><td>$0 < T \le 5$</td><td>2</td></tr><tr><td>$5 < T \le 10$</td><td>3</td></tr><tr><td>$10 < T \le 15$</td><td>6</td></tr><tr><td>$15 < T \le 20$</td><td>1</td></tr></table> The modal class is $10 < T \le 15$, but all 6 values may be close to 15.
Range	It measures how spread out the data is.	It only looks at the two extreme values, which may not represent the spread of the rest of the data.	1, 2, 5, 7, 9, 40. The range is $40 - 1 = 39$ without the last value (40) the range would be only 8.

Exercise 16E

1 Calculate the indicated average for each set of data and explain if that sort of average is sensible or not.

a	2, 3, 5, 7, 8, 10	Mean	**b**	0, 1, 2, 2, 2, 4, 6	Mode
c	1, 4, 7, 8, 10, 11, 12	Median	**d**	2, 3, 6, 7, 10, 10, 10	Mode
e	2, 2, 2, 2, 4, 6, 8	Median	**f**	1, 2, 4, 6, 9, 30	Mean

2 Times (in seconds) to complete a short task are recorded below for 15 pupils:

10.1, 11.2, 11.5, 12.1, 12.3, 12.8, 13.6, 14.4, 14.5, 14.7, 14.9, 15.4, 15.9, 16.6, 17.1

Complete the frequency table and find the modal class.

Explain why the mode is unsuitable for the ungrouped data, but the modal class is suitable for the grouped data.

Time, T (seconds)	Tally	Frequency
$10 < T \le 12$		
$12 < T \le 14$		
$14 < T \le 16$		
$16 < T \le 18$		

3 Calculate the range for each set of data below and decide whether it is a suitable measure of the spread. Explain your answer.

a 1, 2, 4, 7, 9, 10   b 1, 10, 10, 10, 10   c 1, 1, 1, 2, 10
d 1, 3, 5, 6, 7, 10   e 1, 1, 1, 7, 10, 10, 10   f 2, 5, 8, 10, 14

Extension Work

Collect a set of data on the attendances at English Premiership football matches over one weekend. Calculate the mean, median and mode.

Repeat this exercise for the Scottish Premier division.

Compare the differences in the distributions of the data. Explain why the mean is probably more suitable for the English league than the Scottish league.

Experimental and theoretical probability

Look at the picture. Would you say the chance of the jigsaw pieces coming out of the box face up is even or do more pieces come out face down every time?

Example 16.7 Design and carry out an experiment to test whether drawing pins usually land with the pin pointing up or the pin pointing down.

Count out 50 drawing pins, then drop them onto a table.

Record the number with the pin pointing up and the number with the pin pointing down.

Suppose that 30 point up and 20 point down.

We could then say that the experimental probability of a pin pointing up is: $\frac{30}{50} = \frac{3}{5}$.

Exercise 16F

1 Darren says that if someone is asked to think of a number between 1 and 10 inclusive, they will pick 3 or 7 more often than any other number.

a What is the theoretical probability that a person will choose 3 or 7?

b Design and carry out an experiment to test out Darren's prediction.

c Compare the experimental and theoretical probabilities.

2 a What is the theoretical probability that an ordinary fair dice lands on the number 6?

b What is the theoretical probability that an ordinary fair dice lands on an odd number?

c Design and carry out an experiment to test these theoretical probabilities.

3 Five cards, numbered 1, 2, 3, 4 and 5, are placed face down in a row as shown. Cards are picked at random.

a What is the theoretical probability that a person chooses the card with the number 2 on it?

b A gambler predicts that when people pick a card they will rarely pick the end ones. Design and carry out an experiment to test his prediction.

4 a What is the theoretical probability that a coin lands on heads?

b Design and carry out an experiment to test this theoretical probability.

5 Two fair dice are thrown.

a Copy and complete the sample space diagram for the total scores.

b What is the theoretical probability of a total score of 7?

c Design and carry out an experiment to test whether you think two dice are fair.

First dice

Second dice

	1	2	3	4	5	6
1						
2						
3						
4						
5						
6						

Extension Work

Use computer software to simulate an experiment, for example tossing a coin or rolling a dice. Work out the experimental probabilities after 10, 20, 30 results, and compare with the theoretical probability. Write down any pattern that you notice. Repeat the experiment to see whether any pattern is repeated.

LEVEL BOOSTER

5
I can calculate a mean from an assumed mean.
I can compare the range and the mean from two sets of data.
I can decide which average is the best to use in different circumstances.

6
I can construct grouped frequency tables.
I can construct and interpret grouped frequency diagrams.
I can compare experimental and theoretical probability.

1 *2006 4–6 Paper 1*

Hanif asked ten people, "What is your favourite sport?" Here are his results:

football cricket football hockey swimming hockey swimming football tennis football

a Is it possible to work out the **mean** of these results?

Explain how you know.

b Is it possible to work out the **mode** of these results?

Explain how you know.

2 *2000 Paper 2*

a Paula played four games in a competition.
In three games, Paula scored 8 points each time. In the other game she scored no points.

What was Paula's mean score over the four games?

b Jessie only played two games.
Her mean score was 3 points. Her range was 4 points.

What points did Jessie score in her two games?

c Ali played three games.
His mean score was also 3 points. His range was also 4 points.

What points might Ali have scored in his three games? Show your working.

3 *2005 4–6 Paper 2*

Here is some information about all the pupils in class 9A:
A teacher is going to choose a pupil from 9A at random.

	Number of boys	Number of girls
Right-handed	13	14
Left-handed	1	2

a What is the probability that the pupil chosen will be a **girl**?

b What is the probability that the pupil chosen will be **left-handed**?

c The teacher chooses the pupil at random.
She tells the class that the pupil is **left-handed**.

What is the probability that this left-handed pupil is a **boy**?

4 *2007 4–6 Paper 1*

In a bag, there are only red, blue and green counters.

Colour of counters	Number of counters	Probability
Red	8	
Blue		0.5
Green	6	

a I am going to take a counter out of the bag at random.

Copy and complete this table:

b Before I take a counter out of the bag, I put **one extra blue** counter into the bag.

Which of the following statements describes the effect that this has on the probability that I will take a **red** counter?

The probability has increased

The probability has decreased

The probability has stayed the same

It is impossible to tell

FM Questionnaire

Cris created a questionnaire for her Year 8 classmates. She went round asking 40 boys and 40 girls the following questions.

a What is your favourite band or artist? **b** How many CDs do you possess?

c Which is your favourite Wii sporting game?

This is a summary of her results.

Boy/Girl	Music	CDs	Wii Game	Boy/Girl	Music	CDs	Wii Game
Boy	Fall out Boy	12	Bowling	Girl	Kate Nash	17	Bowling
Girl	Arctic Monkeys	17	Bowling	Boy	Foo Fighters	32	Golf
Boy	Panic! at Disco	27	Boxing	Girl	Arctic Monkeys	43	Bowling
Girl	Kate Nash	34	Bowling	Girl	Spice Girls	26	Golf
Girl	Fall out Boy	32	Bowling	Boy	Kate Nash	32	Boxing
Boy	Foo Fighters	29	Boxing	Boy	Foo Fighters	44	Boxing
Boy	Arctic Monkeys	43	Golf	Boy	Arctic Monkeys	53	Boxing
Boy	Foo Fighters	41	Boxing	Girl	Kate Nash	45	Bowling
Girl	Arctic Monkeys	23	Bowling	Girl	Foo Fighters	36	Bowling
Girl	Arctic Monkeys	16	Golf	Boy	Fall out Boy	28	Boxing
Boy	Foo Fighters	26	Boxing	Boy	Arctic Monkeys	16	Tennis
Girl	Fall out Boy	37	Bowling	Girl	Foo Fighters	19	Tennis
Girl	Foo Fighters	24	Bowling	Boy	Panic! at Disco	20	Golf
Boy	Arctic Monkeys	16	Golf	Girl	Fall out Boy	31	Bowling
Boy	Fall out Boy	33	Boxing	Girl	Fall out Boy	40	Bowling
Girl	Kate Nash	45	Bowling	Boy	Arctic Monkeys	43	Bowling
Boy	Foo Fighters	52	Tennis	Girl	Panic! at Disco	55	Golf
Girl	Foo Fighters	37	Tennis	Girl	Foo Fighters	23	Bowling
Girl	Kate Nash	13	Bowling	Boy	Kate Nash	27	Baseball
Girl	Panic! at Disco	31	Bowling	Boy	Arctic Monkeys	35	Boxing
Boy	Kate Nash	50	Golf	Girl	Kate Nash	31	Golf
Boy	Arctic Monkeys	43	Bowling	Boy	Foo Fighters	28	Bowling
Boy	Foo Fighters	25	Boxing	Boy	Panic! at Disco	46	Boxing
Girl	Arctic Monkeys	30	Bowling	Boy	Fall out Boy	34	Boxing
Boy	Fall out Boy	17	Bowling	Girl	Arctic Monkeys	26	Bowling
Girl	Kate Nash	29	Tennis	Boy	Fall out Boy	18	Bowling
Girl	Spice Girls	31	Golf	Girl	Foo Fighters	22	Tennis
Girl	Arctic Monkeys	48	Bowling	Girl	Foo Fighters	40	Boxing
Boy	Foo Fighters	38	Boxing	Boy	Arctic Monkeys	51	Golf
Boy	Panic! at Disco	21	Bowling	Boy	Arctic Monkeys	42	Golf
Boy	Fall out Boy	20	Tennis	Girl	Kate Nash	46	Tennis
Girl	Kate Nash	37	Golf	Girl	Kate Nash	34	Boxing
Boy	Foo Fighters	48	Boxing	Boy	Foo Fighters	50	Boxing
Boy	Foo Fighters	23	Golf	Girl	Arctic Monkeys	43	Bowling
Boy	Arctic Monkeys	19	Bowling	Boy	Foo Fighters	54	Baseball
Girl	Kate Nash	24	Bowling	Girl	Panic! at Disco	23	Bowling
Girl	Arctic Monkeys	52	Bowling	Boy	Foo Fighters	33	Boxing
Boy	Kate Nash	49	Tennis	Boy	Fall out Boy	41	Boxing
Boy	Foo Fighters	38	Golf	Girl	Fall out Boy	37	Bowling
Girl	Panic! at Disco	25	Bowling	Girl	Kate Nash	46	Tennis

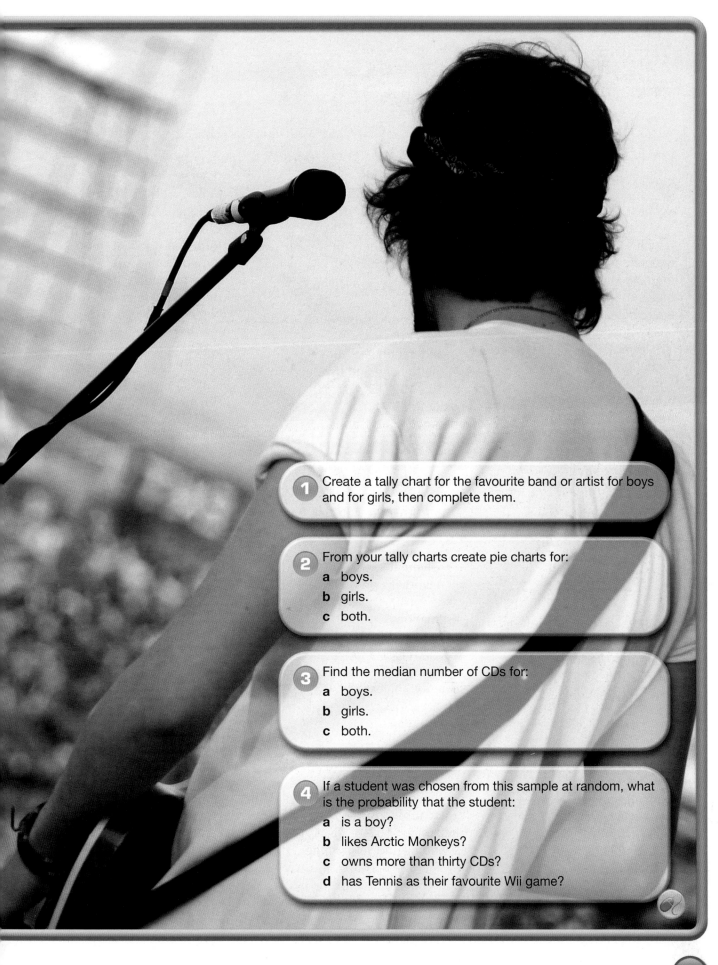

1. Create a tally chart for the favourite band or artist for boys and for girls, then complete them.

2. From your tally charts create pie charts for:
   a boys.
   b girls.
   c both.

3. Find the median number of CDs for:
   a boys.
   b girls.
   c both.

4. If a student was chosen from this sample at random, what is the probability that the student:
   a is a boy?
   b likes Arctic Monkeys?
   c owns more than thirty CDs?
   d has Tennis as their favourite Wii game?

Index

William Collins' dream of knowledge for all began with the publication of his first book in 1819. A self-educated mill worker, he not only enriched millions of lives, but also founded a flourishing publishing house. Today, staying true to this spirit, Collins books are packed with inspiration, innovation and practical expertise. They place you at the centre of a world of possibility and give you exactly what you need to explore it.

Collins. Freedom to teach.

Published by Collins
An imprint of HarperCollins*Publishers*
77–85 Fulham Palace Road
Hammersmith
London
W6 8JB

Browse the complete Collins catalogue at
www.collinseducation.com

© HarperCollins*Publishers* Limited 2008

10 9 8 7 6 5 4

ISBN 978-0-00-726618-0

Keith Gordon, Kevin Evans, Brian Speed and Trevor Senior assert their moral rights to be identified as the authors of this work

Commissioned by Melanie Hoffman and Katie Sergeant
Project managed by Priya Govindan
Edited by Brian Ashbury
Indexed by Michael Forder
Proofread by Amanda Dickson
Design and typesetting by Jordan Publishing Design
Covers by Oculus Design and Communications
Covers managed by Laura Deacon
Illustrations by Nigel Jordan, Tony Wilkins and Barking Dog Art
Printed and bound by Martins the Printers, Berwick-upon-Tweed
Production by Simon Moore

Acknowledgments

The publishers thank the Qualifications and Curriculum Authority for granting permission to reproduce questions from past National Curriculum Test papers for Key Stage 3 Maths.

The publishers wish to thank the following for permission to reproduce photographs:

p.20–21 (main image) © Chris Schmidt / istockphoto.com, p.48–49 (main image) © Sergey Dubrovskiy / istockphoto.com, p.62–63 (main image) © Stephen Strathdee / istockphoto.com, p.62–63 (inset images) © Jovana Cetkovic and Lya Cattel / istockphoto.com, p.102–103 (main image) © Jeff Driver / istockphoto.com, p.118–119 (main image) © Angel Herrero de Frutos / istockphoto.com, p.118–119 (inset images) © Matt Baker, Jennifer Sheets, Milos Luzanin, Mark Evans / istockphoto.com, p.160–161 (main image) © istockphoto.com, p.170–171 (main image) © Chris Howes, Wild Places Photography / Alamy and (inset image) © istockphoto.com, p.184–185 (main image) © René Mansi / istockphoto.com, p.214–215 (main image) © Tetra Images / Alamy, p.228–229 (main image) © Jovana Cetkovic / istockphoto.com

Every effort has been made to trace copyright holders and to obtain their permission for the use of copyright material. The authors and publishers will gladly receive any information enabling them to rectify any error or omission at the first opportunity.

Mixed Sources
Product group from well-managed forests and other controlled sources
www.fsc.org Cert no. SW-COC-1806
© 1996 Forest Stewardship Council
FSC

FSC is a non-profit international organisation established to promote the responsible management of the world's forests. Products carrying the FSC label are independently certified to assure consumers that they come from forests that are managed to meet the social, economic and ecological needs of present and future generations.

Find out more about HarperCollins and the environment at
www.harpercollins.co.uk/green